WHAT YOU DON'T KNOW ABOUT RELIGION (but should)

WHAT YOU DON'T KNOW ABOUT RELIGION (but should)

Ryan T. Cragun

PITCHSTONE PUBLISHING
Durham, North Carolina

Pitchstone Publishing
Durham, NC 27705
www.pitchstonepublishing.com

To contact the publisher, please e-mail info@pitchstonepublishing.com
To contact the author, please e-mail ryantcragun@gmail.com
Cover design by Casimir Fornalski, casimirfornalski.com

Printed in the United States of America

19 18 17 16 15 14 13   1 2 3 4 5

Library of Congress Cataloging-in-Publication Data

Cragun, Ryan T.
 What you don't know about religion (but should) / Ryan T. Cragun.
    pages cm
 Includes bibliographical references and index.
  ISBN 978-0-9852815-3-3 (hardcover : alk. paper) -- ISBN 978-0-9852815-4-0
(pbk. : alk. paper)
 1. Religion. I. Title.
 BL50.C685 2013
 200--dc23
                        2012043541

For my accomplice and my hope, Debi and Toren.

CONTENTS

ACKNOWLEDGMENTS

This book was largely inspired by my wife, Debi Cragun. Through her work, we spent a lovely evening with some of her colleagues at a beautiful house in Eugene, Oregon. As most of the guests helped themselves to their third or fourth glass of wine, the conversation, which had largely focused on their shared interests in public health, turned to me and my work. When I explained to those present that I studied religion scientifically, they wanted to know more. I gave them an example (basically, chapter 8—"All Demons Are from Hollywood"). They seemed intrigued, but I didn't realize the extent of their curiosity until a few days later. My wife told me that, over the next few days, all of the people at dinner that night commented on how interested they were in my explanations of religion. My wife then suggested that most educated people would be equally interested. That led to us discussing this book. I had already been considering something similar, but I realized she was onto something. So, I owe a great deal of credit to my wife for helping me develop the idea for this book.

My wife has also helped me write this book in more practical ways. Most of this book was written during the only time I could find—from about 11:00 p.m. to 3:00 a.m. Saturday nights/Sunday mornings. Given all of my other commitments, that was the only time I could find when I wouldn't be disturbed by e-mails, phone calls, or other issues. That meant I was pretty much useless Sunday mornings for about a year while I worked on this book. My wife accommodated my uselessness.

Finally, she probably knows the contents of this book better than anyone but myself as she's willingly discussed these chapters as I've developed them. She also proofread most of the book and offered helpful feedback. Therefore, I owe a great debt to my wife and thank her for all of the above.

I'm also going to acknowledge my son just because he's awesome. He didn't really help with this book as far as proofreading goes; he's three. But I do tell some stories about him and use him in some examples. Regardless of his contributions, he's the coolest son anyone could ever have. Toren, your dad loves you.

There are others who have been very helpful as well. Kristina Cappello, one of my students at the University of Tampa, spent most of a summer finding news stories on different topics related to religion for this book. Most of those stories never made it into this book, but some did. And those that didn't make it into the book did help convince me that the stories I selected were not isolated cases. Thank you, Kristina.

My mentor, Rhys Williams, who has shared with me innumerable bits of wisdom, is the reason why this book includes stories at the beginning of every chapter. At a conference in Portland he gave a presentation that included several very engaging stories. Afterward he said to me, "If you can make your point with a story, everyone will listen." And, of course, he trained me as a sociologist, which is why I'm even able to write this book. Rhys, thank you.

I am also indebted to Darren Sherkat. His blog, iranianredneck.wordpress.com, covered some of the topics in this book and helped shape my thinking in some chapters. Plus, his blog makes me look like I'm religion's best friend.

I also need to thank Starbucks for providing the caffeine to keep me awake at night. (I would gladly accept free coffee in return for this plug. Hint. Hint.) The manuscript for this book was created using LibreOffice and Zotero, two wonderful pieces of FOSS, running on an Ubuntu machine. Thank you to the programmers who make that software available. I also want to thank the composers of a variety of musical compositions for writing music that inspired me while I wrote. My writing music included the soundtracks of *The Lord of the Rings* series, *Gladiator*, *Gattaca*, *Brokeback Mountain*, *Jurassic Park*, *Memoirs of a Geisha*, the Bourne series, *The Englishman Who Went Up a Hill but Came Down a Mountain*, the Indiana Jones series, *The Last of the Mohicans*, and *World of Warcraft*. Cliché? Perhaps. Epic? Definitely!

Finally, thank you to Kurt Volkan, the editor of Pitchstone Publishing, for taking a chance with this book and providing helpful feedback.

INTRODUCTION

You prayed and God told you that Joseph Smith was his prophet, that the Book of Mormon is true, and that The Church of Jesus Christ of Latter-day Saints is the one and only true church on the planet. If you do not get baptized into our church, you will go to hell.
　　　　　　　　　　　　　　　　　　　　　—Elder Cragun, May 1996

I was nineteen years old when I said the above. The recipient was a middle-aged, lower-middle-class woman in Costa Rica. My companion, Elder Smith, and I had taught her about Mormonism and asked her to pray to god to find out if it was true, and she had done just that. When we returned to see if she had received an answer, she said that she had—god told her that the Book of Mormon and the Mormon Church were true. When Elder Smith asked her if she would get baptized, she said she couldn't because it would cause problems with the rest of her family. That's when I said she was going to go to hell. She cried. I didn't feel bad. I was doing god's work. I was doing what I had been taught my whole life I was supposed to do. I was on a mission for god; convert or condemn—those were the only options.

In addition to believing that praying could actually determine the accuracy and truthfulness of a book and religion, I also believed that I could heal the sick, cast out demons, and get baptized for dead people. I even believed that, with sufficient faith, I could wield the powers of a god to literally move mountains.

Mind you, I was not born in 1900 or even 1950. I was born in 1976. How could I, a public-school educated, moderately intelligent American raised with access to media, books, libraries, and computers (though not the Internet—that became popular while I was condemning people in Costa Rica) be so incredibly naive?

—§—

I was religious.

I thought at the time that I knew enough about religion to not only teach people about my own religion, but also to convince them that their religions were false and of the devil. As I will discuss in a later chapter, religious people tend to be quite arrogant. I should know; I was. I knew very little about religion. I also didn't realize that the tools I was taught to use to manipulate people into taking me seriously as a missionary were largely developed by social scientists.

In retrospect there were two things I didn't know: (1) I didn't know much about the history and doctrine of religions, mine or any others; and (2) I knew nothing about religions as social scientific phenomena. While I have learned a great deal about the former since my mission, this book is almost exclusively about the latter. If you're interested in the doctrines and histories of religions, there are other, better books for you to read. But if you're interested in what the social sciences can tell us about what religion is, what groups of religious people are like, how religious institutions influence their members, and what the future holds for religious people, keep reading. In short, this book will reveal what you don't know about religion (but should).

Let me briefly reiterate what this book *does not* do so that I can better explain what it *does do*. I'm not going to discuss religious doctrine (with the exception of how religious doctrine influences people in important ways). Nor will I point out logical inconsistencies in doctrines, attack belief in god, or discuss the histories of religions.

What this book will cover instead are questions like: What is a religion? Why are people religious? Are religious people more educated than nonreligious people? Are religious people more moral, more humble, or happier? Are women treated well in religions? Are religious people more or less prejudiced than nonreligious people? Is religion good for your health? Are people becoming more or less religious? These questions interest me, but they are also important to ask in light of the fact that religion plays a prominent role in various aspects of our globalized world, from inspiring acts of charity to motivating acts of terrorism. Given the prevalence of religion, wouldn't it be good to know how religion is helping and hurting society?

In fact, I want you to perform a little exercise. Find a piece of paper or, if you're reading this on a tablet or other electronic device, pull up a note-taking application and answer the following questions:

- Are babies born believing in a higher power?
- Why are most people religious?
- Who is more educated, highly religious people or nonreligious people?
- Who tends to be more intelligent, highly religious people or nonreligious people?

- Are highly religious people more or less accepting of science than are the nonreligious?
- Who is more supportive of women's control over their fertility, the highly religious or the nonreligious?
- Who marries at a younger age, the highly religious or the nonreligious?
- Who has more kids, the highly religious or the nonreligious?
- Who employs more scientifically acceptable parenting practices, the highly religious or the nonreligious?
- Who is more likely to commit crimes, the highly religious or the nonreligious?
- Who is more developed in their thinking about moral issues, the highly religious or the nonreligious?
- Who is more arrogant, the highly religious or the nonreligious?
- Who is more misogynistic, the highly religious or the nonreligious?
- Who is more prejudiced toward racial minorities, homosexuals, and women, the highly religious or the nonreligious?
- Who is more wealthy, the highly religious or the nonreligious?
- Who is more environmentally minded, the highly religious or the nonreligious?
- Who is more politically progressive, the highly religious or the nonreligious?
- Who volunteers more, the highly religious or the nonreligious?
- Who is more accepting of violence, the highly religious or the nonreligious?
- Who is happier, the highly religious or the nonreligious?
- Who is physically healthier, the highly religious or the nonreligious?
- Who is better at coping with death, the highly religious or the nonreligious?

Got your answers? Good. Now tuck those away. You'll need them again when you reach the last chapter.

You've probably guessed what I'm going to do in this book based on the above questions: I'm going to answer them. How, you ask? Well, those are all questions I, as a sociologist, study. Sociologists study social life. Included in that are social institutions, or groups of people with relatively stable ways of interacting with each other. Religion is a social institution. We study religion—scientifically. We use the tools of science to understand religions and religious life.

Some religious people might object to my approach under a premise I hear fairly often that goes something like, "If you want to know about *my* religion, talk to a member of *my* religion." Well, it turns out that religious people often don't know very much about their own religions. I know this because I observe it regularly in the college students I teach, who know next to nothing about their religions. I've also observed this in the people I know and have met. But more importantly, I know this because scientific data suggest atheists know more about religion in the United States than do religious people. Just because someone is religious doesn't mean she knows much about her religion.

Just for fun, let's consider applying this objection to other aspects of the universe. If someone wanted to learn about physics, should they go talk to someone who has fallen off a building because they have "experienced" gravity or maybe someone who flew through a windshield in a car accident because they "experienced" momentum? I think they would be better off talking to a physicist, not because the physicist has "lived" physics but because he has studied it. If someone wants to learn about religion as a social phenomenon, they should talk to someone who studies religion as a social phenomenon. If that is of interest to you, you're in luck: I study religion as a social phenomenon.

Assuming you're still interested, you may be wondering where I stand on religion. Am I religious? Do I like religion? Do I want to destroy religion? Technically, those are irrelevant questions. I'm a scientist. I will draw upon data and the research of other experts throughout the book. But you may still want to know my views on religion. Also, if I'm going to be honest, my personal views do influence how I interpret data and other scholars' research. So I'll tell you where I stand.

I was raised a Mormon and remained Mormon until I was twenty-five. After my first year in graduate school studying the sociology of religion, I decided Mormonism wasn't right for me. I shopped around for a while, exploring other churches (e.g., Methodism, Seventh-day Adventism, Presbyterianism, Unitarianism, etc.) and didn't feel at home in any of them. At that point I realized religion didn't really do much for me. I'm still very much interested in religion, but not really for personal reasons. I'm not religious.

Am I out to destroy religion? No.

Well—not really. I'm familiar enough with religion to know that there is a wide variety of religion and some religions are far more objectionable to me (e.g., Christians who believe killing doctors who perform abortions is a good thing) than are others (e.g., religions that encourage pacifism, equality, and service). Religions are diverse and I feel differently about different religions. Religion may not work for me, but some people do in fact benefit from it, as I will make clear. So, no, I'm not trying to destroy religion. But that doesn't mean I'm not critical of religion; I am.

What about the "big" question that other atheist scholars have addressed recently: does god exist?

Not interested!

Really, I'm not interested in that question. That isn't a scientific question. This is a book on the social science of religion. If the tools of the social sciences have been applied to an aspect of religion, I will likely discuss it. Alas, I won't tackle the biology and neurology of religion, despite being greatly interested in those topics. There is a great deal of research that is currently under way in those disciplines and it is fascinating. But it is outside my area of expertise and therefore not the focus of this book.

You may also be wondering if I am going to try to convince you to think about religion like I do. Well, of course! Why else would I write this book? I hold no illusions that I'll succeed, but I will present my best arguments and back them up with data. You may interpret the data differently from how I do. But I think everyone should know what social scientists know about religion. If it doesn't change how you think about religion, so be it. At least you'll know what social scientists who study religion know.

The book is roughly divided into three parts. The first part defines religion and deconstructs it, illustrating that religion is, like all social institutions, socially constructed. The second part explores the characteristics of religious people. This part makes up the bulk of the book as social scientific research on religion has focused extensively on these characteristics. The third and final part of the book explores the future of religion. Social science hasn't developed to the point that we can predict the future perfectly, but current sociological theories offer some insights as to the potential future of religion and the direction of people's religiosity. I also discuss alternatives to religion in the third part and provide some concluding thoughts.

Although there are a lot of chapters, they are relatively short and I have tried to make them engaging. Most chapters begin with a story to illustrate the specific topic under discussion. The stories are followed by a detailed yet simplified explanation of what the current research says about the topic. Most chapters also include data presented in an easy-to-read chart (see the appendix for more information on the methodology). The data help illustrate the point of the chapter. Each chapter concludes with a short summary.

—§—

I do have to explain and possibly even apologize for two things before I conclude this introduction. First, most of the research I draw upon is Christian- and Western hemisphere–centric. I don't discuss religion in the Middle East or sub-Saharan Africa in detail, though some data from countries in those regions are included. There are two reasons I don't focus on those regions. First, most of the research in the sociology of religion is from North America and Western Europe. Second, there is little data on those regions of the world. That means that my conclusions are largely limited to predominantly Christian countries and the West. This is a shortcoming of both my book and the sociology of religion. I have tried to overcome this limitation by including findings from a broad international survey that includes data from countries around the world, from India to Iran and from South Korea to South Africa, as noted in the appendix. Even so, I do not feel confident that I have or can satisfactorily describe the nuances of religion everywhere around the world without writing a book that is several times the length of this one.

The second thing for which I apologize is the limited nuance of the discussions in each chapter. Many of the topics I cover in four to five pages are covered in much greater depth in entire books and hundreds of articles. In any summary geared toward a general audience, nuance will be lost. I mean no disrespect to the scholars whose research I cite and ask them in all sincerity to help me correct any errors they find in my summaries of their work. For those interested in more nuance or the details on any given topic, I provide ample citations, but they are noted in the back of the book to make the book more readable for those who are less interested in references.

Finally, as science is a work in progress, I have had a very hard time considering this book "complete." There are topics I wanted to include, but didn't due to space constraints. There are probably also some chapters that, by the time of the publication of this book, may no longer reflect the latest understanding of the social sciences. Feel free to contact me with corrections or suggestions. I'm excited this book is in print, but I hope this is not the final edition of the book. I have every intention of updating the book as knowledge advances. There is a lot we know about religion, now, but as we learn more, I'll be sure to make that information available to as wide an audience as I can.

1

BUDDHISM IS IN; COMMUNISM IS OUT
DEFINING RELIGION

On June 4, 2002, Brian David Mitchell, who called himself "Immanuel" (i.e., "the chosen one") crept into the bedroom of fourteen-year-old Elizabeth Smart in Salt Lake City, Utah. He held a knife to Elizabeth's throat and told her to get up quietly and do what he said or he would kill her and her family. Elizabeth did as she was told. Brian abducted Elizabeth, took her to a camp he had set up in the nearby woods, and had his first wife, Wanda Barzee, prepare Elizabeth for a ceremony. When Wanda had finished the preparations, Brian entered the tent and proceeded to rape Elizabeth. Elizabeth remained with Brian and Wanda for nine months following the abductions, and was repeatedly raped during that time.

Brian David Mitchell believed he was doing the will of god. In the years prior to the abduction, he claims to have seen angels and had visions in which god told him that he was to lead The Church of Jesus Christ of Latter-day Saints (aka the "Mormon Church") and reintroduce the practice of polygamy. Mitchell wrote down the revelations he received from god and spread them as revealed scripture. Mitchell believed himself to be an angel ordained by god to prepare the world for the return of Jesus Christ.

In 1836, Joseph Smith Jr. was caught by one of his closest followers, Oliver Cowdery, having sex with teenager Fanny Alger, a live-in servant for his family, in Kirtland, Ohio. Joseph Smith was married at the time. Smith had not yet introduced his teachings about plural marriage to his followers, which suggests Smith was, in all likelihood, cheating on his wife, Emma. Smith never denied that he had sex with Fanny Alger, whose family left the area shortly after Oliver Cowdery accused Smith of the affair. Fanny Alger later married a non-Mormon and ceased affiliation with the Mormon Church. Smith later formally married as many as thirty-three women other than his first wife and consummated many of those marriages.

Joseph Smith Jr. believed he was doing the will of god. In the years prior to the affair, he claimed to have seen angels and had visions in which god had told him that he was to found and lead The Church of Jesus Christ of Latter-day Saints (a.k.a. the "Mormon Church"). Joseph Smith was also told to introduce the practice of polygamy later in his life. Smith wrote down the revelations he received from god and spread them as revealed scripture. Smith believed himself to be a prophet, selected by god to prepare the world for the return of Jesus Christ.

I don't know if you noticed it, but the second paragraph in this chapter is almost word-for-word identical to the fourth paragraph, yet they are about two different people who are viewed quite differently. Joseph Smith Jr. is revered by millions of people around the world as a prophet of god who has revealed god's will in the "latter days." His name is spoken with reverence by many and, while not technically worshiped by Mormons, he is held in very high esteem. Brian David Mitchell is serving a life sentence in prison. While Smith's affair with Fanny Alger is obviously not on par with the abduction and rape of Elizabeth Smart by Brian David Mitchell, Smith's philandering and threats against his first wife are pretty despicable. Why is Smith revered and Mitchell in jail? The difference is simple: Joseph Smith Jr. had followers; Brian David Mitchell did not. That difference dictates whether one is classified as a felon or a "religious genius."

Religions are groups of people who hold common beliefs about supernatural things. "Super" means above or beyond. "Nature" refers to the material universe, specifically those parts that can be established to exist. "Supernatural" phenomena are above or beyond the natural universe. They are claimed to exist outside our ability to sense that they exist—by definition. Religions have beliefs, and often rituals, related to supernatural things, like angels, demons, and gods.

Religions have one other key characteristic: they are social institutions, which means they are made up of groups of people. There cannot be a religion of just one person—also by definition. Religions are institutions and institutions are social constructs created by groups of people, not individuals. Religions, therefore, are social; they have to include groups of people with shared beliefs about "supernature."

This is where Joseph Smith Jr. differed from Brian David Mitchell. Joseph Smith Jr. was able to convince other people that his beliefs were credible; Mitchell was not. Ipso facto, Smith is revered as a prophet and Brian David Mitchell is in jail.

There is another interesting point to be made here. While there are certainly many people who would consider the teachings of Joseph Smith Jr. to be bizarre, strange, weird, or even crazy, most would at least recognize that some people take the beliefs seriously and that they cannot be dismissed outright as simply the teachings of a crazy person—because millions of people believe them. The same is not true of Mitchell. No one takes Mitchell's beliefs seriously. Mitchell's beliefs are dismissed as the ramblings of a religious nut, not a religious visionary. While Mitchell was not deemed to be insane, no one finds his revelations and teachings to be credible. Yet, if examined by a skeptical outsider who was blinded as to the source of the different revelations, do you think our hypothetical skeptical outsider would be able to tell which were the writings of the "religious nut" and which were the writings of the "religious visionary"? My guess is no. Both made extraordinary claims. One was just better at gaining followers than the other.

What does this say about religion? In order for a group of people to form a religion they need not have rational, coherent, or even plausible beliefs. All that is required is that multiple people share supernatural beliefs, consider themselves part of the same group, and occasionally get together in some fashion to celebrate those beliefs.

There are other definitions of "religion," but they aren't widely accepted or used in the social sciences and aren't worth discussing in this chapter. What I'd like readers to have clear in their minds as we press forward in this book is what is included given this definition. The five world religions—Hinduism, Judaism, Buddhism, Christianity, and Islam—are all included. They all believe in something supernatural, as do tribal religions and most variants of Paganism and New Age religions. That covers most of what people traditionally consider religions.

What is excluded by this definition? Secular governments would be excluded, along with civic pride and patriotism, as they include no supernatural element. Being a fan of a sports team is excluded, even if you basically worship your team, because there isn't anything supernatural about a sports team or the group of fans. This is the case, despite what the fans of the Chelsea Football Club had put on a banner in the Chelsea stadium during a game I attended. The banner read, "Chelsea is Our Religion." They may hold the team in high esteem and even have rituals, but unless they think of the Chelsea players as supernatural gods, the Chelsea Football Club is not a religion. What about brand loyalty? While it turns out Apple fans think about Apple the same way people think about religions, there isn't actually anything supernatural about Apple, even if Apple's fans think so. So, no, it's not a religion.

As noted, secular governments—meaning governments that do not include religion in their structure and organization—are not religions. This would hold for communism as well. Some authors have suggested that communism is a religion. This claim is usually introduced in an effort to show the evils of communism and to argue that the number of people killed "in the name of communism" is close to the number of those killed in the name of religion (I discuss this in further detail in chapter 22). Don't misconstrue what I'm saying here; I'm not defending or minimizing the deaths that have resulted from communist forms of government. But I do want to make it clear that communism is a form of government, not a religion. The definition I provided above rules it out, along with the "personality cults" that are common in modern dictatorships like Saudi Arabia and North Korea. Yes, these forms of government may utilize some of the tools of religion—e.g., rituals and indoctrination—but they generally do not include a belief in the supernatural that is shared by everyone or is even mandatory for citizens in those countries. These governments may claim that it is god's will that they exist, but the same could be said of many secular governments as well. Yes, some communist countries strongly encouraged atheism, but that does not make communism a religion. In order for communist governments to be religions they would need to claim that the leadership of the country is supernatural or that the government is exclusively guided by the supernatural. Such forms of government have existed in the past (e.g., the imperial cult of Egypt), but they are virtually nonexistent today.

What about nonreligious beliefs, like atheism, agnosticism, or secular humanism? Aren't those groups of people with beliefs about the supernatural? Well, not really. First, secular humanism is a philosophical system that has developed a set of principles to guide conduct. There is very little in that philosophy about the supernatural except to suggest that supernatural entities are unnecessary for deriving morals and values. The fact that secular humanists recognize that some people believe in supernatural entities doesn't make secular humanism a religion, nor does their explicit disbelief in supernatural entities. Some might argue that "disbelief" is still a "belief," and since it is geared toward a supernatural entity, this would make secular humanism a religion. However, the absence of belief is not a form of belief. If secular humanists were to say, "We believe there is no god," then that would be a belief about the supernatural. However, if secular humanists say, "We don't have a belief about god" or "We lack any understanding of what the term 'god' means" or "We lack belief in god," then what they have asserted is not a belief in something supernatural but rather a lack thereof. As that is typically what they assert, secular humanism is not a religion.

Agnosticism is widely understood as being unsure about the existence of a god or gods, though the more technical definition is having no knowledge about a god or gods. The technical definition is individualistic, which rules out a group of like-minded others. Agnosticism is also a disavowal of knowledge, not an assertion of belief. So, agnosticism is not a religion.

What about atheism? Well, this is a bit tricky. If you have a group of people (meaning they have a common identity and feel a sense of connection to each other) and they all reject the existence of a god—which is known as positive atheism—then that comes awfully close to the definition I presented: collective beliefs toward the supernatural. But it is quite rare that atheists feel a sense of unity or togetherness, suggesting they do not identify as a group. If they did, and they regularly met to express their "positive" belief that there is no god, this could arguably be considered a "religious" group. But gatherings of "positive" atheists aren't very common. There is another type of atheism—negative atheism, in which a belief in a god is either lacking or simply suspended. Atheists of this type don't reject or deny the existence of a god; they simply choose not to believe that such a god exists, siding with probability—the existence of such a god is unlikely but not impossible, so they don't believe. That isn't actually the assertion of belief in a god or a rejection, but rather a high probability position that falls between the two: a suspension of belief until the probability increases. Negative atheism, like agnosticism, is the lack of belief, not a form of belief. Lacking a belief in the supernatural is sufficient to disqualify a group as a religion.

In summary, religions are groups of people who share beliefs in supernatural phenomena. Supernatural phenomena are things that are above or beyond the natural world and are therefore not detectable. Religions are social institutions and therefore must include more than one member. The difference between the ramblings of a religious nut and the ramblings of a religious visionary is the ability to gather a following. If someone with beliefs about the supernatural can get followers, that person has created a religion. If they can't, they are often institutionalized. Using the definition I have provided, those institutions that *have* historically been considered religions are in (e.g., Buddhism), while those institutions and philosophies that *have not* historically been considered religions are out (e.g., communism).

2

WITHOUT DATA IT MAY AS WELL BE THEOLOGY
WHY DATA MATTER

I have a friend and colleague who is ambivalent toward god and is critical of religion, but he attends religious services almost every week, does what is necessary to appear to be an observant member of the religion, and even teaches his children to believe in the tenets of the religion he attends. What gives?

His wife is devout and a committed member. His nonbelief, ambivalence, and criticism of the religion nearly ended his marriage. In order to maintain marital harmony, he puts on the trappings of being religious, although he really isn't. My friend isn't alone. Literally millions of people in the United States and around the world do the same thing in order to maintain harmony in their family or among their friends or even to save their lives.

The latter was the situation for Walid Husayin, an atheist blogger in the West Bank who was imprisoned in 2010 for criticizing Islam, which is a crime under Palestinian law. Husayin, a mild-mannered barber in Qalqilya, regularly prayed at the local mosque on Fridays, but he was an outspoken atheist online. When his writings criticizing Islam came to light, he was arrested. As of this writing, he faces the possibility of a life sentence for heresy. His parents are ashamed of his actions and his mother actually favors a life sentence for him to restore the family's honor. Despite calls for his release from local and international human rights groups, Palestinian authorities have refused to release him, claiming his life is now in danger. And, frankly, they may have a point, as people in his town have called for his death.

—§—

The above stories illustrate one of the problems with religion: how do you measure how religious someone is? Both of the examples above are of people who are outwardly religious, putting on the trappings of a religion but denying the tenets of their respective religious cultures inwardly. Are these individuals "religious" or "nonreligious"?

Often cited as the first assertion that religion is multidimensional—meaning there is more than one way to be religious—was a book published in the 1950s by Charles Glock and Rodney Stark. Since then, numerous scholars have developed instruments to try to capture the multidimensional nature of religion. Different dimensions can include things like beliefs (e.g., belief in god, heaven, hell, sin, reincarnation, nirvana, etc.), behaviors (e.g., meditation, prayer, service attendance), influence on everyday activities (e.g., giving donations, volunteering for the religion, etc.), knowledge (e.g., knowing what your religion teaches), and identity (e.g., considering yourself a member of a religion). People can be very religious on one dimension (e.g., attend services regularly) while being simultaneously nonreligious on another (e.g., not believe in god), like my friend and Walid Husayin. The inverse can also be true—people may strongly believe in the existence of a god but never go to church.

You may be asking yourself at this point: okay, I get that people's religiosity may vary along different dimensions, but don't these dimensions tend to go together? Yes, they do. If people regularly attend religious services, they typically believe in a deity and engage in other religious activities. That is true. Of course, there are lots of exceptions, like the two I just noted.

So, religion is multidimensional and there are lots of ways to measure how religious someone is. But are there some ways that are more important or more meaningful than others? The scientist in me wants to say, "No, they are all important." But the pragmatist in me says, "Yes." And those measures are the ones I'll use in this book, despite some resulting loss in specificity.

One way of distinguishing religiosity is along a continuum from fundamentalist to nonreligious, with religious moderates and liberals in the middle. Fundamentalism, historically, refers to a movement within Christianity in the United States to return to the "fundamentals" of religion. In practical terms, fundamentalists today are literalists, meaning they decontextualize their scriptures (i.e., try to interpret them without putting them into their historical time period), and are characterized by black-and-white, us-versus-them thinking. In essence, fundamentalists are one end of a religious-secular continuum. At the other end would be secular individuals—people who reject the tenets of religion and supernatural claims, who do not participate in religious activities, and who live their lives based on science and reason. In the middle would fall religious moderates and religious liberals. Moderates are closer to fundamentalists than are the liberals, but they may not be scriptural literalists and are less likely to exhibit the black-and-white thinking typical of fundamentalists. Liberals are closer to the nonreligious in that they often recognize the problems with the historicity of their scripture, are tolerant of other perspectives on religion and the world, and tend to be more accepting of diversity in areas like gender and sexuality.

Since this isn't a theological treatise but rather a work of science, I'm not allowed to just make shit up. I have to back up my claims. To do that, and to paint accurate pictures of populations, I present data on religious individuals throughout this book. I draw upon several data sets to do this, but use primarily two. For data on people from the United States or Americans, I use the General Social Survey (GSS). And I use the breakdown described in the previous paragraph for the most part, focusing on comparisons between religious fundamentalists, moderates, and liberals. I don't look at specifically secular individuals, but rather those who report their religion as "none" or the nonreligious, largely due to sample sizes (there are more nonreligious than there are affirmatively secular people in the United States and in the GSS). This breakdown is included in the publicly available data set and is based upon participants' self-identified religious affiliation, though I did separate out the nonreligious from the religiously "liberal" category since they really don't belong together. Figure 2.1 shows the makeup of the United States based upon these classifications.

Figure 2.1. Percentage of each religious type in U.S. population

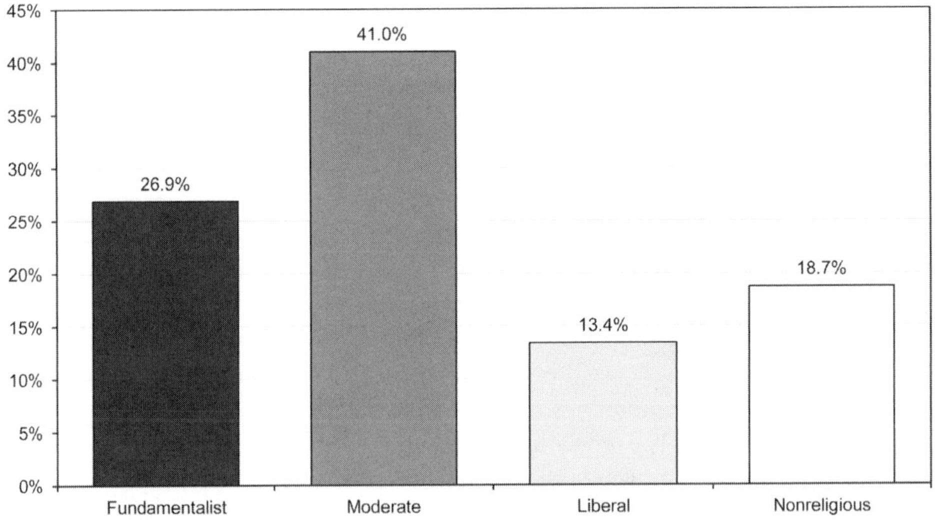

SOURCE: GSS, 2010
NOTE: The sample, excluding those who are missing, includes 1,939 people.

While much of the book focuses on the United States and research conducted in the United States, not all of it does, and many of the findings apply to populations outside the United States as well. To broaden my ability to generalize about the findings in this book to people outside the United States, I draw upon another publicly available data set, the World Values Survey (WVS). The WVS does not include a directly comparable measure to that used in the GSS, in part because the GSS measure of fundamentalism is tied to the religious makeup of the United States. However, there is a similar measure that I will use for most of my comparisons. The question asked participants to rate how important religion is in their life, with the following response options: "very important," "rather important," "not very important," and "not at all important." This question doesn't map perfectly to the question from the GSS about religious fundamentalism, but it does reflect what I am trying to capture: how important religion is to people. Figure 2.2 shows the percentages in the combined waves of the WVS (1981–2008) for each category.

While the WVS does not include data on every country around the world, it does include data from eighty-seven countries that vary substantially in their religious makeup. Aggregating the data loses some nuance, but when the overall trends hold both within the United States and outside the United States in the countries reflected in the WVS, I believe it is safe to say that the relationship represented is likely robust. Some additional information on the GSS and the WVS and these variables are included in the methodological appendix.

The above approaches allow for comparisons to be made across spectra of religiosity, either from nonreligious to fundamentalist or not at all important to very important. These are the primary approaches used throughout the book (though others will occasionally be employed). I believe the resulting analyses are generally accurate and fair comparisons. However, this approach is not without its problems. As noted above, religiosity is multidimensional. The variables I use for my analyses are based largely on single dimensions—religious identification and importance of religion. That could be a problem and may cause some of the nuance in the relationships I am exploring to be missed. I'm willing to accept that risk in order to keep the analyses simple enough for a general audience to understand the figures I present, despite the noted limitations.

Unlike theologians who get to make up their subject matter, sociologists have to use data to make assertions about the social world. Going forward you'll see that this is a data-heavy book. I noted in this chapter that it is important to recognize that religiosity is a complex idea that is difficult to measure well. Some people are

FIGURE 2.2. Collective percentage of each religious type in WVS countries

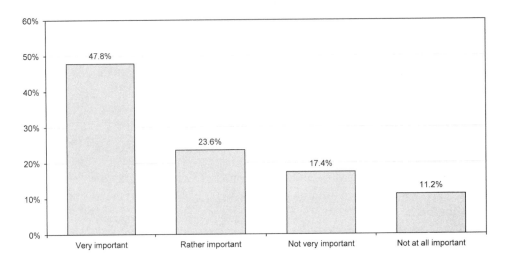

SOURCE: WVS, 1981–2008
NOTE: The sample, excluding those who are missing, includes 232,538 people.

religious in one way but not in another. Using single measures to compare people is not ideal. However, due to data constraints and my desire to make this book accessible to a general audience, I use simplistic but satisfactory measures of religiosity from the General Social Survey and the World Values Survey to reflect on relationships between religiosity and other constructs in the United States and the world, respectively. The resulting analyses are not perfect representations of the multidimensional nature of religion and its nuanced relationships with other aspects of the social world, but they are reasonably good approximations of overall patterns.

3

ALL BABIES ARE ATHEISTS
WHY BELIEF IN A SPECIFIC GOD IS NOT INNATE

Have you heard of Bobario? No?

Let me introduce you to him.

I was watching the movie *Rio* with my then two-year-old son, Toren, one day. The movie is about a blue macaw, Blu, whose owner takes him to Rio de Janeiro, Brazil, to mate him with another blue macaw. Of course an adventure ensues; it's a feature-length movie. As part of that adventure, Blu and the other birds fly around Rio de Janeiro, and in a rather beautifully executed animation sequence, they fly past the Christ the Redeemer statue. My son had at that time quite an extensive vocabulary, including such words as Harry Potter, trampoline, computer, tablet (he has an Android tablet), Granmary (that's what he calls my wife's mom), and Uncle Richard (the neighbor). He did not, however, know any religious words. He had not heard the words god, Jesus, religion, church, pray, or heaven often enough to have picked them up or to know what they meant. As the birds flew past the statue of Christ, Toren turned to me and said, "Who is that, Dad?"

You can call me a bad parent if you'd like, but I thought this would be a perfect opportunity to conduct an experiment. I am a scientist! Rather than try to explain that the statue was of a possibly mythical character named "Jesus" who supposedly walked on water, turned water into wine, was brutally murdered because he wanted to be, brought himself back from the dead, and then floated up into heaven, I had a different idea. I told him the statue was of a guy named "Bob."

Toren said, "Bob?" as though he wasn't quite sure if that was his name.

I replied, "Yep, that's Bob from Rio."

Toren nodded that he understood, then said, "Bobario." (He used to contract full sentences into single words.)

Laughing, I repeated it back to him, "Bobario."

And that's how "Bobario" was born. Now, whenever Toren sees a picture of

Jesus, I remind him that the person in the picture is named "Bobario."

During one of our trips to see family in Utah just after I told him about Bobario, we drove past a very prominent church. Toren, ever inquisitive, asked what the church was. I told him it was Bobario's house. Again, Toren nodded in understanding, and during the rest of the trip, whenever we drove past that church, Toren pointed to it and said, "Bobario's house." Several times there were family members in the car. Luckily, they couldn't make out what he was saying, so we didn't have to explain my experiment. During that same trip Toren saw a picture of Jesus on the wall at my mother-in-law's house and excitedly pointed to it and said, "Dad, look! Bobario!" Again, no one was around so we didn't have to explain why our son was calling Jesus "Bobario."

I'm sure some reading this think I'm a terrible father. Maybe I am. But my experiment with my son serves as a perfect illustration for this chapter: what Toren learns about the world and about religion is colored by his parents. He isn't born with religion any more than he is born a Republican or a Communist. He has to learn to be religious. He has to be taught to believe in god or gods or goddesses. Of course, in the case of my son, he won't be taught any of that. I'm sure at some point he'll learn about what his dad studies, and what his grandparents, aunts, uncles, and cousins and many others believe. He'll probably come talk to me about it at some point as well. We'll have a frank talk about religion, during which I'll likely hand him a copy of this book. Whether or not he'll choose to look into religion will be up to him.

Whether or not my son shows interest in religion at some point in the future doesn't change the fact that, at two, "Jesus" was just as meaningful to him as was "Bobario." My son perfectly illustrates that all babies are, in fact, atheists.

I really like saying, "All babies are atheists." It grabs peoples' attention and forces them to think about their taken-for-granted assumptions about religion. I think one of my students characterized peoples' responses accurately in a class discussion on this topic when he said, "The contrast of innocent, cute babies who everyone adores with irascible, immoral atheists is just too much; people can't take it when you put the two together in a sentence." Saying "All babies are atheists" bothers people. It bothers people not because it isn't true but because they don't want it to be true. In the United States in particular, atheists are a very hated minority. And they are hated because people distrust them and consider them immoral. Thus, the reason people don't like it when you say that babies are atheists is because it makes it seem like babies shouldn't be trusted and are immoral, and that's just a funny thought . . . unless you're Catholic.

Okay, so the statement gets under peoples' skin. But is it really accurate?

Yes, it is. With some clarification.

First, what does "atheist" really mean? While there have been a number of efforts to define and redefine the term, if you go to the etymological roots, it can easily be broken down. The prefix "a-" means "without" or "lacking." "Theos" is god. "Theism" is belief in a god. So, atheism is "without a belief in a god." When I explain this to people, they often find it surprising as they believe that "atheists" are god deniers—that is, atheists are believed to run around pointing at people's gods and declaring, "Your god doesn't exist. Na na na na na. There are no gods anywhere, ever, at all. Zip. Zero. Zilch." And then they punch you in the face, steal your kids, and, um, rape your horses.

Well, that's not really accurate. There are some atheists who deny the existence of a god or gods. As noted in chapter 1, such atheists are called "positive" atheists, as they make a positive assertion about the nonexistence of a deity. There are others who don't deny the existence of a deity; they simply lack a belief in that deity. These atheists are "negative" atheists, as they do not make a positive assertion of nonexistence but rather a negative assertion of nonexistence, or something like, "I don't know that there is no god." Some would consider this to be the equivalent of agnosticism. It's technically not. Agnosticism means you lack any knowledge about an entity called "god." Again, "a-" means "without." "Gnosis" means "knowledge." Thus, an agnostic is someone without knowledge, typically without knowledge of a god.

With these definitions laid bare, you should be able to make the next connection: being a negative atheist does not preclude one from being an agnostic. In fact, I'm guessing most of the people reading this right now are both negative atheists and agnostics toward Njörðr. What that means is that you (1) lack a belief in Njörðr as a deity but you also (2) have no knowledge of such a god (if you do have knowledge of this god, kudos to you for knowing your Norse pantheon). You can, quite accurately, say, "I am an agnostic and an atheist toward Njörðr." This doesn't prevent you from simultaneously being a theist or believer in, say, Jehovah or Allah or Aphrodite or, my personal favorite, Ba'al from *Stargate SG-1*.

This discussion of, as one of my colleagues put it, "the denominations of atheism," brings us back to the original point, that all babies are atheists. Now that you understand that atheism does not necessarily mean "denier of all gods everywhere and anywhere at all times and in all places" but rather can mean something as simple as "lacking belief in a god," it's pretty obvious that all babies are, in fact, negative atheists and also agnostics, just like you were toward Njörðr before reading this chapter. Babies lack a belief in a god. And, as my story above illustrates, they never need believe in a god either. In order for babies, who eventually become abstract-thought-capable children, to believe in a god, they must be taught to believe in a god, which is the subject of the next chapter. The point of this chapter is simply to illustrate that belief in a *specific* god is not innate.

There is a potential counterargument here that I have come across in previous discussions of this point. In expressing the sentiment that all babies are atheists in a peer-reviewed article that I published, one reviewer suggested that this assertion was not true because babies do not have a clear concept of self and therefore any discussion of their beliefs is moot. He argued that once babies develop a self, a process that involves the internalization of their respective culture, then discussions of what they believe can take place. Since culture exists prior to the "self" existing, then the self is always going to be the result of the culture in which the self is socialized. In the mind of this reviewer, babies can't be atheists because they don't know the term and they could only become atheists once they can explore the possibility of atheism. In his mind, you have to be taught about god and atheism before you can *not* believe in a god. This individual would be correct if atheist only meant "positive atheist." This reviewer obviously didn't know what you and I both know now, did he? Had he understood the "denominations of atheism" I outlined above, he might have realized that there are multiple ways of not believing in a god, including ignorance. Just like most readers of this book were ignorant of Njörðr before reading this chapter, babies are simply ignorant of the very concept of god. And they definitely do not have knowledge of any specific deities. Thus, all babies are negative atheists and agnostics: they lack a belief in any and all gods and have no knowledge of such gods.

I have also encountered another objection to this idea. In a discussion I had over this issue with one of my brothers, a devout Mormon, he noted the Mormon belief that all people are born with the "Light of Christ." In Mormon theology, the "Light of Christ" is defined as the power of God, through Jesus Christ, that gives life and light to all things and influences humans to do good. It is basically the supernatural equivalent of the human conscience. Thus, Mormons believe all children are born with an innate urge to become Christians because God dwells inside them through Christ—except, I guess, people with antisocial personality disorder (aka psychopaths). They don't have a conscience. Oops! If they don't have a conscience, is it because god made a mistake or because god is mean? The "Light of Christ" claim also falls short when you consider that some cultures have held values that contradict Mormon teachings, like the Mangaia who were taught to masturbate at about the age of eight and were encouraged to have as many sexual partners before marriage as possible. Because they were taught this was normal, they didn't feel guilt over it. How do you explain different cultural mores, Mormons?

In short, there is no biological proclivity toward any given religion or conception of god. All babies are atheists.

—§—

In summary, the default state of humans is nonbelief and ignorance toward all supernatural entities. People only believe in specific supernatural entities if they are taught to. Children can just as easily be taught to call any man with long hair and a beard "Bobario" and believe he lives in churches as they can be taught to call him "The Christ" and believe that he was a savior god. What all this means is, and you can say it with me this time: "All babies are atheists."

4

THE RELIGIOUS CLONE WARS
HOW MOST PEOPLE BECOME RELIGIOUS

In May 2010, Josh McAuley, a well-liked fifteen-year-old, was preaching on the streets of Smethwick, which is a suburb of Birmingham, in the United Kingdom. Josh decided to take a break from his evangelism to purchase some candy. On his way into the store the driver of a car lost control, slammed into Josh, and pinned him against a wall. The wall collapsed and Josh, still alive but horribly injured, was pulled from the rubble and flown by helicopter to Selly Oak Hospital in Birmingham. Doctors immediately began working on him, but when the doctors tried to give him a blood transfusion, Josh refused. As a minor, his parents could consent to the transfusion for him, forcing him to receive it. His parents did not force him. In fact, they supported Josh's decision to refuse the blood transfusion. Josh was a Jehovah's Witness, and that is why he refused the the procedure. He died from his wounds.

Josh is a victim of religious socialization.

"Socialization" is not the same thing as "socializing." "Socializing," in how it is typically used, is basically the equivalent of the modern phrase, "hanging out," as in, "I'm going to go socialize with friends." When people are socializing they are spending time with others; they are being "social." Socializing, in sociology and in the context of this chapter, means something different. It is part of socialization. Socialization is the process by which individuals become members of groups.

Think about a group you have joined. It can be something like starting a new job, joining a sports team, moving into a retirement home, or joining a nudist colony. In each of these situations there is a preexisting group with established norms, beliefs, values, and behaviors or a "culture." When you join a group, socialization is the process by which you learn the culture of that group. And learning the culture is how you become a member of the group. It is, in fact, a requirement of group membership. It can be a formal process, like the training new employees undergo at, say, Subway or Burger King. It can also be more informal, like learning the subtle nuances of how your teammates expect you to act in a recreational soccer league. The point is, there is a process by which people learn the culture of a group. The existing group members are the "agents" of socialization; they teach the new member what he/she needs to know in order to join the group.

Sociologists often divide socialization into two types: primary and secondary. Primary socialization is the initial socialization a child receives from her parents in order to become a member of the family and the broader society. It includes training in acceptable forms of behavior, language, beliefs, values, rituals, and other norms. Secondary socialization is more along the lines of the examples I gave above—joining a group after you've already experienced primary socialization. It's secondary in the sense that individuals undergoing secondary socialization have already been socialized into society; they are just learning the additional expectations for a specific group.

Religious socialization is basically the same. It can be primary or secondary. Most commonly, it is primary, which is to say, religion is typically passed on from parents to children. There are, of course, many people who join religions later in life and undergo secondary socialization into religion, but, in this chapter, I'm going to focus on primary socialization.

Religious socialization is pretty effective. The single best predictor of a child's religion is his or her parents' religion, and that continues throughout adolescence and even into adulthood. Figure 4.1 illustrates this. The figure contrasts adults' recollections of their religious affiliation at age sixteen (i.e., when they were adolescents) with their recollection of their parents' religious affiliation when they were growing up. For instance, someone could report that he was a Catholic at sixteen, as was his mother, but his father was a Jew. The figure shows that the concordance between parents' religious affiliation and their children's religious affiliation varies by religion, but, on average, teenagers have about an 85 percent chance of having their parents' religion. To be even more clear, here's how you can interpret this figure. Looking at the first two columns, you could say, among adults who recall being Protestants at age sixteen, 84.7 percent recall their fathers also being Protestant and 94.5 percent recall their mothers being Protestant as well. While this is retrospective data, it falls in line with data from other longitudinal sources that support this conclusion: children are likely to have the same religious identity as do their parents.

Figure 4.1. Percentage of Children Adhering to Parents' Religion as Teenagers

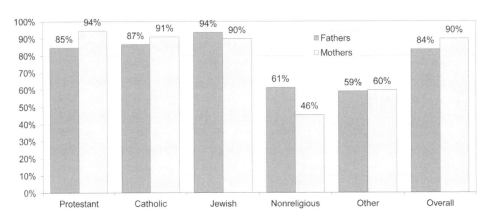

SOURCE: GSS, 1991, 1998, AND 2008; VARIABLES: MARELKID, PARELKID, & RELIG16

Religious socialization, then, is quite effective. Children are very likely to be religious clones of their parents. The figure also shows that, with some exceptions, there is greater concordance with mothers than with fathers, which is not surprising given that women are generally more religious and do more of the child rearing in the United States. Religious socialization is even more effective when both parents share the same religion. When they do not, research suggests children are more likely to adopt the religion of the more devout parent. Since that is typically the mother, mothers often win the religious clone wars.

Figure 4.2 is very similar to figure 4.1, except, instead of contrasting respondents' recollection of their religious affiliation at sixteen with their parents' religious affiliation, it contrasts respondents' current religious affiliation. In effect, figure 4.2 shows how likely adults are to retain the religious identity of their parents later in life. The concordance drops by about 10 percent overall, which suggests people grow more distant from their parents, religiously, as they age. However, socialization into religion appears to be pretty effective even later into life.

These figures illustrate that religious socialization is effective. But they also raise some interesting and important questions. Why is religious socialization so effective in passing religion on to children? What are the ramifications of parents socializing their children into religion? And should parents socialize their children into a religion? I'll take these in turn.

There are a number of reasons why religious socialization is so effective. The first is largely biological. There is some evidence that children have evolved to accept what their parents tell them as being true. This makes sense from an evolutionary stand-

FIGURE 4.2. Percentage of Children Adhering to Parents' Religion as an Adult

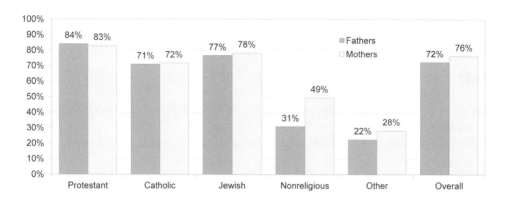

SOURCE: GSS, 1991, 1998, AND 2008; VARIABLES: MARELKID, PARELKID, & RELIG

point, as it can easily mean the difference between life and death. Telling a young child to stay away from a decrepit, abandoned house because it is haunted is a lie—and we all know it is. But there is a practical reason for doing this: abandoned homes can be dangerous for a variety of reasons. There could be loose flooring, walls, and ceilings, wild animals could have moved in, etc. Taking advantage of the gullibility of children is fairly common in parenting.

Maybe I should be ashamed about this, but I've taken advantage of my son's trust and obedience, though it's typically for his benefit. I've lied and told him things like "the cookies are all gone" so he'll stop looking for them and will eat healthier food. At about a year and a half, he didn't question me when I said things like that. But at two and a half, he started to get suspicious and would occasionally double-check.

Lying about the cookies being gone is a little different from teaching kids about god. In the cookie lie, I'm claiming something is gone that is not, and it's empirically verifiable. In teaching children about god, parents are teaching their children to believe in something for which there is no evidence, and there is no way to gather evidence (i.e., it's not empirically verifiable). In both cases, children typically believe their parents. In the former they can verify what their parents are claiming; in the later they cannot. Given their biological proclivity to do so, children typically do believe their parents.

This is precisely why religion is so easily passed on to children from parents, particularly lazy parents. When children are old enough to start asking questions about how the world works, they are also not sufficiently cognitively developed to question what their parents tell them. When a child asks what causes the rain and a parent says, "God," kids literally believe that is true. And when parents tell their kids, "God is watching you, so you better behave," the kids literally believe a god is watching them. Whether it is moral or kind to do this is a different question, which I won't address. My point is that parents say such things, socializing their children into religion as a result.

In addition to the biological explanation for why children believe what their parents tell them, kids typically idolize their parents, want to be like them, and want to please them. Kids also learn from observing and imitating their parents' behavior. If kids witness their parents praying regularly, kids will learn that this is what adults do and it will become part of their regular routine. To the extent that religion is encouraged by parents, children respond accordingly. If parents strongly encourage religious beliefs and behaviors in their children, they will have more religious children, on average. If parents do not encourage such behaviors, their children are likely to be less religious. Thus, in addition to the biological imperative, children are directly and indirectly taught how to be their parents' religious clones.

But why does it stick? Humans are creatures of habit. Some might argue that this is because we are lazy, but it's really an efficiency issue—if we can habitualize behaviors, we don't need to spend cognitive resources on these behaviors and instead can spend those resources on other issues. One of the best illustrations of this is the shower routine. Every person I have asked has a shower routine. Of course the routines vary from person to person, but each has a routine. People know they have a routine, but they don't typically think about either the routine or the fact that they have a routine until the routine is interrupted or someone annoying like me points out that they have a routine. Because the actions taking place in the shower are routine, we don't have to spend cognitive resources on them and instead can think about things like: what we have to do at work, what we're going to do on our day off, or what we need to do to get laid that night. We habitualize as many parts of our day as possible, allowing us to conserve cognitive resources for the parts of our day that require them. What does our habitualizing of everyday life have to do with religion? Lots of people go to church and are religious because it is just what they do. They grew up doing it; they continue doing it. They don't think that much about it. It may not even be all that important to them, but they still do it, because that's just what they do.

Religions know that humans are creatures of habit! If they can get kids socialized into the religion early on, the odds go up that they will keep the kids later in life. In order to get children engaged with religion early, religions have introduced ideas like limbo, baptism, and confirmation. While not an official doctrine, limbo, combined with original sin, has a strong motivational effect: it urges parents to involve their children in the religion as infants. While there are similar ideas and rituals in other religions (e.g., bar mitzvah in Judaism), Catholic rites like confirmation and communion serve a socializing function, drawing children into the religion.

Religions aren't the only institutions that attempt to socialize people into their groups. Corporations do the same thing. When I was in graduate school at the University of Cincinnati, I observed firsthand how Microsoft used this tactic. The University of Cincinnati had an arrangement with Microsoft to sell its software to faculty and students at a huge discount. I was able to buy a copy of Windows XP in 2002 for twelve dollars. The entire Office Suite, which typically sold for close to two hundred dollars, was also twelve dollars. Why would Microsoft agree to sell its software for so little? First, it was likely still making money off the software—the CDs it came on did not cost twelve dollars to produce. But second, and far more importantly, it knew that if it could get faculty and students used to using its software, they would be reticent to switch from it in the future. Selling it for cheap to students would likely reap substantial long-term profits once the students graduated, as they would have developed familiarity with and habits specific to the software.

That we become accustomed to things like software and religion is, in fact, quite logical. We have invested time into learning something. When that thing we have invested time into is religion, we develop and accumulate "religious capital." Religious capital functions like any other type of capital. Unless someone has more than she could ever really need, once she has accumulated capital, she won't want to just throw it away. Thus, when it comes to the socialization of children into religions, it is well worth the time, effort, and money religions put into things like Sunday School, summer Bible Camps, youth groups, and other activities geared toward children, as these activities translate into religious capital that people want to conserve. The end result is that children, as they age, are reticent to throw that capital away, which means they are likely to stay in the religion where they have capital. Religions target young people for precisely this reason.

Thus, religious socialization is effective because it typically starts very young, when kids believe pretty much everything they are told by adults. Children want to be like adults and learn from adults. And children, like adults, develop habits, and those habits turn into religious capital, which adults don't want to throw away. If you think about this from the perspective of religions, targeting kids is one of the smartest things they can do for their long-term success. I mean, who doesn't want an army of clones? If it was good enough for the Republic, it's got to be good enough for the pope, right?

What are the consequences of parents socializing their children into religion? While there are lots of consequences, as will be laid out in the other chapters in this book, I focus here on just two. First, their kids are religious. And that means they get all the positives *and* negatives that come with religion. Second, children are not typically given the chance to consider alternatives. This second consequence has actually been established through surveys and interviews. Basically, nonreligious individuals, when asked how they are going to raise their children, almost universally say that they will let their kids decide whether or not they want to be religious and, while they'll talk to them about alternatives, they will support them in whatever their decision is. The same cannot be said of religious fundamentalists, who have every intention of indoctrinating their children to think exactly how they do (religious moderates and liberals fall between these positions). In fact, religious fundamentalists go so far as to report that, if they met a young person raised in a nonreligious home who was questioning her beliefs, they would happily try to convince her to become a religious fundamentalist like themselves. Nonreligious people say they would treat them the same as their own kids—encourage them to explore all their options but not try to persuade them one way or the other. Religious fundamentalists literally want religious clones, which makes my literary allusion all the more disturbing.

I'm reminded here of my time spent as a Mormon missionary. In hindsight I realize just how naive I was when I embarked on my mission. I knew virtually nothing about any other religion when I started my mission in 1996. By the time my mission ended in 1998, I still knew next to nothing about most other religions (I learned a bit here and there). Yet, I spent two years trying to convince people that my religion was right and their religions were wrong, without knowing jack shit about their religions. You'd have to try to be more naive than I was! Naivety is probably why young Mormons are willing to serve missions. If they knew more about their own religion and other religions, they'd probably come to the conclusion that trying to convince other people they are wrong and that Mormons are right is a colossal waste of time and resources. I didn't know about other religions because I was socialized into a religion in such a fashion that alternatives were only presented as evil.

Finally, should parents socialize their children into their same religious or nonreligious views?

Yes.

You did read that correctly. I said "Yes." I'm sure some readers will wonder why I said yes in light of what you just read. Here's my logic: there is no way to stop religious socialization without opening a massive can of legal worms. If you suggest that parents should not socialize their children into their own religion, what other things can parents not teach their children? Can they not discuss politics with them? What about parents' views on race or sexuality? Should parents be disallowed from teaching their kids either that homosexuality is immoral (the traditionally religious position) or that it is moral? With few exceptions, I don't think there should be regulations placed on what parents can or cannot teach their kids. I'm pretty libertarian in this sense. Parents should have the right to teach their kids pretty much what they want. I say that primarily out of self-interest. If the majority in the United States got to dictate what I could and could not teach my son, I'd probably have to teach him that he should be a Christian. I don't want to do that. Since I don't want to be forced to do that, it seems only fair that I can't force other parents to teach their kids my values and beliefs. That means I'm in favor of religious indoctrination, but only because I'm also in favor of irreligious indoctrination.

What about claims by people like Richard Dawkins that religious indoctrination is a form of child abuse? This is an area where Dawkins is extreme in his views and fails to recognize that religiosity ranges along a continuum, from extreme religious fundamentalism to strident atheistic secularism. If you sat Richard Dawkins down with a Quaker mother and her ten-year-old daughter and let Dawkins listen in while the mother explained how her religious beliefs inspired her social activism toward peace and equality, I don't think Richard Dawkins would scream, "Abuse!" He'd probably say that supernatural beliefs are not required to support equality and pacifism, but, because he would presumably agree with what is being taught, just not the justification, he'd be in an awkward situation. It would begin to look like he's saying that teaching kids anything with which he disagrees is child abuse. I find that a much scarier proposition than letting religious parents socialize their kids into their religions. No one should be able to dictate what parents can and cannot teach their children about religion.

But aren't some forms of religious indoctrination akin to child abuse? Sure. But couldn't parents threatening to disown their kids if they believe in a god also be considered a form of child abuse? The real issue here is not religious indoctrination but rather abusive parenting. While abusive parenting is far more likely to occur among the religiously fundamentalist than the nonreligious (see chapter 12), it could also occur among the nonreligious. In short, religious socialization can be abusive. Typically, it is not.

Primary religious socialization is the process by which children are taught the necessary elements of culture to become members of religions. It's very effective, as children have very high odds of retaining the religion they were taught, even as adults. Religions want parents to turn their children into religious clones, and religiously fundamentalist parents try hard to accomplish that. Socializing children into religion is highly effective for a variety of reasons, from our biological imperative to trust our parents to the accumulation of religious capital that makes it hard to leave religions. One of the main consequences of religious socialization is that it results in children not being presented with religious/irreligious options. Children raised by nonreligious parents seldom have this problem and are more likely to expose their children to multiple ideas or at least less likely to push certain beliefs over others. Despite the problems with religious socialization, it is hard to argue against it, as that is a slippery slope. Drawing a line between protecting children from abuse and protecting children from learning what their parents believe isn't easy. However, generally speaking, religious socialization is not abusive.

5

WHY YOU DON'T KNOW WHY YOU'RE (NON)RELIGIOUS
WHY SOCIAL NETWORKS MATTER

While on my Mormon mission in Costa Rica I regularly went out knocking on doors to try to interest people in converting to Mormonism. While engaged in this activity one day with my companion, we walked up to a rather nice house on one of the nicer streets in a suburb of San José called Desamparados. A middle-aged man was just walking out of the front door. We greeted him and he responded with a look of disdain. Before we could even give our standard spiel about us being representatives of The Church of Jesus Christ of Latter-day Saints with a really important message for him, he said, "You're wasting your time. I was born a Catholic and I'll die a Catholic."

Intrigued—which is a pretty common state of being for me—I asked him why he would say that. He didn't initially want to engage with me, but I convinced him that I was actually sincere since I had never heard anyone say that before. He succinctly explained that he was raised Catholic, that Catholicism was part of being a member of his family, and that he saw no need to consider alternatives, as Catholicism suited him just fine. That was the first time someone said to me, "I was born a member of religion X and I will die a member of religion X," but not the last.

In the previous two chapters I explained two important points. First, we are not born believing in the supernatural. Second, we have to be taught to believe in the supernatural and religious dogma. The question of concern in this chapter is why we continue to believe in religious teachings and supernatural ideas. Said in another way, "Do you know why you remain (non)religious?" I've interviewed and spoken with thousands of people about their religion. They all seem to think they know why they hold the religious views they do. I'll bet you have a reason, too. But it's probably not the real reason why you are what you are, or at least not the entire explanation. Humans don't always know why they do what they do or think what they think. Really, we don't.

First, for those who were raised in a religion and remain a member of that religion, which I showed is a pretty substantial percentage of people, the answer as to why many are what they are is simple—they never question their beliefs. I don't mean that to be insulting. I'm not suggesting that these people aren't intelligent or thoughtful in other ways. They very well may be. But they honestly don't think much about their religious beliefs.

They are socialized into a religion and never really see a reason to question what it is they have been taught all their life. But it isn't just because they have no reason to question their beliefs. It's also because of their social environment. They are surrounded by and surround themselves with people who think and believe just like they do. They marry someone with the same beliefs. They go to church with people they think share their beliefs. And their religious worldview is sufficiently explanatory to address all of the concerns they have throughout their life: Why am I here? What happens when I die? Why should I not rape sheep? Why does god have a beard? etc.

While I am quite critical of religion, I do respect it. Religions are still around because they have developed what appears to be a credible perspective on the world. From an evolutionary perspective, this makes perfect sense. If you assume that institutions, like living things, compete for scarce resources to survive, then those institutions best able to reproduce themselves in a competitive environment will succeed. In a competitive environment, religions must evolve, just like living things do. The major religions around today are the ones that have outcompeted other religions by evolving to a state that is credible to at least some people. They succeeded because they are fairly well adapted. Even if you are not a fan of religions, at the very least you should respect them because they have fought, some literally for millennia, to survive. The result is that they seem, at least under superficial inspection, to be credible and compelling.

For the individual who rarely or never questions his beliefs, the pat answers provided by his religion will typically suffice. But how many never question? Since you are obviously interested enough in religion to read this book, you're probably thinking that most people question their religious beliefs—because you have probably questioned your religious beliefs. But . . . you'd be wrong.

Prior research suggests that anywhere from 50 percent to 75 percent of believers never doubt their religion or religious faith. This varies by the cause or source of doubt; some issues are more likely to cause doubts than are others. This is illustrated in figures 5.1 through 5.4, which come from the GSS.

Figure 5.1. Percentage Doubting Faith because of Evil in the World by Religious Group

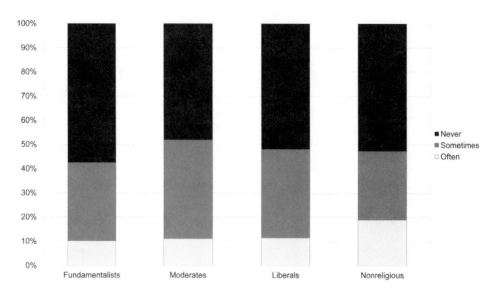

SOURCE: GSS, 1988 AND 1998

Figure 5.1 suggests that close to 50 percent of people in the four religious groups we have been examining—fundamentalists, moderates, liberals, and the nonreligious—have questioned their faith because there is evil in the world, though religious fundamentalists are the least likely to ever do so and the nonreligious do this the most often. Figure 5.2 is very similar; the source of doubt in this figure is suffering in the world.

In figures 5.3 and 5.4, there is a slightly different pattern. In figure 5.3, which shows the results of doubts based on science, the percentage who have *never* doubted their religious faith increases dramatically for the three religious groups, particularly religious fundamentalists but also religious liberals, though likely for different reasons. Religious fundamentalists are unlikely to question their religious faith over science because they reject science (see the next chapter), while religious liberals are unlikely to question their faith because their faith has conceded ground to science, resulting in their faith and science being less likely to contradict each other. The nonreligious are the most likely to report questioning their religious faith based on science, though the survey doesn't specify whether those questions occurred before leaving a religion or whether they are occurring in the present, which makes the data for the nonreligious somewhat difficult to interpret.

FIGURE 5.2. Percentage Doubting Faith because of Suffering in the World by Religious Group

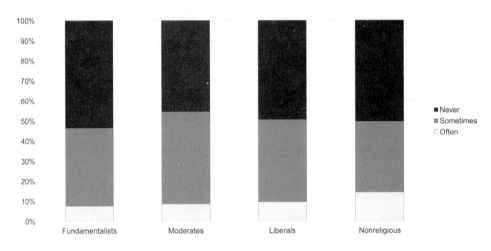

SOURCE: GSS, 1988 AND 1998

FIGURE 5.3. Percentage Doubting Faith because of Science by Religious Group

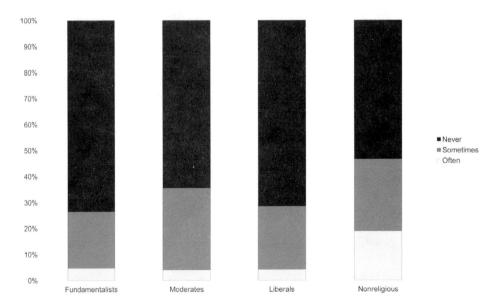

SOURCE: GSS, 1988 AND 1998

Figure 5.4 depicts a slightly different pattern. The cause of doubt in figure 5.4 is over meaninglessness in the universe. This issue results in increasingly higher levels of doubt as religiosity declines—over 80 percent of fundamentalists have never doubted their faith because of meaninglessness, while just over 60 percent of the nonreligious have never done so. Just 3 percent of the religious often doubt their faith over this issue.

Figure 5.4. Percentage Doubting Faith because of Meaninglessness by Religious Group

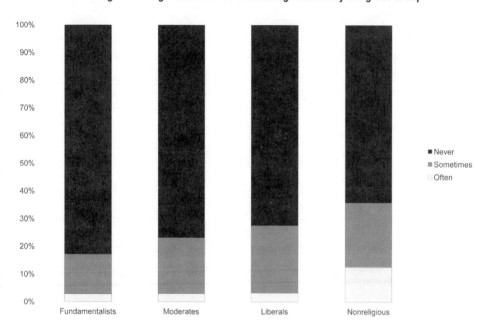

SOURCE: GSS, 1988 AND 1998

While there is a lot of information in the above figures, the primary point I want to make with them is that somewhere between 50 percent and 75 percent of people never—*never*—question their religious or supernatural beliefs. That's a pretty large number of people who pretty much coast through life believing what they were taught from infancy through childhood. Clearly people don't need to question their religious beliefs, but never wondering about such important questions seems like the very life not worth living that Socrates warned us against a couple thousand years ago. Such individuals are like the Catholic individual I met in Costa Rica—they are born with their religion and they'll likely die with it. Unless some traumatic event comes along to shake them up and force them to examine their beliefs, they are unlikely to ever seriously consider these issues.

Okay, but what about those who do doubt and question their beliefs? Current evidence suggests that there are some biological or psychological differences between those who don't believe and those who do. For instance, there is some evidence that atheists are more liberal and more intelligent. What does that have to do with biology? Liberals are biologically predisposed to change and embracing the unknown. Conservatives are, by definition and biological nature, opposed to change. They are neophobes; they do not like the unknown and prefer to play things safe. They prefer the status quo and are not fond of risk. Nonbelievers are less averse to risk. In short, believers and nonbelievers may be "wired" differently. It's not that the nonreligious don't want any security; they are just satisfied with the security provided by government or some other "worldly" source, while the religious turn to religion and god for an existential source of security. It is, therefore, possible that some people reject religion because they are biologically predisposed to do so. I believe such biologically predisposed people are the vanguard of secularization; they are secular innovators for whom religion just never worked.

But biology is not the only factor in the rejection of religion. Genetic inheritance studies suggest that social factors are more prominent and significant. And, guess what? That just happens to be my forte!

So, think about it like this. . . when people have doubts they turn to the people around them. If the person who is doubting is surrounded by believers—or at least people who pretend to believe—they are likely to resolve their doubts in favor of belief and retain their religion. Those surrounded by nonbelievers are likely to resolve their doubts in favor of skepticism and nonbelief and drop their religion. This is not unlike other aspects of peoples' lives. If those close to you are overweight, your odds of being overweight go up. If those close to you engage in criminal behavior, your odds of engaging in criminal behavior go up. If those close to you belong to a specific political party, your odds of belonging to that political party go up. Religion is no different. If those close to you belong to a specific religion, your odds of belonging to that specific religion go up. In fact, people are recruited into religions through social networks, and social networks help keep people in religions. Thus, if someone's social network transitions from being made up of largely believers to largely nonbelievers, the odds of that person becoming a nonbeliever go up as well. This obviously requires some people to be nonbelievers before they can have an influence on others. I just argued that some are biologically predisposed toward rejecting religion. Thus, the biologically predisposed may start the process by influencing some to leave, who then influence others, and so on. Some leave because their biology encourages it, but most leave because they don't have sufficient reasons to stay and are surrounded by people who are out of religion. The inverse could, of course, also be true.

What does all this mean? It means that people join and leave religions, not because they have thought or reasoned themselves in or out of religion, with some exceptions, but because that's what their friends and family are doing. But who wants to admit that they are just following the herd? In our remarkably individualistic society, admitting that you're a follower or suggesting you converted or deconverted because of your friend, spouse, parent, or child makes you seem, well, weak. So, people make up really compelling stories to justify what they have done, and those stories typically paint people in the best possible light.

I'll use myself as an example. Here are two possible stories I could tell about my decision to leave Mormonism. You choose the one you think I prefer to tell people.

Story #1: I lost my faith because I began to meticulously research Mormonism. As I studied my faith, I began to examine one key aspect of the religion—the Book of Mormon. Because the Book of Mormon can be interpreted as making factual claims (e.g., there were chariots, steel swords, horses, and elephants in the Americas prior to the arrival of Europeans), those claims can be investigated using the tools of science. I examined the archaeological evidence for the claims of the Book of Mormon and found that they were not true. There were no chariots, no steel swords, no horses, and no elephants in the Americas prior to the arrival of Europeans. Through this, along with many other intellectual discoveries, I became convinced that Mormonism was not true. I lost my faith through reason, intellectual inquiry, and science.

Story #2: I moved to Cincinnati, Ohio, for graduate school from Utah. In Utah, almost all of my friends and all of my family were Mormon, as was my wife and her family and friends. I spent a great deal of time socializing with my Mormon friends and family while in Utah. In fact, I rarely spent appreciable amounts of time with anyone but Mormons. As an active, believing, devout Mormon, I spent hours every week in church or in church-related activities. When I moved to Cincinnati, I had to develop a completely new social network. My wife and I did make connections with a local Mormon congregation and developed some fairly close friendships with some of the younger couples in that congregation. But we also became very good friends with many non-Mormons. In particular, one of my wife's classmates was a semidevout Catholic and her husband was a nondenominational Christian. One of my classmates, to whom I grew very close, was an Evangelical Christian, and he soon married another Evangelical Christian. Most of the faculty and other students in our programs were either nominally religious—with a few exceptions—or were not religious at all. During our first year in Cincinnati, we spent far more time with our non-Mormon friends than with our Mormon friends. In particular, I spent hours and hours with my classmate, Dean, who also happened to be struggling with doubts about his own faith. Dean and I engaged in many conversations about religion, and his non-Mormon perspective strongly influenced my views. Within a year, Dean and I had both decided that our conservative religious views were not defensible, and within another six months, we were both atheists. My wife, who was not an observant Mormon before I met her (she had been dating a Catholic) and had largely worked her way back into Mormonism during the time we were courting, was not a particularly devout Mormon. When I discussed the concerns I mentioned in story #1 with her, she agreed that they were insurmountable problems with Mormonism. We left together, and became nonreligious at the same time as did Dean and his wife. We fit right in with many of our professors, classmates, and new friends. In other words, our social network shifted from being mostly Mormon to mostly non-Mormon and largely nonreligious. As a result, so did we.

Story #1 makes me seem like I'm smart, rational, and inquisitive. It also makes me seem like I pursue truth wherever I find it and that I thought my way out of religion. It's much more respectable than the second story. In story #2 I end up seeming like I left religion because those around me were not religious and I was giving up religion just to fit in. The reality is a combination of the two stories, of course, but most people are oblivious to the social influences on their lives. By changing my social network, the barriers to exiting religion, which are quite high for Mormons, were substantially reduced. If I left, yes, I would have to face the wrath of my still-Mormon family, but they lived 1,600 miles away and I communicated with them only infrequently. The people immediately around me were not religious and did not reject me when I decided to leave but rather embraced my decision. Social networks are a major factor influencing religious belief and nonbelief.

So, why are you (non)religious? If you're like most people, it's because you've never questioned your beliefs. Some people, however, may reject religion or pursue religion because of a biological predisposition to do so. But for many people, whether they are or remain religious or nonreligious is tied to their social network. If they are enmeshed in a religious social network and have doubts, the doubts will likely be resolved in favor of religion, and they will remain religious. If they are enmeshed in a nonreligious social network, the doubts will likely be resolved in favor of non-religion, and they will likely exit religion. People tell self-aggrandizing stories to justify why they are religious or nonreligious. While some aspects of those stories are likely true, it's unlikely the case that the stories people tell encapsulate all of the relevant factors. In reality, most people are quite oblivious to why they are religious or nonreligious.

6

SUNDAY F~~S~~CHOOL
WHY RELIGION AND EDUCATION DON'T GO TOGETHER

In late 2008, Shamsia Husseini, a seventeen-year-old Afghan girl, was walking to school with her sister. A man pulled up to her and her sister on a motorcycle and asked her if she was going to school. Shamsia replied that she was. With no hesitation, the man pulled Shamsia's burqa from her head and sprayed her face with acid. The acid disfigured her face. It also affected her vision, leaving it blurred and making it difficult for her to read. The damage was so severe doctors in Afghanistan could not treat her and Shamsia had to leave the country for additional medical attention.

Despite the horrific attack on her, Shamsia continues to attend school, and her parents support her efforts. Her mother, like many women in Afghanistan, cannot read or write. And that is precisely how the Taliban want it to be. With limited education, Afghan women are highly dependent upon men. Likewise, many Afghan men with limited education do not have the knowledge and critical thinking skills to question Taliban leadership.

Shamsia understood why this random stranger sprayed her with acid, "The people who did this to me don't want women to be educated. They want us to be stupid things." She left two elements out of her explanation. First, the Taliban want women to be uneducated to control them. Second, they justify their behavior with religion.

—§—

Education has long been seen by some religions as an enemy. Some, even today, openly disparage education. This is obviously the case among the Taliban in Afghanistan. But even in the United States, Jehovah's Witnesses disparage higher education and recommend Christian education instead of college—that is, Sunday school lessons prepared by the Watchtower Society. Yet, if the educational attainment and incomes of Jehovah's Witnesses are any indication of how successful their Sunday school training is, it really is more accurate to call it "Sunday fool training," because Jehovah's Witnesses rank dead last in educational attainment and income.

Why have religions opposed education, and why do some continue to do so? Education increases peoples' ability to think critically about religion and expands people's knowledge of other religions. Comparative religion and critical thinking are anathema to religious indoctrination; they substantially increase the odds of leaving religions.

The results of religions disparaging education to varying degrees can be seen in the educational attainment of members of the different religious groups in question. Figure 6.1 shows the average years of educational attainment by religiosity in the United States; twelve years of education is the equivalent of a high school diploma, sixteen years is the equivalent of a college degree; eighteen years or more is the equivalent of a graduate degree. The more religiously fundamentalist people are, the lower their educational attainment, though religious liberals do have the highest levels of education, with the nonreligious coming in second.

FIGURE 6.1. Years of Education by Religious Group

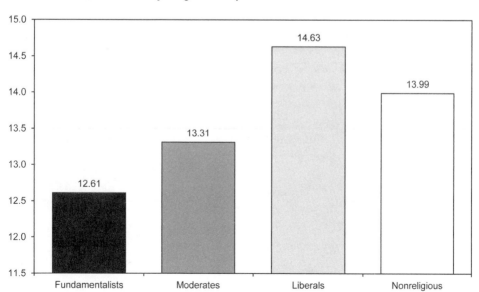

SOURCE: GSS, 2010

FIGURE **6.2. Educational Attainment by Importance of Religion**

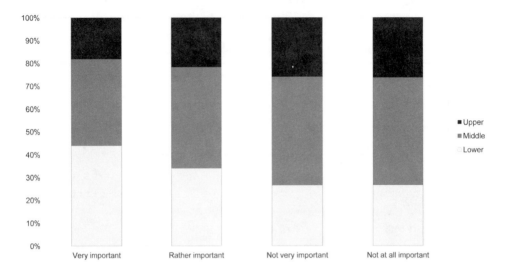

SOURCE: WVS

Figure 6.2 shows a similar relationship between education and religiosity outside the United States. Using WVS data, figure 6.2 breaks down educational attainment into three groups—those with upper, middle, and lower levels of educational attainment relative to the specific country—for each level of religiosity. As the percentages show, individuals who report that religion is very important to them report the lowest levels of educational attainment, while those who say religion is not very important or not at all important report the highest levels of educational attainment.

Prior research has shown that the lower educational attainment of the most religious is largely the result of parents and religious leaders disparaging education. Research has also shown that increases in religiosity reduce desire to continue one's college education.

It is also possible that the causal relationship is somewhat reversed as individuals with lower levels of education may find religion more appealing. Likewise, less intelligent people may find religion more appealing. The most highly educated people in the United States, scientists, are substantially less religious than is the general population, and the more elite the scientists, the less religious they are. While the causality between intelligence and religiosity is complicated by education, evidence for the idea that less intelligent people may be more attracted to religion can be seen in scores on intelligence and reasoning tests included in the GSS.

FIGURE 6.3. Scores on Vocabulary Test by Religious Group

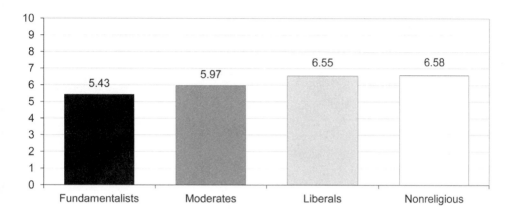

SOURCE: GSS, 2010

Figure 6.3 compares the scores of the four religious groups on a vocabulary test. Fundamentalists have the lowest average score and the nonreligious have the highest (the difference is 1.15, but, on a 10-point scale, that's an 11.5 percent difference; also, the difference between fundamentalists and the nonreligious is statistically significant, meaning it is not due to chance).

On a slightly different measure examining reasoning ability, a similar pattern is observed and is shown in figure 6.4. Religious fundamentalists have the worst reasoning ability, with 38 percent getting the test completely wrong, while the nonreligious appear to have the best reasoning ability, with 31 percent getting the test completely wrong and 43 percent getting the test completely right.

Of course, the differences in vocabulary and reasoning scores between the religious and nonreligious above are not enormous, but they are in the direction we would expect (and, again, statistically significant). Research has also shown a similar relationship between religiosity and intelligence at the country level; countries with higher average IQs are less religious.

It is also worth noting that college education may not uniformly reduce religiosity. Because college education increases civic engagement, individuals who make it through college with their faith intact attend religious services more frequently. However, college does appear to reduce religious orthodoxy, which means it does appear to reduce religiosity, generally, even though it may increase participation in religion for some.

Figure **6.4. Scores on Reasoning Tests by Religious Group**

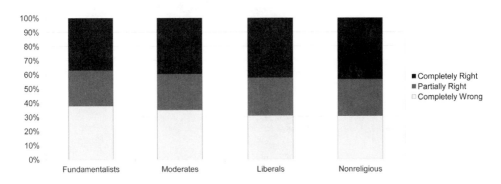

SOURCE: GSS, 1972–2010

—§—

What, then, can we say about religion, education, and intelligence? The more religious individuals are, the lower their IQ and their educational attainment, though to what extent the relationship between these three variables is causal is not clear. Far from educating members, then, Sunday school turns the religious into " fools," which is rather ironic considering the Bible calls atheists " fools" (see Psalm 14:1). What can be concluded from this chapter is that more fundamentalist religions play prominent roles in impeding the educational attainment and even the educational aspirations of their members.

7

I'LL BE A MONKEY'S COUSIN
RELIGION AND SCIENCE

I remember very clearly the first time science and religion conflicted for me. I was sitting in a classroom on the first floor of the now-demolished Morgan Middle School in Morgan, Utah, my hometown. The classroom was just around the corner from the principal's office and the windows were to my left. It was a fifth grade class on American history. The teacher was discussing the settlement of the Americas and said that Native Americans were descendants of Asians who came across the Bering Sea during an ice age when there were glaciers covering most of North America. The ice age lowered ocean levels, exposing a land bridge, allowing humans to cross from the far reaches of Siberia to the Americas. I remember very clearly listening to this explanation from my teacher and thinking to myself, "She can't really believe that! She's a Mormon, just like me. We know where the Native Americans came from. They were Jews and they were led to the Americas by God in a boat. It says so in the Book of Mormon. And if it says so in the Book of Mormon, it has to be true!"

I was eleven or twelve years old at the time. I was a very devout and obedient little kid. I took the directions of my religious leaders and parents seriously. When Ezra Taft Benson, the Mormon prophet during most of my formative years, urged all Mormons to read the Book of Mormon, I did. And then I read it again, and again, and again. Unfortunately, it didn't get any more interesting the more times I read it. But I now realize why I was told to read it so often: if I spent all my time reading the Book of Mormon, I wouldn't be able to read other books that were actually filled with useful information, which is pretty much any other book. It's a brilliant strategy to keep members of your religion ignorant. Even today I regret having spent so many hours poring over scripture as though something magical would occur after the tenth reading and the heavens would suddenly open to me, revealing all of god's secrets. As I talk with my colleagues in sociology and other academic disciplines, it's apparent that most of them spent much of their childhood reading popular children's books and their adolescence and teens reading classic literature. Some even dug into popular science. All the while I was rereading the Book of Mormon.

Granted, it's really not all bad that I took this religious advice seriously. I'm one of probably just a handful of people on the planet who has read the Bible from cover to cover *and* all of the books of Mormon scripture from cover to cover. That's a total of 2,476 pages of text, and a lot of begetting, violence, bigotry, misogyny, and remarkably implausible stuff. Plus I reread the Book of Mormon another eleven or so times from cover to cover (about 5,841 additional pages). Just to put that into context, *The Harvard Classics*, compiled by Charles W. Eliot, contains about 21,600 pages, or just slightly more than double the pages of scripture I read. Had I been reading that instead of Mormon scripture, I would have been reading Plato, Francis Bacon, Benjamin Franklin, Adam Smith, Charles Darwin, John Stuart Mill, Thomas Hobbes, Jean Jacques Rousseau, David Hume, and Blaise Pascal, among many others.

The conflict I experienced over the scientific and religious explanations I was taught about the settling of the Americas was not the only time science and religion conflicted for me. I thirsted for knowledge and took every advanced placement class I could in high school. One of those was AP Biology. I ran into the classic evolution-creationism issue during that time. Amazingly, this conflict was decided in favor of evolution rather quickly. I had a remarkable biology teacher in high school, Gary Mowery, who built such a compelling case that creationism didn't really stand a chance. It was at that point that I realized I really was a monkey's cousin, and that that was nothing to be ashamed of.

Strangely, my parents didn't discourage my pursuit of education and my fascination with science. In fact, they encouraged it, but probably without being fully aware of the potential ramifications. Both my parents have bachelor's degrees—from Brigham Young University, the flagship school of the Mormon Church. My mother has a nursing degree and my father has a business degree. While they both took science classes, they are not scientists and were taught science largely in a context where science was often coupled with religion in ways that either reconciled the two or put religion first. As a result, I don't think my parents ever saw any threat to my religion because I was studying science. They viewed science as a means to an end for me—a successful career that would facilitate my continued participation in religion. Um, yeah. . . not so much. But their attitude toward education and science

FIGURE 7.1. Percentage Who Know Correct Answer on Science Questions by Religious Group

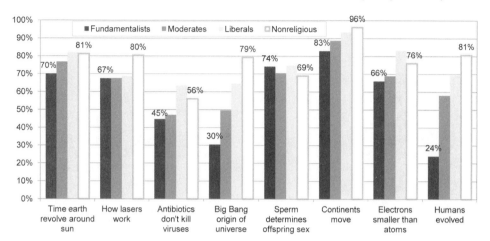

SOURCE: GSS, 2010

is fairly common among the religious, most of whom do not really feel they are or need be in conflict with religion.

However, the more religious you are, particularly the more religiously fundamentalist you are, the more you oppose science and the less you know about it. This is clearly illustrated in this chapter's figures. Figure 7.1 shows the percentage of Americans in 2010 in each religious group who gave the correct answer to scientific questions like, "How long does it take the earth to revolve around the sun?" or "Electrons are smaller than atoms, true or false?" With just one exception, religious fundamentalists know the least about science. Generally, the most knowledgeable about science are religious liberals and the nonreligious.

Figure 7.2 gives a slightly different view on this issue. It shows the percentages of Americans in 2010 who agree or strongly agree with two questions. The first is whether we put too much emphasis on science rather than faith. The second is whether science makes our way of life change too quickly. These questions basically reflect antiscience attitudes. On both, the nonreligious are clearly the most accepting of science.

Conveniently, the WVS included two similar questions, though participants were asked to rate their responses along a scale ranging from 1 to 10, with 1 being complete disagreement and 10 being complete agreement. The two questions are nearly identical to those in figure 7.2. The first asks if we depend too much on science and not enough on faith. The second asks how strongly participants agree

Figure 7.2. Attitudes toward Science by Religious Group

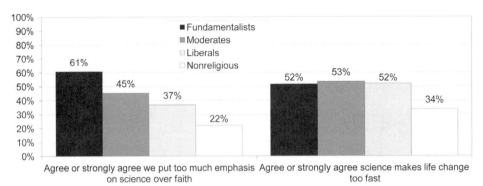

SOURCE: GSS, 2010

that science makes our way of life change too fast (see figure 7.3). The relationship between religiosity and the responses isn't quite as distinct as it is in the United States, but a similar pattern emerges: the least religious are the most accepting of science.

All three figures illustrate that more religious individuals tend to be more opposed to and less knowledgeable about science, with religious fundamentalists generally being the most ignorant and most opposed to science. Nonreligious individuals tend to be the most knowledgeable and the most in favor of science.

Two additional points are worth mentioning in this chapter. First, I'm a scientist. As such, it's kind of hard for me to be even remotely objective on this issue. It really bothers me that people oppose science, especially given all of the wonderful things science has provided us: modern medicine, computers, smartphones, cars, airplanes, knowledge in lots of areas, etc. Sure, there are risks and concerns with science. I've been to Hiroshima and Atomic City, Idaho; I'm well aware of the dangerous potential of science. But my general view is that science is a net positive for humanity. What's more, most of those who oppose science do so in theory, but in practice they are *all* beneficiaries of science and they all use it in their daily lives. Even groups that claim to reject modern technology, like the Amish, don't reject all of the benefits of science. They simply chose to stop accepting scientific advances after a rather arbitrary point in time.

Those who oppose science are also, unfortunately, slowing science. The primary reason people oppose science is religion. Some religious people aggressively oppose science, working to reduce education and increase ignorance. As I noted, I have a bias here. That leads me to say forthrightly that this is one of the things I really, really hate about religion. Granted, not all religions and religious people

FIGURE 7.3. Attitudes toward Science by Importance of Religion

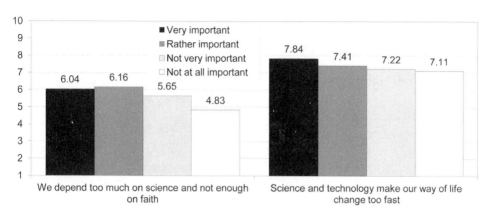

SOURCE: WVS, 2010
NOTE: 1=COMPLETELY DISAGREE; 10=COMPLETELY AGREE

oppose science. To those, I say, "Thank you!" To the many, many religious people who oppose science on religious grounds, I say, "You don't deserve to benefit from science, you fucking hypocrites!" Did I mention this issue bothers me?

What about the objection that religion plays an important role in holding science back from doing bad things? This is not an uncommon objection put forth by some ethicists who argue that scientists cannot evaluate the morality associated with their science and therefore must draw upon religion as a guide for what science should be done. They have a point in the sense that scientists are not trained ethicists. But there are two simple responses to this point. To begin with, scientists are not automatons; they are thinking, feeling, responsible individuals. Sure, sometimes they do objectionable things. But scientists rarely pursue knowledge with no regard for the consequences. Additionally, why would religion-based ethics be required for this when secular philosophy (i.e., secular ethics) is perfectly suitable? Religion brings little more to this discussion than principles based on the archaic writings of people who knew next to nothing about science.

This leads to my second and final point. Stephen Gould, a quite famous evolutionary biologist, argued that religion and science are "non-overlapping magisteria." The basic idea he was suggesting is that religion addresses questions that science can't answer, while science answers questions that religion can't answer. For instance, scientists are unable to gather data on what happens after we die. Religion can conveniently step in when such questions arise and offer an answer. It's a completely baseless answer, but it's an answer, and it's not something science can do. Thus, in Gould's framework, religion is limited to answering questions that science cannot answer.

That's all well and good if you limit what you mean by religion to liberal, non-literalistic, relatively modern religions. If you don't limit your definition of religion to very specific religions that have, in fact, embraced modern science (like most mainline Protestants), but instead expand it to all religions, what you get is a very different picture. Religions have, historically, claimed to answer not only the questions science cannot answer today, but also many of the questions that science has now answered. For example, religions have claimed to answer: the age of the earth (Genesis 1:31), whether the earth revolves around the sun or vice versa (Psalms 93:1), the shape of the earth (Job 38:13), the origins of humans and other living things (Genesis 1 and 2), the origins of different languages (Genesis 11:5–8), and the characteristics of animals (see Leviticus 11:19 and Leviticus 11:22). These are just a few topics where religion claimed to have an answer and has since been shown by science to be completely and utterly wrong. Historically, then, many religions answered questions that eventually became the domain of science.

However, as science advanced, some religions retreated. This is, in fact, part of why some religions are called "liberal," because they became less orthodox in light of modernization. Those religions are likely the ones Gould was thinking of when he suggested his non-overlapping magisteria idea. But not all religions retreated. Some religions, specifically more fundamentalist religions, have tried to hold their ground. Religions in the Pentecostal tradition and Southern Baptists are largely literalistic in their interpretations of scripture and make religious fact claims that fall squarely into the domain of science. It is these religions that tend to oppose science and work actively to limit science funding. Gould was wrong. Religion and science are, depending on the religion, overlapping magisteria. They don't have to be, but for many people (i.e., close to one-third of Americans and billions around the world), they are. For these people, science contradicts their beliefs. Additionally, some of these religious people believe that a scientific understanding—particularly of humans, but also of nature generally—reduces the importance of humans as it minimizes the influence of God and his plan in everyday life. The result of these beliefs is active opposition to science education and scientific research.

In summary, religious people, particularly religious fundamentalists, tend to be less knowledgeable about and more oppositional toward science than are nonreligious individuals. They are so concerned about being "direct descendants" of monkeys (i.e., "monkeys' uncles") that they fail to realize they are actually distant "cousins"

of modern-day monkeys. Although evolution is perhaps the most vehemently opposed scientific topic, antiscience rhetoric is not limited to evolution. Religion and science have historically overlapped and, for many religions and religious people today, they continue to overlap. As a result, many religious people and many religions actively—even proactively—oppose science education. This active opposition to science has both resulted in poorer science education than might otherwise be the case and reduced funding for science. Religion is at least partially responsible for slowing the pace of technological advancement and the development of scientific breakthroughs that could potentially be very helpful to humanity (e.g., stem cell research). If someone you know dies because scientific advances have been slowed down due to lack of funding or other restrictions, don't blame scientists. Blame fundamentalists.

8

ALL DEMONS ARE FROM HOLLYWOOD
HOW MEDIA CREATED THE POSSESSION FAD

Terrance Cottrell Jr. was a challenging eight-year-old. Many eight-year-olds are. But Terrance was autistic. Autism is characterized by difficulty interacting with people in socially expected and appropriate ways. Autistic children, depending on the severity of the condition, don't make eye contact, don't show much affection, may not talk, and may ignore commands or directions. As a result, caring for a child with autism can be challenging and requires substantial patience. We don't know the exact cause of autism at this point, but it is believed to be a combination of genetic and environmental factors. Terrance's mother, Patricia Cooper, was either unaware of the scientific research on autism or had disregarded it. She believed Terrance's autism was due to demonic possession.

To solve her son's behavior problems, Patricia took him to an exorcist (aka "deliverance minister"). The exorcist, Ray Hemphill, agreed to perform an exorcism on Terrance. The exorcism lasted two hours and involved Hemphill kneeling on Terrance's chest, with one hand on his head and another between his legs. Terrance's mother and another woman held Terrance's legs. Hemphill prayed over Terrance and commanded the demons of autism to leave.

At the end of the exorcism, Terrance was not breathing and had extensive bruises on his neck and back. Cardiopulmonary resuscitation (CPR) was of little use to Terrance by the time those performing the exorcism realized he was unresponsive. Terrance died because his mom believed autism was caused by demons . . . in 2003.

—§—

Before you read the rest of this chapter I want you to do something. Put aside this book and find a business directory for your local area. Search for "Deliverance."

If you live in a large metropolitan area, you'll probably find half a dozen or more churches or ministries with "deliverance" in the name. When I wrote this chapter in the fall of 2011, I found eight such ministries in Tampa, where I live. Many ministries or churches with "deliverance" in the title offer a unique service: exorcisms. You could phone pretty much any one of these ministries and, for a relatively small donation (anywhere from $20 to $200), get an exorcism.

How is it possible that demonic deliverance is just a phone call away in most major American cities in the twenty-first century? This is all the more interesting since prior to about 1970 it would have been next to impossible to get an exorcism in the United States, at least not since the early 1900s. How then did we get from no exorcisms to deliverance ministries in the yellow pages?

While not the first book on the topic, William Peter Blatty's *The Exorcist* is largely responsible for the current demonic possession fad. It is a *completely* fictional book that was claimed to be based on a true story. However, every detail of the book has been thoroughly refuted. The book was made into a movie in 1973 and made hundreds of millions of dollars as people flocked to see it. Since that time, there has been a dramatic increase in belief in demonic possession in the United States. This is all detailed in an excellent book titled *American Exorcism*, by sociologist Michael Cuneo. Cuneo compellingly illustrates that modern belief in demonic possession is the direct result of media portrayals of exorcisms. He shows that, prior to the release of Blatty's book and the subsequent movie, very few people believed in demonic possession and no religions had trained exorcists waiting to help those in need. After the release of the book and movie, consumer demand for exorcisms drove a corresponding increase in supply—plenty of pastors signed up to take people's money to perform rituals to rid them of the demons they suddenly believed were everywhere.

How pervasive is the belief in demonic possession? According to the Barna Group, a Christian surveying outfit that appears to be the only group interested in this question, belief in demonic possession is pretty pervasive. Figure 8.1 shows that Christians in the United States are more likely to believe in demonic possession (64 percent) than they are to believe that Jesus Christ was sinless and divine (55 percent). Incredibly, Americans are only about half as likely to believe Satan exists (35 percent) or that the Holy Spirit is an actual living force (34 percent) than they are to believe in demonic possession.

What figure 8.1 illustrates is the remarkable power of media to shape the beliefs of people. A search on the Internet Movie Database (IMDb) for the keyword "exorcism" returns just over 200 films, almost all of which were made after 1970.

In researching his book, Cuneo observed dozens of exorcisms. Guess what he never saw? Not once did he observe the elements of demonic possession made

FIGURE 8.1. Percentage of U.S. Christians with Specific Christian Beliefs

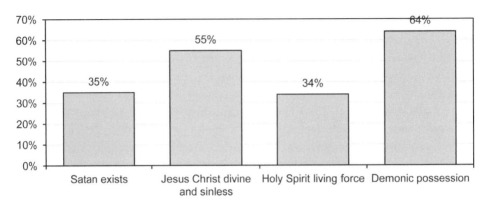

SOURCE: BARNA, 2009

famous by Blatty's movie: heads turning 360 degrees, levitation of either beds or humans, super-human strength, projectile vomiting of green goop, or little girls jamming crucifixes into their vaginas—all of which are in the movie (yes, even the last one). In fact, Cuneo never saw anything he could even remotely claim was supernatural in origin. He saw many things that could be considered disturbing, but not because they indicated the presence of demons. His findings are disturbing because they represent the remarkable gullibility of Americans and the pervasive and sometimes pernicious influence of media. Cuneo observed hundreds of people buying into the myth of demonic possession and blaming demons for all sorts of problems. People claimed to have demons of lust that drove them to cheat on their spouses. People claimed to have demons of anger that drove them to yell at their children. And, of course, parents claimed children had demons that made them misbehave, like poor Terrance Cottrell Jr. In many cases demonic possession has become just another way for people to not accept or take responsibility for their problems. And exorcisms are just one more easy, quick fix that desperate people pursue.

Interestingly, one thing Micheal Cuneo did not observe was nonbelievers seeking exorcisms. The only people who were asking for deliverance were Christians. There are a couple of possible explanations for this. It could be that demons pursue only Christians because god wants to test the faith of his "true" followers. That's kind of a shitty thing to do to the people who believe, but not out of character for Jehovah. Alternatively, it could be that nonbelievers are possessed and they simply don't know it. However, the most logical explanation is that only Christians get possessed because believing is a prerequisite for demonic possession.

Given that there is such a fascination with exorcism today, it is rather surprising that there are no videos of "real" exorcisms on video sites like YouTube depicting supernatural feats. Given the popularity of these sites and the potential to profit from posting videos online, anyone with incontrovertible evidence of demonic possession would likely post it for all the world to see. YouTube should be filled with videos of levitating, vomiting, and head-revolving masturbators rather than videos of babies, pets, and musicians. So, where are those videos?

The lack of evidence hasn't kept young people from believing in demonic possession. For the past few years in my sociology of religion course I have had my students read Michael Cuneo's *American Exorcism*. Before we read the book, I show my students the original film version of *The Exorcist*. Many of the students are reticent to watch the film as they have been told by others that it is terrifying and depicts *real* events. I've had students try to get out of watching the movie for fear that something similar could happen to them just by watching the movie. I even had one parent accompany her daughter to class the day I showed the movie, just in case! More than thirty years after this fictional movie was released, it retains a remarkable ability to penetrate the psyche and fill people with fear. Yet, after they watch it, my students universally find it laughable, ludicrous, and lewd. The reputation of the movie is far scarier than the movie itself.

Demonic possession and its antidote, exorcism, are creations of modern mass media. Demons really do come from Hollywood. According to Michael Cuneo and the Roman Catholic Church, there has never been an authentic case of demonic possession. In other words, there are no demons. Yet, people around the world are firmly convinced that demons do exist and that demons have nothing better to do than to take control of their bodies, leading them to fits of anger, to cheat on their taxes, and to play with their genitals. And, unfortunately, some people's belief in demonic possession has resulted in the death of their loved ones.

9

GOD OWNS YOUR UTERUS
RELIGION AND THE RIGHT TO CHOOSE

In 2009, a nine-year-old Brazilian girl was impregnated by her stepfather, who repeatedly raped her and her fourteen-year-old sister. The girl reported the sexual abuse only when stomach pain related to the pregnancy forced her to seek medical attention. In trying to discern the cause of the stomach pain the doctors discovered she was carrying twins. Given her age, the doctors immediately asked who had impregnated her, which ultimately led to the girl revealing the stepfather's abuse. When the doctors, in the interest of saving the girl's life and with the consent of the girl's mother, aborted the fetuses, the doctors and the mother, all Catholics, were excommunicated by the Catholic Church.

The stepfather, who secular authorities arrested, was not excommunicated. Catholic Cardinal Giovanni Battista Re defended the excommunication of the doctors and mother by the regional archbishop, Jose Cardoso Sobrinho. He also justified not excommunicating the father, noting that, while the father had committed "a heinous crime . . . the abortion—the elimination of an innocent life—was more serious." Archbishop Sobrinho said in relation to this case, "God's law is above any human law. So when a human law . . . is contrary to God's law, this human law has no value."

In many religions a woman's sole value is her uterus, which she does not control. God owns her uterus and he, through his male mouthpieces of course, dictates how, when, and why that uterus should be used.

—§—

Opposition to abortion is heavily motivated by religion. This is clearly illustrated in relevant survey data. Figure 9.1 shows that, regardless of the context or motivation for an abortion, religious fundamentalists are the most likely to oppose abortion,

FIGURE 9.1. Support for Abortion by Reason and Religious Group

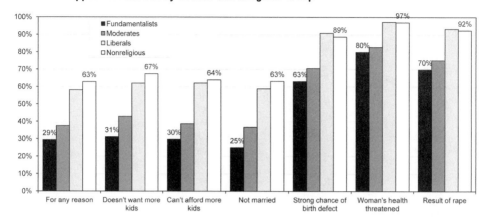

SOURCE: GSS, 2010

followed by religious moderates, then liberals. In almost every scenario, the nonreligious are the most supportive of a woman's right to control her uterus. However, religiously liberal individuals are very similar to the nonreligious on the issue of abortion.

Figure 9.1 also shows that opposition to abortion varies by the reason behind the abortion. When there are physical complications, like birth defects or the mother's health is endangered, support for abortion rights increases. The same is true in the case of rape. When the reasons are not directly health related but are more for social or economic reasons, like a woman not being married, support for access to abortion decreases among all four groups. Two disturbing statistics in figure 9.1 are at the far right of the figure. First, 20 percent of religious fundamentalists would force a woman to put her life in danger or jeopardize her health, prioritizing the possible life of the unborn child over that of the woman; only 3 percent of nonreligious Americans would do so. Second, 30 percent of religious fundamentalists would force women to have their rapists' children; just 8 percent of nonreligious Americans would do so. If anything illustrates the value put on the lives of women, it is the views of different religious groups toward abortion and how unborn fetuses are valued over women.

A similar pattern is observed internationally. Figure 9.2 shows that those who consider their religion very important are the most likely to oppose abortion in all situations. However, like attitudes in the United States, the context matters. When the mother or child are physically in danger, opposition declines. When the reasons are more social, opposition increases.

Figure 9.2. Support for Abortion by Reason and Importance of Religion

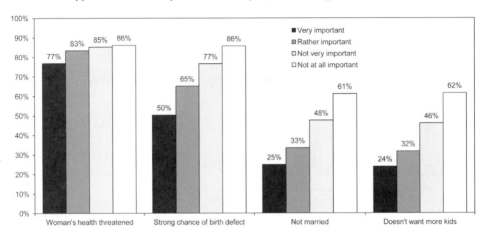

SOURCE: WVS, 2010

Given that some nonreligious people oppose abortion, and opposition varies by context, it must be the case that opposition to abortion is not exclusively rooted in religion. There are other reasons to oppose abortion. However, the figures in this chapter illustrate that religion plays a powerful role in opposing abortion rights around the world.

If emptying a pregnant uterus prematurely runs counter to god's will in some religions, it shouldn't be surprising that so, too, does preventing the uterus from becoming pregnant. In the twenty-first century there is still opposition to birth control in the United States, particularly for teens. Opposition to birth control is tied to religion. While the benefits of birth control to women's autonomy and health is well established, nearly 50 percent of religious fundamentalists in the United States remain opposed to allowing teenagers access to birth control, as shown in figure 9.3. Similar differences by religiosity exist for birth control generally.

The message so far is pretty straightforward: the more religious someone is, the more opposed he or she is likely to be to birth control and abortion. While that is the primary point I want to make in this chapter, I thought it might be interesting to ask one more question: what about actually getting abortions? Neither the General Social Survey nor the World Values Survey have data on having abortions, but I did find a data set that asked American women about abortions and also asked about religion. The survey is the National Survey of Family Growth (Wave 6, 2002). Figure 9.4 shows the average number of abortions per woman by

FIGURE 9.3. Percentage Who Agree or Strongly Agree Birth Control Should Be Made Available to Teens Aged 14–16 by Religiosity

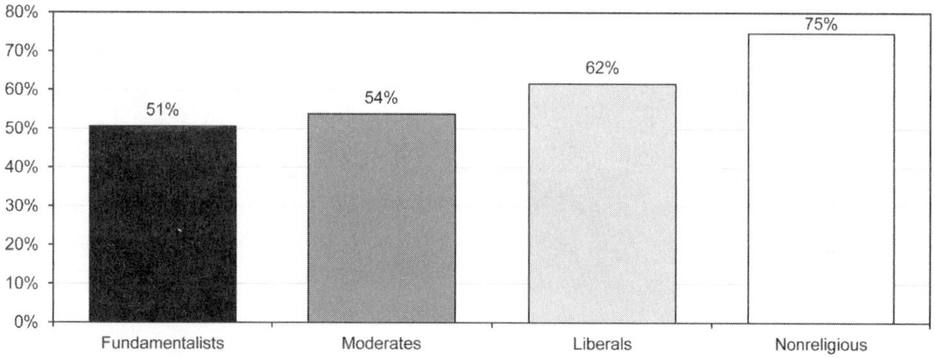

SOURCE: GSS, 2010

religion, with just four religious categories shown: the nonreligious, Catholics, Protestants, and other.

Figure 9.4 illustrates that having an abortion is also related to religion. The nonreligious are more likely to have an abortion than are Catholics or Protestants, but not more likely than members of other religions. However, it is kind of interesting to point out that, given the relative sizes of these populations, the nonreligious only account for 14 percent of abortions in the United States; Catholics account for 30 percent; Protestants account for 51 percent, and other religions account for 5 percent. In other words, 81 percent of abortions in the United States are performed for women from the religious groups who most strongly oppose abortion. That would be ironic if it wasn't so disturbing.

You may be asking yourself at this point: why should people care about women's control over their uteri? When women have control over their fertility, they want and choose to have fewer kids. The children they do have are better cared for and are more likely to survive to adulthood. Additionally, while perhaps not causal, it is the case that in countries where women have control over their uteri they also tend to be better educated and more affluent.

Reproductive rights are inseparable from women's rights. Opposition to reproductive rights is simultaneously opposition to women's rights and gender equality. Forcing women to have children often makes them more dependent on men and reduces women's autonomy. I don't mean to suggest that children are a curse or burden. To the contrary, I believe children are precious and, of course, they are

FIGURE 9.4. Average Number of Abortions per Woman by Religious Affiliation of the Woman

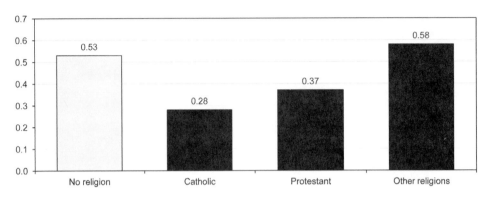

SOURCE: NSFG, 2002

the future of humanity. But forcing women to have more children than they want carries with it numerous negative consequences, including reductions in women's autonomy, education, and economic status, not to mention negative affects on their mental and physical health. When women are forced to have children, they lose control of their lives. They are subordinate to men. Opposition to birth control and abortion is also opposition to gender equality.

This is, in all likelihood, precisely the reason why religions and, in particular, the male leadership of those religions, oppose abortion and birth control. By controlling women's uteri, religions gain more followers, and the men in the religions retain their positions of both responsibility and authority. The women in those religions are too busy taking care of the children to get involved in self-governance. And because they have as many children as they do, they are heavily dependent upon men. In patriarchal religions, opposition to birth control and abortions is an indirect way of retaining male power and authority. This isn't about kids; it's about controlling women!

In summary, opposition to birth control and abortion varies by religiosity, with the most religious being the most opposed to both. Religion is not the only influence on peoples' attitude toward birth control and abortion, but it is the strongest influence, both in the United States and around the world. Opposition to reproductive rights is also opposition to women's rights. Given the gender inequality that is pervasive in religions, it isn't all that surprising that male-dominated religions, which typically have all-powerful male gods, want to lay claim to women's uteri. Having control of a woman's uterus is an effective way to control her.

10

MARRY NOW, STAY FOREVER
WHY RELIGIONS ARE "PRO-FAMILY"

My anniversary is December 31, 1999. I married at 23; my wife, Debi, was 25. The average age at which men married in 1999 was 26.9; for women it was 25. I married four years earlier than the average male and I probably would have married sooner, but the two years I spent in Costa Rica as a missionary set me back a bit. Why did I marry so young?

The honest answer is a mixture of good reasons and, well, not-so-good reasons. First, and most importantly, I found someone I loved who was smart enough to challenge me intellectually, shares a lot of interests with me (we met at a ballet studio, both love sci-fi, and are both science geeks), and is beautiful. But I also was horny as hell and wanted to get laid. I've only ever had sex with my wife; as a faithful Mormon I was strongly discouraged from almost all intimacy, and sex was anathema. There was no way I was going to have sex before marriage (though lots of Mormons do). Marriage was a gateway to sex for me, which made it quite an attractive option.

You may be thinking that I was an idiot for actually taking my religious beliefs seriously. Maybe you're right. But that's not really my point in telling you this. Have you ever asked why religions are so opposed to premarital sex and why they encourage marriage at such a young age? An encounter with one of my sisters should give you a hint. . .

Debi and I left Mormonism at the same time. We talked about our concerns at length and, luckily, agreed that we no longer wanted to actively participate in the religion in the summer of 2002. We formally resigned our membership a couple of years later so we could, in good conscience, say that we were no longer Mormons, much to our parents' chagrin. Shortly after we left Mormonism I was visiting with my family in Utah, which was still trying to come to terms with our decision to leave. During one of the conversations about our decision to leave, my older sister

FIGURE 10.1. Age of First Marriage by Cohort and Religious Group

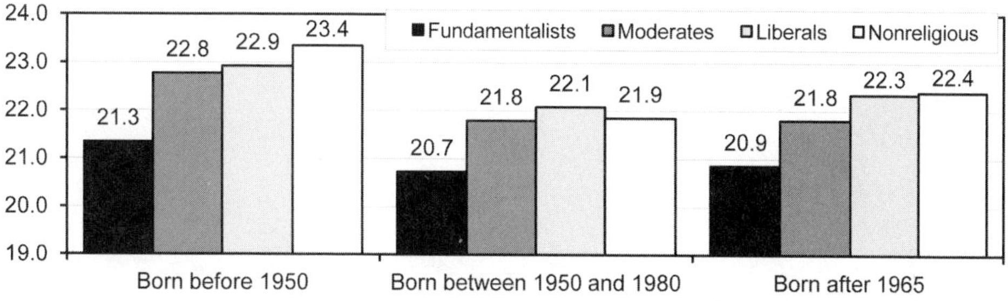

| | Fundamentalists | Moderates | Liberals | Nonreligious |

Born before 1950: 21.3, 22.8, 22.9, 23.4
Born between 1950 and 1980: 20.7, 21.8, 22.1, 21.9
Born after 1965: 20.9, 21.8, 22.3, 22.4

SOURCE: GSS, 1972–2006

pulled me aside and began grilling me about what had transpired. Because being strong willed runs in my family, my sister wanted to know whether I had pressured Debi into leaving Mormonism with me. I told her that I had not and that Debi makes her own decisions. My sister's response has stayed with me. She responded to my assertion about Debi's independence by saying, "But I just don't get it. Whenever I have a problem at church, my husband is there to help me. Whenever he has a problem, I'm there to help him. That's what spouses are for—to bring you back when you start to doubt."

I don't think she realized how sociologically adroit her insight was.

—§—

It's not all that surprising, but the more religious someone is, the younger they are when they first marry, as is illustrated in figure 10.1. Figure 10.1 breaks down age at first marriage by the year people were born (referred to as "cohort") and by their religious groups, as the age at which people have married has changed over time. The personal narrative I shared explains the primary reasons why fundamentalists marry younger. The first reason is that more conservative and fundamentalist religions tend to be opposed to premarital sex and consider it a sin. One way to reduce the risk of committing the sin of premarital sex is to marry young. The second reason more conservative and fundamentalist individuals marry younger is because they are encouraged to do so by the leaders of their religions.

Acceptance of premarital sex is increasing (see figure 10.2), though a majority of fundamentalists (63 percent) still consider it wrong. However, what young religionists don't realize is that the motivation of religions in advocating early marriage has nothing to do with benefiting those who follow this advice. Demographers have

Figure 10.2. Percentage Reporting Premarital Sex Is Not Wrong At All by Religiosity

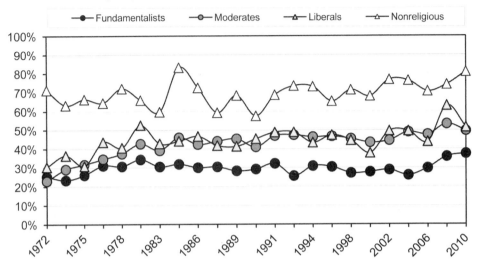

SOURCE: GSS, 1972–2010

long known that couples who marry younger are more likely to divorce. The primary benefit of encouraging couples to marry young accrues to the religions themselves. How? Why? Because early marriage substantially reduces the odds of young people leaving the religion.

Are religions really so callous that they would encourage young people to behave in ways that may not be in the best interest of their younger members but that are in the best interest of the religion? Sure! They do it all the time. Priests and rabbis have regularly tried to cover up sexual abuse by keeping victims from pressing charges. Once religions become structured institutions, institutional inertia—in the form of self-interested leaders who want to retain their lucrative jobs—begins to influence how they behave. Leaders act in the best interest of keeping the institution alive rather than in the best interest of the members.

What's more, religions today know that marrying young reduces the odds of young people leaving their religion. How do they know this? They know this for the same reason I do—they have academically trained social scientists working for them. Their scientists read all of the same books and articles I read. I know a number of them because they attend the same academic conferences I attend. If I know that marriage increases the odds of retaining members, the religions know this as well!

The fact that marriage reduces religious exiting (aka apostasy) is well known, though few have tried to explain why this is the case. My best guess is that it has to do with network ties. A hypothetical example may be the best way to illustrate this.

Meet Brad, who has just turned eighteen and graduated from high school. Brad is a member of a conservative religion and has been raised in that religion his whole life by his father and mother. Brad also has a younger sister. At this point in his life, Brad is facing a crossroad. Let's pretend that path A will take Brad off to a "secular" state university, away from home. On path A, Brad does not marry right away but instead decides to wait until he finishes his education. Path B is different. On path B, Brad follows the advice of his religious leaders, finds a girl, Amber, who is also a member of the religion, and marries at age nineteen. The important element to consider at this point is the variation in social networks that result from each of these paths. Figure 10.3a below shows Brad's ties to his religion and religious congregation as an adolescent.

I have somewhat simplified the ties to church friends and other church members just so the lines aren't overwhelming. Even so, using this simplified model, Brad has at least three direct ties to the religion—a direct connection with the pastor or clergy person in his church, a direct connection with his friends at church, and a direct connection with the adult members of his church. These connections will be of varying levels of strength, of course, but they exist. Additionally, Brad has indirect connections to the church through his sister and his parents, who are also connected to all of the people in his church. The minimum number of indirect connections Brad has is nine (three from his sister and from each of his parents). Thus, even in this simplified model, Brad has at least twelve relational ties to the religion of his upbringing. This helps explain why adolescents tend to be pretty similar, religiously, to their parents—they are enmeshed in their parents' religious social network.

FIGURE **10.3A. Brad's Ties to Religion during Adolescence**

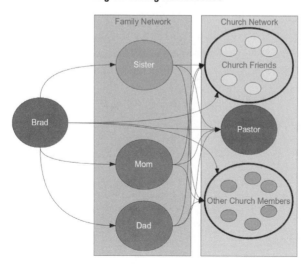

Figure 10.3b. Brad's Ties to Religion via Path A

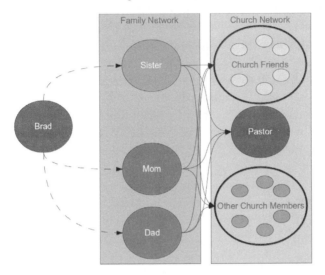

What happens to Brad's connections to the church if he follows path A? His direct ties to the pastor, his church friends, and the other church members basically disappear (see figure 10.3b). He is no longer directly connected to his religion. What's more, his relationship with his family grows less immediate. Even if he stays in contact with them, they are likely hundreds of miles away. Thus, his only ties to the religion are indirect ties through family members whom he is only occasionally around. In short, Brad finds himself growing away from the church of his upbringing because the social connections are no longer there. Without strong connections to the religion, his odds of leaving increase.

Now consider path B. In path B, Brad marries right out of high school. Whether or not he then goes away to college is less damaging to his ties to the religion because he now has an extra set of indirect ties to the religion that are not through a family member who is far away but through his wife, who is very close, as shown in figure 10.3c. He also has even more ties to the religion, as his wife, Amber, has ties to all of the same people, plus indirect ties through Brad's sister and parents, and indirect ties through her own family (not shown in the diagram). In other words, by marrying Amber, Brad has basically tripled his ties to the religion: he retains his ties, Amber has ties through his family, and Amber has ties through her own family.

What's the point of all of this? Humans are social animals. That is our primary evolutionary advantage—well, that and our big brains, which coevolved with our sociality. We are strongly influenced by those around us. We surround ourselves with people like us, but we also conform to those around us. If you have a social

FIGURE 10.3c. Brad's Ties to Religion via Path B

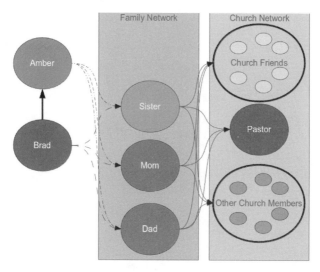

network made up of deviant individuals, the odds are you'll be deviant. If you have a social network made up of fat individuals, the odds are you'll be fat. And if you have a social network made up of religious individuals, the odds are you'll be religious.

In the interest of emphasizing this point, let me reiterate what I said above: *religions know this!* They know about social networks and the importance of social connections to the religion. Why do you think so many religions oppose premarital sex and encourage young people to marry? And why do religions encourage people to marry other members of the religion? You know the answer now: they do it because it increases ties to the religion and reduces the odds of people leaving. This is also why religions are pronatal and advocate having lots of kids, preferably at a young age: every kid increases the number of ties to the religion, thereby reducing the odds that someone will leave (see chapter 11).

The leaders of religions aren't stupid. Dishonest, manipulative, conniving, and immoral? Many, yes! Stupid? No. Leaders of religions have every incentive to keep people in the religion as they are only able to continue in their positions so long as they have a flock to fleece. If they can keep the people someone cares about in the religion, they have pretty good odds of keeping that person in the religion as well. This is basically the long version of what my sister said to me and why she is a better sociologist than she realizes.

Keep in mind that religions today do this despite knowing that it increases the odds of the marriages being unhappy and ending in divorce, which is a well-known consequence of marrying young. This can actually be seen in marriage statistics. If

FIGURE 10.4. Marital Status by Religious Group

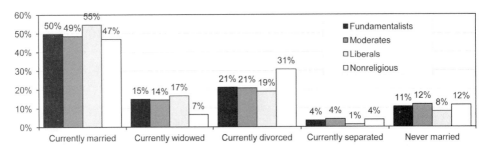

SOURCE: GSS, 2010

you just look at current marital status, it looks like the nonreligious are a bit more likely to be divorced, as figure 10.4 shows.

But current marital status is a bit misleading. Figure 10.5 shows the percentage in each religious group that has ever been divorced. As figure 10.5 illustrates, fundamentalists in the United States have a slightly higher divorce rate than do moderates and liberals, though the difference with the nonreligious is negligible. And if you look back at figure 10.4, you'll see that fundamentalists are about as likely as all the other groups to be currently married, suggesting that emphasis on marriage translates into divorcées quickly remarrying.

FIGURE 10.5. Percent Ever Been Divorced by Religious Group

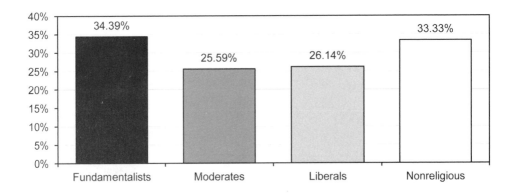

SOURCE: GSS, 2010

FIGURE 10.6. Marital Status by Importance of Religion

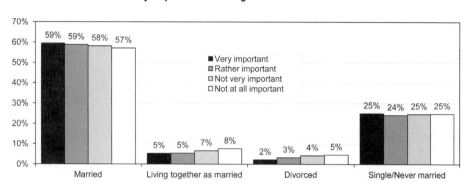

SOURCE: WVS, 2010

Internationally, the differences in marital status are pretty minimal, as figure 10.6 illustrates. Given the emphasis on marriage in religions, particularly conservative and fundamentalist religions, the religious should be substantially more likely to be married and the nonreligious should be much more likely to be something other than married. But that isn't what the statistics show, either in the United States or internationally.

In reality, while religions often claim to be family focused, their advocacy of marriage at young ages actually works against the realization of that value. This suggests that religions care less about marital happiness and stability than they do about retaining members, though, of course, they would never, ever admit that.

Some readers will no doubt note after reading this chapter that there is some research suggesting premarital sex is associated with negative outcomes, like increased odds of marital dissolution or poor educational outcomes, so marrying young is a way to alleviate this problem. Yep, there is some research that says that, mostly written by religious scholars with the aim of supporting their religious beliefs. The preponderance of scientific evidence suggests that adolescent sexual activity is basically benign. Even when research finds statistically significant negative outcomes (i.e., there is a mathematical relationship), the relationships are practically meaningless; premarital sex, including among adolescents, is highly unlikely to ruin lives, particularly if the sex is with a future spouse and the participants are knowledgeable about safer-sex practices. What's more, simple logic suggests claims of negative outcomes are absurd. Roughly 75 percent of both men and women have sex before marriage, and close to 50 percent of high schoolers have had sex. If there were dramatic and notable negative outcomes resulting from premarital or adolescent sex, we would see all sorts of problems in society directly related to that sexual activity. For instance, teen pregnancies and the divorce rate would both be up. Surprise, surprise! Teen pregnancies and divorce rates are down from the 1980s and 1990s. Premarital and adolescent sex make basically no difference in terms of life outcomes.

The more fundamentalist the religion, the younger age at which the members typically marry. This is the result of two factors—the desire to have sex without sinning and the emphasis placed on marriage by the religions. Some of that emphasis may be genuine concern for preventing sin by the leadership of the religion, but much of the emphasis on marriage is in order to increase the retention of members, which is a self-serving action on the part of the religions. The emphasis on marriage does translate into slightly higher rates of marriage among the religious, but also higher rates of divorce among fundamentalists, which they conceal by quickly remarrying. If religions cared about the happiness of their members, they would encourage them to wait until they are ready to marry rather than push them into marriage at young ages. That isn't what motivates religions, however. Religions want bodies in pews to maintain the cash flow, and by getting young people to marry, religions increase the odds of keeping those bodies in the pews forever.

11

MULTIPLY AND REPLENISH THE PEWS
WHY RELIGIONS ENCOURAGE PROCREATION

Vyckie Garrison was basically a run-of-the-mill conservative Christian living contentedly in the United States. She was married to a fellow conservative Christian, Warren, and had three children. Her pregnancies had all been difficult, resulting in Cesarean sections, but she was happy to have her kids and her life seemed satisfactory. Then she and her husband came into contact with the literature and ideas that make up the Quiverfull movement. Quiverfull is a collection of beliefs and practices, found largely among conservative Christians, that advocates for maximum fertility—couples try to have as many children as possible.

Vyckie's doctors had discouraged her from having more children because of the difficulty of her earlier pregnancies, and Warren had already had a vasectomy. Regardless, they found the ideas of the Quiverfull movement compelling and embraced it. Along with maximizing fertility, Quiverfull advocates homeschooling and a strict patriarchal authority structure in the family. Shortly after embracing the movement, Warren had his vasectomy reversed and Vyckie became pregnant. The pregnancy was difficult and complicated by preeclampsia. While modern medicine has some treatments to help with preeclampsia, Quiverfull is also opposed to modern medicine, making Vyckie's pregnancy even more dangerous and difficult. The child eventually arrived and was healthy. The complications with the pregnancy didn't prevent Vyckie and Warren from continuing down their newly chosen path.

Over the next few years, Vyckie and Warren had three more children. The last child, their seventh, nearly died during labor. In accordance with her new beliefs, Vyckie was planning a home birth, but she felt like something was wrong with the pregnancy and went to the hospital instead. The doctors diagnosed a uterine rupture, which necessitated an emergency Cesarean section. Both Vyckie and the child were saved, but the complications along with all of the other stresses she was dealing with at the time had exhausted Vyckie.

Despite all these challenges, Vyckie and Warren's family was named Nebraska Family of the Year in 2003. The excitement of that award was short-lived. Vyckie's oldest daughter, Angel, was not doing well in the highly restrictive, patriarchal family arrangement. Her acting out got her sent to live with a friend in Nashville, Tennessee. Shortly after she moved there, Vyckie received a call from a social worker at the Vanderbilt University Medical Center informing her that Angel had attempted suicide. Angel survived, but this was enough of a shock to Vyckie to raise some doubts about her new beliefs.

Angel's suicide attempt helped Vyckie to notice that her other children were growing distant. They were increasingly afraid to talk in the home for fear of upsetting Warren, who had become oppressive and patriarchal. Warren's increasingly abusive behavior, which was directed toward her and the kids, along with the pervasive depression among her and her kids, eventually convinced Vyckie that something had to change.

She left the house one day and started driving. She ended up driving to a nearby town and walked into a church, where a stranger noticed her and let her talk. That conversation, and a conversation that played out with her nonreligious uncle, Ron, ultimately convinced Vyckie that her beliefs and her husband were the problems that were making her life unbearable. Not long after her chat with the stranger in a random church, Vyckie divorced Warren.

While Vyckie continues to attend religious services, she now describes herself as largely a nonbeliever who enjoys religious community. The change in her children, who were eventually allowed to go to public school, was dramatic. They were finally happy, freed from the oppressive environment of their parents' pronatalist religious beliefs and their father's patriarchy. One son, Andrew, who had harbored anger for years but kept it bottled up for fear of triggering his father's rage, wrote in a school assignment about how his life changed when his mother divorced his father and stopped pursuing biblically based teachings about fertility. His talk, which received a spontaneous standing ovation from his class, noted that he was finally starting to like himself because he was able to learn things. For the first time, he liked his life.

Having kids is hard. I know, I didn't actually carry my child in a womb for nine months or give birth to him, though I did live with my wife during that entire time and observed how hard it was for her. But I do know firsthand that raising kids is difficult. I love my son, but he can be really aggravating at times, as he, like all kids, pushes boundaries and doesn't always listen. He takes up a lot of time, too, though

FIGURE **11.1.** Average Number of Kids by Religiosity

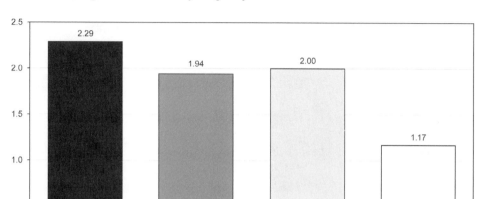

SOURCE: GSS, 2010

that part I don't regret. And the money! I manage the finances in my family and am a little anal about keeping track of expenses. My wife and I spend about $600 a year on diapers for my son. We spend almost $10,000 a year on daycare alone. Now, I'm well aware of the fact that I shouldn't be complaining about these things—there are kids starving to death who have never worn a diaper or seen the inside of a daycare. I get that. I'm just trying to suggest that even for me, a father in a developed country with lots of advantages who tries to be engaged, having a child is exhausting. Now multiply that by seven, like Vyckie did, or nine, like my mother did! I have no idea how people have more than one kid, let alone half a dozen or more. But some people do have lots of kids and, more likely than not, they are motivated to do it by their religion.

The data on number of children by religiosity is unequivocal—the more religious or more fundamentalist you are, the more kids you are likely to have. Nonreligious individuals tend to have the fewest. Figures 11.1 and 11.2 illustrate this in the United States and internationally, respectively.

There is obviously a connection between pronatalist doctrines and having lots of kids. But there are also other factors at play here. To begin with, why are religions pronatalist? Religions have developed a variety of theological justifications for why people should have lots of kids. But arguing that religions are pronatalist because

Figure 11.2. Average Number of Kids by Importance of Religion

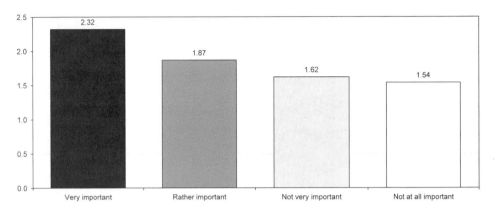

SOURCE: WVS

of their theology doesn't explain why their theology is pronatalist. There are two possible arguments for why religions are pronatalist, both of which are compelling. As noted in chapter 10, religions are aware of the fact that having children increases the odds of retaining members, likely due to network ties (similar to the function of marriage for religions). Thus, member retention may help explain the pronatalist policies of religions.

But there is another possible explanation. Religions that advocate many children will, if they can convince their members to have those children, outcompete religions that don't advocate having many children. As a result, pronatalist religions are likely to grow (or at least maintain their numbers) and be more widespread. The higher fertility rates of conservative Protestants in the United States helped them grow in absolute numbers in the 1980s and 1990s as compared to the mainline Protestant religions in the United States, which demonstrates the importance of fertility in fueling religious growth. An obvious counterexample is the Shakers, who advocated sexual abstinence. As of January 2011, there were five Shakers in the world. Thus, religions may be pronatalist because pronatalism increases the number of members and/or because pronatalist religions are more likely to grow.

Pronatalism has another function in religions: it supports a patriarchal power structure. As the story that began this chapter illustrated, when women are kept continually pregnant and have lots of kids, their ability to stand up to their husbands is severely limited. Not only is all of their time consumed with child-rearing responsibilities, but they are also typically financially dependent upon their husbands. Pronatalism is a tool of patriarchy—it keeps women subservient to men because it keeps them dependent upon men. While some women really do want large families, most women want few kids, especially in developing countries where the odds of the kids surviving to adulthood and the cost of having kids are increasing. Women with few or no kids are less dependent upon men, as are women who work outside the home. Thus, religions may be pronatalist to increase members or because they outcompeted other religions that are not pronatalist, but being pronatalist carries with it the subservience of women to men, whether that is intended (probably) or not.

Some recent research has suggested that the long-term consequence of the higher fertility rates of religious individuals means that religiosity is going to increase over time rather than decrease. This claim is based on the fact that the highest birth rates are in the most religious countries, which also happen to be the least developed. On its face that seems like a reasonable claim. However, there is reason to be skeptical. Such a claim really requires the contrasting of two numbers. The first is the overall rate of increase among the religious versus the nonreligious. The second requires the calculation of the rate of religious exiting or secularization. If people are exiting religions faster than the religious can give birth to new members, meaning they are not retaining their offspring, then the religious will not "inherit the earth." If, however, the religious are giving birth at higher rates and their offspring remain religious, the percentage of the world's population that is religious may increase. I have yet to see anyone compellingly calculate whether or not the world is growing more or less religious, but my inclination at the moment would be to conclude that the world is close to an equilibrium. Lots of people, particularly in the developed world, are leaving religions. However, due to higher birth rates in less developed countries, religions do not appear to be experiencing a decline in the overall percentage of people who are religious. What direction this will tip is unclear at the moment; we'll just have to wait to see.

More religious people have more kids. Religions are pronatalist because pronatalism retains members, because pronatalist religions outcompete religions that are not explicitly pronatalist, and possibly because pronatalism keeps women subservient to men. Whether the higher fertility rates of the religious will translate into religious growth around the world is uncertain. In order for that to happen, religions will have to start doing a better job retaining the offspring of members to replenish their pews, particularly in developed countries and in countries that are rapidly developing.

12

SPARE THE ROD? NOT WITH GOD!
PARENTING AND RELIGION

A few years ago I was at an academic conference on religion when one of the presenters, Bronn, shared this story.

Bronn was raised by parents who were members of the Christian Science religion. At about the age of ten he developed an abscess in one of his teeth. His parents, not believing in modern medicine, read to him from the Bible night and day in an effort to cure him. It didn't work. The abscess worsened.

Eventually Bronn grew so sick he couldn't leave the house or even his bed. A concerned relative who was not a Christian Scientist called a doctor and asked him to stop by Bronn's house. The doctor did. The parents, somewhat surprisingly, let the doctor in to examine Bronn. The doctor told the parents that he had to take the child to the hospital immediately or the child wouldn't likely survive for another twenty-four hours. The parents, still devoted to their beliefs, put the decision on Bronn. They told him that he could stay and let them continue their efforts or he could go with the doctor. However, if he went with the doctor, he wasn't welcome to return to their home; he would be disowned.

Bronn went with the doctor.

He was forced to choose between his life or his parents that day—he chose life. Modern medicine saved his life; religious fundamentalism cost him his parents.

—§—

While it's possible some nonreligious parents might disown a child who decides to become religious, it's highly unlikely. Most of the research on this topic finds that nonreligious parents are very open to their children exploring all of their options. Also, as chapter 7 noted, the nonreligious are more accepting of science, so choosing between science-based medicine and nonreligion isn't really much of an issue

FIGURE 12.1. Percentage Who Agree Spanking Is a Good Discipline Method by Religious Group

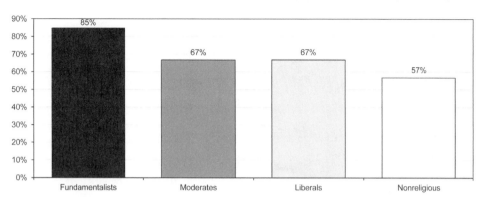

SOURCE: GSS, 2010

for the nonreligious. What happened with Bronn is almost guaranteed to never happen in a nonreligious household.

Are there differences in how religious people think about and raise their kids from how nonreligious people think about and raise their kids? Yes! Religious fundamentalists in the United States are much more likely to favor spanking children than are nonreligious people, as shown in figure 12.1—85 percent of religious fundamentalists in the United States agree or strongly agree that spanking is a good way to discipline a child, compared to 57 percent of the nonreligious.

FIGURE 12.2. Percentage Reporting Desired Characteristics in Children by Religious Group

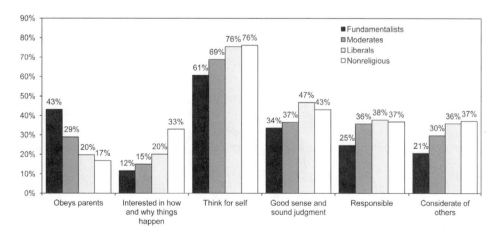

SOURCE: GSS 1973, 1975, 1976, 1978, 1980, 1983

FIGURE 12.3. Percentage of Adults Reporting Desired Characteristics in Children by Importance of Religion

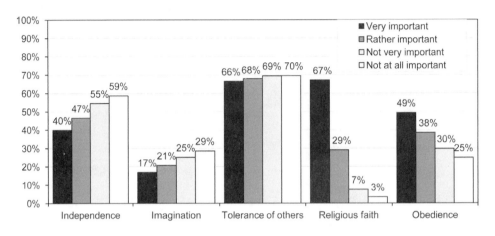

SOURCE: WVS

Additionally, religious fundamentalists want different characteristics in their children than do nonreligious individuals. Religious fundamentalists want children who are obedient; nonreligious and more liberally religious individuals want children who are considerate of others, interested in how the world works, and are able to think for themselves. These differences are shown in figure 12.2. Data in this figure come from a question in the GSS that asks respondents, "Which three qualities listed would you say are the most desirable for a child to have?" Respondents choose their three most desired qualities, and the figure shows what percentage of each religious group chose that characteristic as one of their top three.

International data from the World Values Survey shows the same pattern—those who consider religion very important in their lives want obedient children while the less religious want children who are independent, as shown in figure 12.3. In the WVS respondents chose the five values that were most important to them, in contrast to three in the GSS.

So, why might highly religious parents want obedient children? This is probably a reflection of two factors. The first factor is that religious fundamentalists tend to exhibit an authoritarian personality. What that means is they like rigid structure with clear power differentials. They don't mind being in power, but if they are not in power, they want someone to clearly have power. Thus, religious fundamentalists are fond of respecting authority and obedience—it's part of their personality. The second factor relates to the nature of fundamentalist religions themselves. Fundamentalist religions typically emphasize obedience to the will of god and to

FIGURE 12.4. Percentage of Children Reporting Ability to Make Own Decisions by Importance of Religion

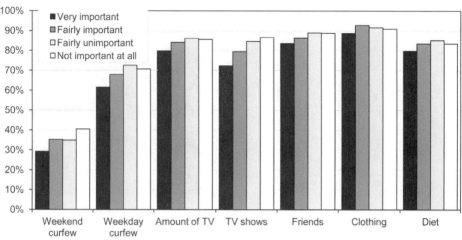

SOURCE: ADHEALTH, WAVE 1

religious leaders. Religious fundamentalism is not known for encouraging people to think about their beliefs. Rather, it is known for encouraging people to follow the beliefs they are taught. In contrast, liberal religions tend to encourage careful consideration of religious doctrine and are much less likely to enforce rigid adherence to orthodox doctrine and statements of faith. Thus, the personalities and religions of highly religious parents encourage obedience in the parents, leading the parents to want similar traits in their children, while the personalities of less religious individuals and the religions of the liberally religious parents do just the opposite.

Lest readers think these statistics are just reflecting desired characteristics in children, it turns out that children report differences in how their parents treat them based upon their religion. Data from a different survey (the Adolescent Health Survey) show that kids who consider religion very important in their lives are also less likely to make their own decisions on everything from their curfew to what they eat and who their friends are. Their parents are more likely to make those decisions for them. This is shown in figure 12.4.

Readers familiar with research on parenting will likely recognize that the characteristics highly religious parents desire in their children fall into the parenting style delineated by Diana Baumrind as being authoritarian. Authoritarian parents tell their kids what to do, demand obedience and respect from their children, and

Figure 12.5. Percentage of Adolescents Reporting Feeling Very or Quite Close to Mother and Father by Importance of Religion

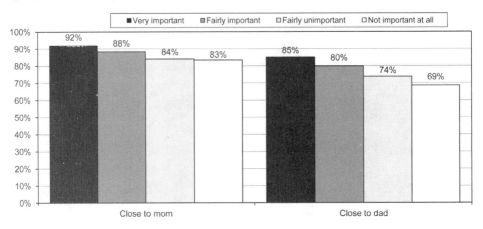

SOURCE: ADHEALTH, WAVE 1

are very strict in their punishments. In contrast, authoritative parents, while they set boundaries and have rules, are more likely to reason with their children and negotiate. (I'm leaving out the third and fourth types—parents who don't set boundaries and parents who are neglectful.) Research suggests better long-term outcomes in education and social adjustment when children are raised using an authoritative style rather than an authoritarian style.

Yet, here's the strange thing. In the same data set from which I drew figure 12.4, the children who report religion being very important also report feeling significantly closer to their parents than those who report religion not being important, though the difference is not large (see figure 12.5).

How can that be the case? I don't actually know the answer to this, but I'm going to offer two possible explanations. The first could be as simple as having something important in common—religion. We tend to view those who share characteristics with us more favorably just because we have characteristics in common. However, it could also be the case that children raised in authoritarian homes confuse "emotional closeness" with "dependency." When they were asked how "close" they were to their parents, they could have been reporting that they were very close, but only because their parents basically ran their lives for them and did not give them much freedom. In contrast, children in homes where religion was not very important were encouraged to think for themselves and their parents gave them greater freedom. As a result, when asked how "close" they were to their parents, they might have been reporting that they weren't as close (though still quite close), because their parents have encouraged them to be more independent. Additional evidence in favor of this interpretation comes from other variables in the same data set that find that there are no differences in the percentage of religious and nonreligious kids who have talked to their parents about someone they are dating or about parties they have attended in the past month. This supports the second explanation—that more religious children confuse dependency with closeness.

What can we conclude about the relationship between religion and parenting? Highly religious parents favor spanking as a form of punishment far more than do nonreligious parents. To what extent that translates into actually spanking isn't perfectly clear, but it is likely the case that religious fundamentalists don't spare the rod with their kids. Highly religious parents also want obedient and respectful children, while less religious parents are more likely to want children who are considerate, interested in the world around them, and able to think for themselves. It appears that parents are getting what they want as highly religious children report less freedom in decision making then do less religious children. These differences in parenting suggest that nonreligious and liberally religious parents employ an authoritative style of parenting while religious fundamentalists and the highly religious employ a more authoritarian style of parenting. Highly religious children do report being slightly closer to their parents, but it's possible the difference reflects dependence on parents, not emotional intimacy or time spent with parents.

13

THERE ARE NO ATHEISTS IN. . . PRISON CELLS?!?
RELIGION AND CRIME

Matt Baker was a pastor of a Baptist congregation in Waco, Texas, in early 2006. He had a wife, Kari, and three daughters, Kassidy, Kensi, and Grace. To most of those who knew Matt, he was a dedicated family man. As a Baptist pastor in Texas, no one really questioned Matt's ethics. His privileged position in his community opened doors—and apparently vaginas—that would not have been available to him otherwise. Matt used the power of his position to seduce one of his parishioners, a divorced mother who had recently joined his congregation, Vanessa Bulls. Of course, today in the United States it is not a crime to have an affair. Having an affair was unethical, but not illegal.

However, Matt's story doesn't end there. On April 7, 2006, Matt gave his wife, Kari, sleeping medication, handcuffed her, then smothered her with a pillow. He then typed up a fake suicide note and called the police, claiming that he had found his wife unresponsive and that he thought she had committed suicide. Matt's story was initially accepted by law enforcement, probably because of the esteem associated with his position as a Baptist pastor. But Kari's family, who knew Kari was not suicidal, didn't believe him. They hired a private investigator who eventually uncovered the affair, leading law enforcement to reopen the case. Eventually investigators found sufficient evidence to try Matt for the murder of his wife. A jury found him guilty in July 2010.

Fact: Matt Baker was a Baptist pastor.

Fact: Being a Baptist pastor did not prevent Matt Baker from killing his wife or from trying to cover it up.

—§—

The best data available suggest that religious people are no less likely to commit crimes or engage in deviant acts than are nonreligious people. There is some research that suggests young people in high-risk neighborhoods who spend a lot of time in churches are less likely to engage in crime. That's a finding in favor of religion and perfectly reasonable as well. Why? Because if young people are spending their time in church, they can't be on the streets committing crimes, can they?

Does this mean religion reduces criminality? Not at all. When you use a different measure of religiosity—like how important religion is to these young people—there is no difference in crime rates. So, considering religion important to you doesn't reduce criminal behavior, but spending time doing something other than engaging in criminal behavior does. Seems kind of obvious, doesn't it?

The scientific evidence also suggests that religion is not a deterrent to criminal behavior, as the introductory story suggested. Prison inmates are disproportionately religious and atheists are significantly underrepresented among convicted felons in the United States. The countries with the lowest crime rates in the world also have some of the lowest rates of religiosity. Countries that have higher crime rates, including the United States, also have some of the highest levels of religiosity. If religiosity reduced criminality, then the reverse should be true. Since it is clearly not true, the obvious conclusion is that religiosity, depending on how you measure it, doesn't reduce criminality. Let me state that again for emphasis: the higher the religiosity in a country, the higher the rates of criminal behavior, which is just the opposite of what many religious people claim.

Why might this be the case? Some advocates of secularism have claimed a causal relationship here. They suggest that religion increases crime rates and secularization reduces them. I don't think that is actually true. I think this is a great example of what statisticians refer to as a "spurious" relationship. Yes, religiosity and criminality are correlated, but, in all likelihood, the relationship between the two is the result of modernization, which leads to higher levels of education, fewer economic disparities, better social welfare programs, and lower poverty rates. As societies modernize, they become less religious. One major contributor to that is education. But another is social welfare programs, like universal healthcare, retirement programs, unemployment benefits, etc. Most modern and developed societies—the United States being a prominent exception—have complex and robust social welfare programs that go a long way toward reducing poverty. When peoples' needs are largely met, the need to engage in criminal behavior is substantially reduced. As a result, most of the highly developed countries around the world have lower rates of criminal behavior than less developed countries (and the United States). And since they also have lower rates of religiosity, there is a correlation. But lower religiosity likely isn't the major factor in reduced crime rates; it's modernization.

Figure 13.1. Percentage Engaging in Criminal Behaviors by Religious Group

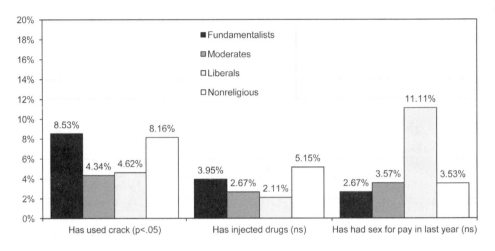

source: GSS, 2010

Why would I suggest that there is no causal relationship? Because there does not appear to be much of a relationship between criminal behavior and religiosity at all—religious and irreligious people commit crimes. Data from the General Social Survey support this. While there are some minor differences between our four religious groups in some areas, only one difference in figure 13.1 is what statisticians call "statistically significant," meaning there is a meaningful mathematical difference, and that is in crack cocaine use. Both fundamentalists and the nonreligious are more likely to have used crack cocaine than are moderates and liberals.

There is not a significant difference between the religious groups in whether or not they have ever injected drugs or had sex for pay, though religious liberals appear to be getting it on! As figure 13.1 shows, religiosity does not reduce criminality.

Now, I have a question for you: why might being religious reduce criminality?

Scientists regularly come up with theories and then test them. Can you think of a logically consistent, rational reason why religious people would be less likely to engage in criminal behavior than nonreligious people?

One possibility would be something like, "Well, religions encourage people to be moral, which should reduce criminality." That would be nice if it were true. I address the issue of morality and differences in morality by religiosity in the next chapter at length. (Spoiler alert: there is no difference in moral behavior!)

Turning this around, I would actually argue that there is reason to believe that religious people would be more likely to engage in criminal behavior than nonreligious people. Many religious people think about the law in a rather disturbing way. Basically, they are fine following the laws of the land. . . until or unless the law runs counter to their religious beliefs. At that point, their religious beliefs trump the law. This can and does happen. Hutterites in Canada, while typically law abiding, have refused to follow the law in instances where it runs counter to their religious views, like getting a photograph for a driver's license (not really a big deal) or not paying income tax because their religion does not believe in private property and they therefore cannot receive personal income (a bigger deal). Catholic clergy, while typically law abiding, have not followed the law when it comes to reporting sexual abuse by priests and have even tried to cover up sexual abuse by clergy. Brigham Young, the second prophet of the Mormon Church, sent a militia of soldiers to harass federal troops who were on their way to Utah, believing the troops were going to attack his followers. When religious people believe there is a conflict between what their god wants them to do and what the government wants them to do, typically they side with their god, leading them to engage in criminal behavior. Religions and religious people can and sometimes do put "God's laws" above secular laws. Of course, in the modern world, where religious people are subject to secular governments and religions only exist because secular governments give them the right to exist, religious people typically follow the law. Regardless, theorizing that religion makes people more likely to behave legally because religions encourage moral and legal behavior isn't very compelling. Religions can actually encourage civil disobedience and illegal behavior!

Some readers might object to the assertion of this chapter that religion doesn't reduce the odds of criminal behavior based on their interpretation of their religion. This train of thought typically goes something like this: "You can't be a Christian if you commit crimes. So, people like Matt Baker aren't 'true' Christians." As soon as someone adds a qualifier to religious membership beyond self-declaration (i.e., "I'm a Catholic because I say I am."), they have started down a slippery slope to the land of logical fallacies. This fallacy is known as the "No True Scotsman" fallacy. The flaw in this logic lies in the fact that the person making the argument is changing the definition of what it means to be something in order to rule out those he does not want included in that category.

An absurd example will help illustrate this. My parents had a lot of kids—nine, to be exact. Of those, most have brown hair, myself included. If for some really stupid reason I wanted to define a member of my family out of the family, I could say something really asinine like, "Only those with brown hair are 'true' Craguns." That, of course, would be ridiculous, especially considering my dad had red hair (alas, his hair is now white). In this example, the fallacy is obvious—I've simply defined into a group those I want to include in the group and defined out those I want to exclude. No reasonable person would really believe that the hair color of a member of my family would play a role in determining membership in my family.

Those trying to rule criminals out of their religion are committing the same fallacy. Just because a member of a religion does something stupid, criminal, or horrendous doesn't mean they are no longer members of that religion. People want to define them out of the religion to make themselves feel good about their own religion. No one wants to feel like they belong to a group that includes really terrible people. Joseph Stalin had brown hair. Because he and I both have brown hair, does that mean I'm a terrible person? Or should I rule him out of the group of brunettes by saying, "Joseph Stalin was no 'true' brunette!" See how silly that sounds when I use something like hair color? Just because someone shares a characteristic with you does not mean their behavior reflects upon you.

But religious people do this all the time when their coreligionists do bad things. Because they believe, erroneously, that their religion should lead people to behave in positive ways, when someone does not behave in such a fashion, they claim that person is not a "true" member of the religion. There is a much easier way to deal with the poor behavior of some people—admit that religion does not keep people from behaving in illegal or unethical ways. Scientific data back this up. Logic backs this up. And millions of religious prison inmates back this up as well.

Religion doesn't keep people from committing crimes. Religions may encourage legal behavior, but only when secular laws do not contravene god's laws. While some might go so far as to say that being religious increases the likelihood that people do commit crimes, I don't think the evidence is solidly suggestive of that either. Religiosity has very little influence on criminal behavior, though there are far fewer atheists in prisons than there are in foxholes and more secular countries have lower overall crime rates than highly religious countries.

14

MORAL DEVELOPMENT—WIN FOR ATHEISTS
MORAL BEHAVIOR—DRAW

When I was seventeen, two of my closest friends did something unethical. I grew up in a small town in Utah called Morgan. Despite being a small town, it had two prominent trade routes running through it—a railroad and Interstate 84, which connects Utah with Wyoming and everything east of Utah. When we were seniors in high school, I-84 was being resurfaced, resulting in substantial construction throughout the county. A couple of miles before the exit to Morgan the traffic on the eastbound side of I-84 was being redirected to the westbound lanes, which were divided with concrete barriers. Running between them was a temporary lane paved with asphalt. Large orange barrels had been set up to help guide cars from one side to the other.

My two friends, I'll call them Mack and Tim, decided to take advantage of the construction for their own amusement. They stopped by my house before they went out and asked if I wanted to go. For some reason I bowed out that night. Around 1:00 a.m. they arrived at the section under construction, pulled their car off the road so it was well hidden, then proceeded to move the orange barrels. They tried a variety of arrangements, from a straight line across the interstate to a gradual line pushing cars off to the right into the grass and gravel. Once they had an arrangement complete, they would hide in the grass on the side of the road to see what would happen. Some cars and trucks plowed right through the barrels, others slowed and slowly worked their way around them, trying to figure out what they were supposed to do.

After several hours of amusing themselves doing this, they left and returned to my house, probably around 4:00 a.m., where they recounted their adventures to their and my amusement. We then fell asleep and thought nothing of it. Several days later there was a story in the local paper about an accident on I-84 on the night Mack and Tim were out messing around with the barrels. A car had run off the road and had suffered some minor damage. No one was hurt, but the paper included an advert for a $1,000 reward for information leading to the arrest of the individuals responsible for the accident.

All three of us were fairly devout Mormons at the time. Does our behavior reflect poorly on our religion? Would you have done something like this when you were seventeen? And was I morally obligated to turn my friends in to the police?

I'm going to be completely up-front about not wanting to write this chapter. I'm not an ethicist. I don't claim to be an expert on ethics. But social science does have something to say about ethics and there are some data on this question, so I'll do my best.

However, there are some things I'm not going to do in this chapter. I'm not going to engage in a lengthy discussion about whether or not religion is necessary for morality. That has been done at length by other people who are much better qualified to discuss it. The short answer is that religion is not necessary. I'm also not going to debate whether an ethical system based on religion is superior to an ethical system not based on religion. That, too, has been addressed elsewhere by people who are more knowledgeable about such things.

What does this chapter do then? Two things. First, I'm going to take as my starting point that there are better and worse ways of thinking about what is right and what is wrong. While not without its criticisms, the most widely cited social scientific ideas in this area are Lawrence Kohlberg's stages of moral development. The basic idea is that, during human development, people move from more simplistic ways of thinking about what is right and wrong to more complex ways. In evaluating someone's stage of moral development, the key isn't what the person would do but rather what motivates the action. Thus, someone at the most basic stage of moral development could do the same thing as someone at the most developed; the difference in development is in how they arrive at concluding whether an action is right or wrong.

Kohlberg's approach suggests there are six stages of moral reasoning. Starting with the most basic, which is common in children, people are primarily concerned with the direct consequences of their actions on themselves. In other words, if they will get punished if they do something, they will try not to do it. The second stage involves acting out of self-benefit rather than avoiding punishment. The third stage is a recognition that there are social norms and expectations and that you should live up to them. The fourth stage involves behaving morally because it is the law. The fifth stage attributes moral behavior to a social contract with others. Rules aren't immutable, but they should always be geared toward the greatest benefit for the greatest number. The final stage of moral development involves applying moral reasoning based on universal ethical principles. In this stage, people can disregard laws if the laws are unjust. This stage of reasoning also requires the individual to take on the role of others in order to understand all of the factors that influenced their behavior before deciding how to evaluate their behavior.

What may not be clear from the above is that Kohlberg's stages largely reflect a move from black-or-white, right-or-wrong type thinking to a more relativistic thinking about morality. In the black or white worldview, something is either right or wrong. There is no middle ground. The source of determining whether something is black or white isn't really questioned. As people progress through the stages of moral development, they do not think in absolutes and they question the source of morality. What may be right in one situation may not be right in another. Some things may be morally ambiguous and that is perfectly acceptable. Sometimes there are not clear right or wrong answers.

Let me take this from the abstract to the concrete. I've mentioned my son before. He was two when I was writing this. I do not tell my son at this stage in his life that it's sometimes okay to hit. I don't think he would understand that it is okay for Anderson Silva or Georges St. Pierre, mixed martial artists, to hit someone in a match, but not okay to just punch random strangers or even people you don't like. Instead of trying to explain the difference, I find myself saying things like, "We don't hit, Toren." To reinforce this, if he hits, he gets a time-out. My son's level of cognitive development doesn't allow him to consider the possibility that there are different expectations in different contexts.

Now contrast my son with my college students. I take great pleasure in trying to confuse them as to what is morally correct. For instance, in a class I teach on human sexuality, I raised the question as to whether consensual, nonprocreative sex between siblings is morally wrong. So long as there are no offspring, which addresses the concern about higher incidences of birth defects due to consanguinity, and the sex is consensual (typically experimental), the scientific evidence seems to suggest that there are no long-term psychological consequences to such sex. If all of the above is true, is consensual, nonprocreative sex between siblings for experimental sexual exploration morally wrong? Framing it that way, I was able to convince a class of thirty college students that such sex was not immoral. Don't get me wrong. I'm not advocating consensual sibling sex. I'm simply using it as an example of the type of situation that requires more complex moral reasoning.

So, where am I going with this? Well, the evidence seems to suggest that the more religious you are, the less developed your moral reasoning is. In fact, one of the characteristics of religious fundamentalism is that such individuals engage in

Figure 14.1. Views on Morality *Not* Being Black and White by Religious Group

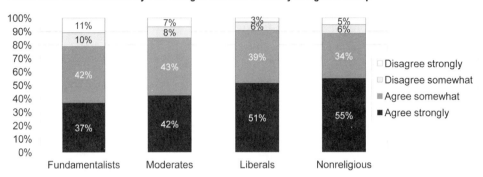

SOURCE: GSS, 2010

black-or-white thinking. In the limited data I found readily accessible on this from the General Social Survey, the relationship is quite clear. In figure 14.1 you can see that the more fundamentalist someone is, the less likely they are to say that right and wrong is not black and white. Nonreligious individuals are the most likely to say that right and wrong is not black and white.

What does this mean? The above doesn't mean that nonreligious people are "better" than highly religious people. This isn't about evaluating the worth of individuals. What it means is that nonreligious people are more developed in their moral reasoning. The obvious follow-up question is: does that translate into nonreligious people engaging in more moral behavior?

Here we run into a problem, a problem that has long plagued the social sciences. The issue is that highly religious people see some things as immoral while nonreligious people see other things as immoral. For instance, for some religious groups, drinking alcohol is immoral, as is watching pornography, having sex before marriage, using drugs, and swearing. The nonreligious are much more likely to consider all of the above perfectly fine, within reason. So, if you use the morality of the highly religious as your basis for judging moral behavior, then of course the nonreligious are less moral than the highly religious. But you have also started from a highly biased position. You're basically playing a game in which one person gets to set the rules and they set the rules to favor what they do.

If you turn the tables and instead use the morality of the nonreligious as your basis for judgment, you get very different results. Nonreligious individuals are more likely to consider it immoral to: not allow homosexuals to marry, not recycle, not allow homosexuals to adopt children, prohibit interracial marriage, have huge disparities in wealth, and not allow women to have equal rights. If you use these as the basis of your comparisons, not surprisingly, highly religious individuals come out looking pretty immoral.

So, what's the solution? In the limited research that has tried to step above these loaded issues and focus on something that both groups can agree is immoral, like cheating on a test or a spouse, or moral, like helping those in need, there are no notable differences between the nonreligious and the religious. Religion doesn't make people more or less moral.

For those wondering what I did when I found out there was an accident as a result of what my friends did, I did not report them. At the time, my allegiance to my friends and the limited severity of the crash were the two factors I weighed when considering what I should do. Did I do the right thing? I'm not sure, but my religion did not factor into my decision and I'd likely make the same decision today, as an atheist.

There are different ways of reasoning about morality. Lawrence Kohlberg argued that some ways of reasoning were "superior" to others. Nonreligious people are more likely to reason about morality in those "superior" ways. However, their "superior" moral reasoning does not seem to translate into morally "superior" behavior when using objective measures of moral behavior, like cheating on a test or a spouse. The religious and nonreligious tend to behave about the same from a moral standpoint. Fearing a god's wrath or not recognizing the existence of a god doesn't seem to matter when it comes to moral behavior.

15

IF YOU'RE HUMBLE AND YOU KNOW IT. . .
RELIGION AND ARROGANCE

Do you remember where you were and what you were doing on April 7, 2004, from 11:42 to 11:53 a.m.? Most readers probably don't. I do. I remember it very clearly. I was chatting with my younger brother, Josh, via an instant messaging client. (It helps that I keep my chat logs.)

I left the Mormon religion in the summer of 2002. The fallout of that decision continued for several years as I had to negotiate a new relationship with my still-Mormon family. Part of that negotiation was dealing with my family's version of why I left the religion. The motives they attributed to me and my decision were and, frankly, still are, hurtful. In retrospect, I should have expected something like this (for reasons I'll explain later), especially since I was being trained as a sociologist at the time. But actually going through it is far different from simply studying it.

Josh was serving as a missionary for the Mormon Church when I left the religion. I'm sure it was hard for him and my other younger siblings as we were all close and, I believe (in part because they have told me so), they had looked up to me as a faithful member of the religion. My brother had the courage to discuss my decision to leave the religion on several occasions despite warnings from church leaders not to associate with "apostates." We had discussed my leaving several times before the conversation reported below, but this conversation was the culmination of those discussions.

Here is basically how it went (edited for spelling, grammar, and flow, but still in chat format):

Josh: So you tell me, once and for all, completely honestly, was there sin involved or not? . . . And I'll believe you (not that I didn't before. . .).

Ryan: I left because I do not believe what Mormonism teaches, not because of sin. Of course, it helps that I no longer believe in sin, but based on your definition of sin, I left not because of sin.

Josh: But what I'm getting at is: did you come to that conclusion because of sin?

Ryan: If doubting the existence of god is a sin, then I obviously sinned. If not reading your scriptures every day is a sin, then I obviously sinned. If believing prayer is ineffectual, then I sinned. If being critical of the church and its leaders is a sin, then I sinned. But in the sense you mean, no I was not a sinner.

Josh: Well that answers that. The rumors are circulating, and, much as you said, they tend to lean toward saying you sinned and were too proud to repent.

Ryan: Um, who said this? Because that is a bunch of shit.

Josh: Someone came to the conclusion that you slept with someone while you were out here away from Debi [my wife] and that's when you went AWOL, which I thought was laughable, but I didn't really know the truth. So, I didn't refute anything.

Ryan: Sick, wrong, delusional, and typical Mormon bullshit.

Josh: LOL. Yeah, I thought you would like that.

Ryan: Um, who came up with this? I have never had sex with anyone other than Debi—end of story!

Josh: I don't know. Shortly after I came home [from his LDS mission in Spain], that was the rumor circulating among the family—not necessarily that you slept with someone, but that a mixture of sin and *pride* led you away.

Let me summarize just to be clear. After I informed my family that I was no longer going to be attending or participating in the Mormon religion, someone in my family suggested that the reason why I had decided to leave was because I had an affair and was too *proud* to repent. And, yes, it was an immediate family member who suggested this, either a sibling, one of my siblings' spouses, or one of my parents (I still don't know who).

The accusation of adultery is, in fact, a brilliant accusation. If they had accused me of, say, piercing my scrotum or getting a tattoo on my ass, I could have easily dispelled that rumor. But accusing me of adultery is smart because, while I can deny it, there is no way I can prove that I did not commit adultery.

But the point I want to emphasize here is not that my family accused me of committing adultery, which is a really terrible thing to do. The point is they accused me of being too *proud* to repent of my sin. While I no longer think my family believes I committed adultery, I'm fairly certain they remain convinced that my pride is keeping me out of the religion. I recently had a Mormon friend confirm to me that he thinks that is the major impediment keeping me from returning to the religion—I am too learned and arrogant in my "worldly" knowledge (i.e., science and scholarship), preventing me from seeing the truthfulness of religion. Accusations of pride are a common weapon in the arsenal of the religious. This chapter will remove that weapon from their arsenal (and give it to the nonreligious).

—§—

Pride is a tricky concept to tackle. Pride, in one sense, is actually an important element of positive mental health. Everyone should be proud of who they are in the sense that they have a reasonable sense of self-respect. Not being proud of who you are and lacking self-respect is actually an indication of poor self-esteem and poor mental health. Used in this sense, pride isn't bad at all and really is something to be sought after.

However, the religious typically don't think about pride this way. When they level their accusations of pride at those who disagree with them (because you can't disagree with them on logical or reasonable grounds), what they really mean is more along the lines of either conceit, which is an excessive appreciation of one's own worth, or arrogance, which is an attitude of superiority that is often manifested by making presumptuous claims or assumptions. Alleging pride in nonbelievers is quite common among the religious and appears in scripture regularly, like the following verses:

> Proverbs 16:5—*The LORD detests all the proud of heart. Be sure of this: They will not go unpunished.*

> Proverbs 16:18—*Pride goes before destruction, a haughty spirit before a fall.*

While the religious mean arrogance and conceit when they accuse people of being proud, what they are really doing is accusing people of dissenting. Religious people don't actually hate that some people are arrogant or conceited (else they would hate themselves). What they hate is when someone challenges them or disagrees with them. To curtail dissent, they call it "pride" or "arrogance" and they use this to demean those who question. In a remarkable manipulation of language, the religious have completely inverted the meaning of pride. When the religious say you should be humble, they actually mean "claim to know stuff you don't." And when the religious say it is bad to be proud, they are actually criticizing those who question and doubt.

To question something isn't arrogant; it's exactly the opposite. Those who question are unsure of what they know or believe. What they are exhibiting is humility, not conceit. Yet it is those who question who are accused of being proud. Confusing, isn't it?

Among the most common recipients of accusations of arrogance by the religious are people with advanced education who question or don't believe. Believers assert that those with "worldly" education believe they know more than the leaders of religions (which, not surprisingly, is often true).

I have had several friends and family members accuse me of being arrogant because of my education. There is a great deal of irony in this. When I was a Mormon, I was an arrogant asshole. I condemned people to hell, regularly. I refused to associate with people who I believed were sinners. In fact, one of my closest friends in high school did not disclose to me that he was having sex with his girlfriend because he thought I would stop hanging out with him. It pains me to admit it now, but he was probably right—I would have pitied him for having no self-control and for sinning, and would have cut him off so I would not be tainted by his sinfulness. And, more relevant to the point at hand, I thought I knew everything there was to know about Mormonism and I was certain that what I believed and did was right without question. As I noted in the story that began this chapter, I left Mormonism because I learned more about it, not because I was too proud to repent (for a sin I didn't commit, no less). When I was religious, I was proud and arrogant, yet called myself humble. Now that I've left religion, I'm accused of being proud by the religious, yet I'm much more humble. I now admit that there is a hell of a lot I don't know about most things. My wife has even pointed out that the nickname she gave me when we met, "Arro" (short for "arrogant"), no longer fits.

Before I left Mormonism, I had a lot of people come to me when they had doubts or questions. I frequently answered them, thinking I had all the answers. Yet, now that I actually have more knowledge and information about Mormonism, most Mormons refuse to talk to me. They don't consider me trustworthy anymore. Religious believers will turn to someone with virtually no formal education for answers so long as the answers validate their existing beliefs, but will shun someone with formal education who has evidence that doesn't validate their beliefs. Which of these two informants is proud: the uneducated person claiming to know things he doesn't, or the educated person who provides the limited information available to him bounded by the limits of probability?

What the above suggests is that, based on objective definitions of arrogance, pride, and conceit, it is highly likely that nonreligious individuals will be less arrogant than religious individuals. Arrogance includes making presumptuous claims. Claiming to *know* things when you don't know them is arrogant. While many liberal religious people phrase their beliefs in tentative terms, more fundamentalist people do not. They insist that the things they believe are real. In fact, they typically will not say things like, "I believe in a god" or "I hope there is a heaven." What they will say is, "I know there is a god" and "Heaven is real." They assert that these beliefs are facts with no evidence. Is that humble?

Contrast religious assertions with scientific assertions. Science is, at heart, a tentative endeavor. Scientists may assert that they "know" certain things, but they only do so once the evidence for those things is overwhelming! For example, a scientist could assert that earthquakes are due to shifting tectonic plates and say, "Earthquakes result when the plates that make up the earth's crust move." The evidence behind this claim is compelling enough at this point that no scientists question it. It is a defensible assertion given the mountains of evidence that exist to support this claim (pun intended). What you will rarely, if ever, hear a scientist say is that she knows something is true when she has no evidence to support the assertion.

This is basically how social scientists frame everything we write. We know there is discrimination against racial minorities in the United States. But we don't know how extensive it is or to what extent the discrimination accounts for the higher rates of poverty among many racial minorities. We can assert that discrimination against racial minorities contributes to higher rates of poverty among those groups, but you will not find a reputable social scientist who would say, "I am 100% certain that racial discrimination accounts for 53.748534% of the difference in poverty rates between blacks and whites." We just aren't that certain. We make estimates, but those estimates are always couched in various levels of uncertainty. We don't speak in definitives. We speak in probabilities, despite having evidence to support our assertions.

Contrast these two positions. The religious person, without any evidence, asserts that certain things are true. This is done purely on faith. Scientists, who have evidence to back up their claims, typically couch their claims as tentative and probabilistic (i.e., more or less likely). If arrogance is making presumptuous claims or assertions, which of the two groups is more arrogant: those who definitively claim to know things without evidence or those who suggest they may know something based on evidence? I'll help you: it's the religious who are arrogant, not scientists.

I don't mean to suggest that all nonreligious people are scientists or think scientifically (though many do and a large percentage of scientists are nonreligious). But nonreligious people are much less likely to assert that they *know* things than are religious people. The empirical evidence bears this out. Figure 15.1 displays the results of several questions from the World Values Survey that illustrate various aspects of arrogance.

FIGURE 15.1. Characteristics of Pride by Importance of Religion

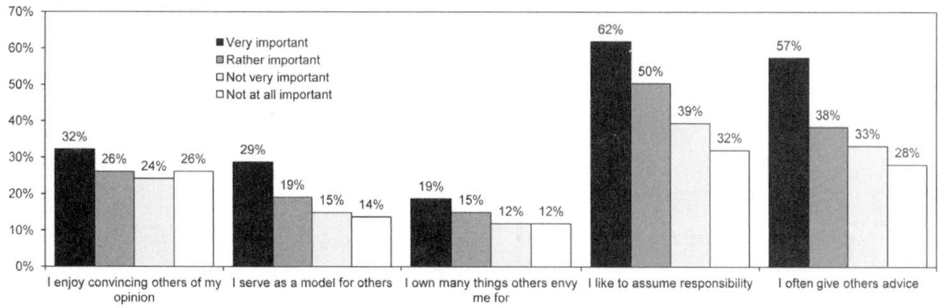

SOURCE: WVS

The questions depicted in figure 15.1 ask whether the respondent considers him or herself to have specific characteristics. The first question asked respondents if the following statement described them, "I enjoy convincing others of my opinion." The most religious individuals around the world are the most likely to agree with that statement. They are also the most likely to agree with all the others shown in the figure, including, "I serve as a model for others," "I own many things others envy me for," "I like to assume responsibility," and, the coup de grâce when it comes to arrogance, "I often give others advice." The most religious score almost 20 percent higher than the next most religious and 30 percent higher than the nonreligious. In other words, if anyone has an inflated sense of self-importance, indicative of conceit, it is the highly religious. The nonreligious are, on most measures, the least conceited. Other researchers have arrived at the same conclusion using other data—highly religious people are the least humble and the most arrogant as they claim to know things when they don't, while the least religious do just the opposite.

There may be some readers who are surprised by this finding. I don't find it surprising at all. Many people turn to religion precisely because it gives them a sense of importance and significance. Think about it this way: the modern world is a big, scary place. It is virtually impossible today to not be aware of your insignificance. Very few people have the influence and fame to be considered actors on the world stage. Most of us are bit players in local productions with no chance of ever making a name for ourselves outside of our family, let alone our neighborhood or our city. Modernization breeds a sense of insignificance.

Religion, particularly exclusive, strident, fundamentalist, monotheistic religion, offers an antidote to insignificance: a personal relationship with a supreme, supernatural being. The world may pass you by; your family may even reject you.

But your god knows you, cares about you, and will alleviate all of your problems in the afterlife. What's more, this "personal" god will actually listen to you when no one else will. He (sometimes she) is always listening—literally, always. How better to make someone feel significant than to give them an omnipotent, omnibenevolent, always approachable, and always supportive buddy?

Additionally, for monotheists, the god they worship epitomizes arrogance. He is (allegedly) self-described as jealous, supreme, superior, all-knowing, all-powerful, and perfect. If you met someone who described himself/herself as having just one of these characteristics, let alone all of them, wouldn't you consider that person to be arrogant? Worshipers of an arrogant god who hypocritically demands humility happen to be arrogant. Is anyone surprised by this?

Of course, it's not just the god of monotheists who is arrogant or proud. Any religious leader who claims to be able to interpret god's will better than any other person can only be considered to be arrogant as he/she is claiming to have superior knowledge to others—ironically by claiming superior knowledge about the unknowable.

Gods are proud. Religious leaders are proud. And highly religious people are proud. This is not pride in the "pride-is-good-for-your-self-esteem" sense but in the "we're-better-than-you-and-claim-to-know-shit-we-don't" sense. It seems, then, that the cornerstone of religion is not humility, but pride.

Religions' use of pride is a brilliant bit of marketing and doublespeak. Religions and religious people decry pride as being a terrible thing. They assert that pride will lead people out of religion or keep people from becoming religious. And yet, the more religious you are, the prouder, more arrogant, and more conceited you are. Religious people consider themselves to be more righteous than nonreligious people; religious people consider themselves to be better than nonreligious people; and religious people claim to know more than nonreligious people. Religious people exhibit all the characteristics of pride, but they call it humility. They're humble and they *know* it.

16

'CAUSE JESUS HAS A PENIS
RELIGION AND GENDER (IN)EQUALITY

Sansa was raised Mormon in a very devout family. She was taught her whole life what her role was supposed to be as a Mormon woman—to be a faithful wife and mother. She did her best to make that dream a reality. She attended Brigham Young University, the flagship university of the Mormon Church located in Provo, Utah, and after just a single year she met a faithful Mormon who had just returned from his mission, Joffrey. They married shortly after meeting and kids followed quickly—seven of them.

To those outside their family, Sansa and Joffrey seemed like the perfect Mormon couple—they had lots of kids and were active participants in the religion. But all was not as it seemed. Joffrey was abusive. He beat Sansa regularly. He also insisted that she was lazy, despite Sansa's many activities. Sansa played the piano quite well, so she taught lessons to bring in extra income. She played the piano at a local Episcopal church to bring in even more money, despite the internal conflict she and Joffrey felt about her helping members of a different religion. In addition to her musical talents, Sansa knew how to sew; she sewed all of the childrens' clothes and mended other peoples' clothes. She also managed a paper delivery route. She did all of this on top of having responsibilities in the local Mormon church and while managing a large household of active children. Yet it was never enough for Joffrey, who criticized her relentlessly and beat her mercilessly.

Sansa wasn't happy, but her religious indoctrination made it difficult for her to figure out why. She thought the problem was with her—that she was simply not doing enough for her husband, and that it was her responsibility to make him happy. She began to question that one day when Joffrey turned his wrath on one of the children, punching, kicking, and battering him in their garage. Realizing something was wrong, Sansa turned to the resource she had always been taught held the answers—her local religious leader. This leader, Bishop Lannister, listened to

Sansa's concerns, then told her that the fault did, in fact, lay with her. If Joffrey was beating her and the kids, it was because Sansa was not living up to her responsibilities as a good Mormon wife. She was told to go home, cook Joffrey a cherry pie, and be more humble and subservient.

Sansa tried. It did not work. The more she submitted to Joffrey, the more domineering and abusive he became. Sansa continued to believe that there were problems, and even packed up and left for a few days, hoping it would teach Joffrey a lesson. It did, but not the lesson she intended. Joffrey, in consultation with Bishop Lannister, decided that there was a problem with Sansa and that she needed counseling. Little did they realize that counseling was precisely what Sansa needed to give her the strength to do what she should. Talking with a counselor helped her realize that the problem was not with her and that spousal abuse was never justifiable. The counselor also suggested that this may be a marriage that needed to end, even though he had been told specifically by Bishop Lannister to save the marriage.

Sansa started to save up money and make photocopies of important documents. She contacted an attorney. Once she threatened divorce, Joffrey finally started to ease up, but that, of course, was a ploy. Once he realized she was serious, the abuse returned, forcing Sansa to get a protective order against him. She served him with divorce papers the same day she got the protective order. Sansa followed through with the divorce, leaving her abuser. Bishop Lannister excommunicated Sansa for leaving her husband shortly after the divorce.

The above story was posted on a Web site geared toward helping those who have left the Mormon Church deal with the resulting trauma. It was posted anonymously and didn't include any names, so I added some fake names and rewrote the story to make it more concise. Since the story is anonymous, some might question whether it is true. Maybe it's not. But even if this particular story is not real, there are plenty of others that are. Both my wife and I have met people who have experienced very similar events—women who were abused by their spouses and by their church leaders. While these examples may be somewhat rare, they illustrate quite well the patriarchal nature of religion at three levels: the submissiveness taught to women, the domination and aggressiveness taught to men, and the support of this hierarchy reinforced by the religion.

I want to make three points in this chapter when it comes to the relationship between religion and gender equality. My first point relates to the issue of how women are treated in religions. One half of the Christian denominations in the United States today do not allow women to be ordained. That number will vary by country, but there are discriminatory religions in pretty much all countries (Catholics are every-where!). The reasons given for not allowing female ordination are pretty ridiculous. For example, priests are supposed to be representatives of Jesus, and since the essential feature of Jesus that made him a god was that he had a dick, only men can be priests. Seriously, that's the primary rationale used by the Catholic Church for not allowing women to be ordained. Here's a quote illustrating this from the 1976 Declaration on the Question of the Admission of Women to the Ministerial Priesthood,

> The Christian priesthood is therefore of a sacramental nature: the priest is a sign, the supernatural effectiveness of which comes from the ordination received, but a sign that must be perceptible and which the faithful must be able to recognize with ease. . . . When Christ's role in the Eucharist is to be expressed sacramentally, there would not be this "natural resemblance" which must exist between Christ and his minister if the role of Christ were not taken by a man.

The real reason why these religions don't ordain women is because they are trying to recruit members who are conservative and antimodern; they are targeting a specific type of religious consumer—misogynists. By emphasizing their misogyny, they are distinguishing themselves from religions that are not stuck in the Dark Ages.

But what about the religions that do ordain women? Are women treated well in those religions? Actually, not really. In pretty much every religion in which women are allowed to be ordained, female clergy make less money than male clergy, are less likely to get jobs (when they do get jobs they are in smaller, less prestigious churches), and are less likely to be head pastors than are men. In short, female clergy are not treated all that well. Admittedly, gender disparities exist outside religion as well. But shouldn't religions actually follow their own teachings, particularly about

FIGURE 16.1. Sex Differences in Religiosity

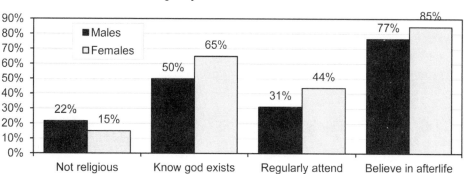

SOURCE: GSS, 2010

FIGURE 16.2. Sex Differences in Religiosity around the World

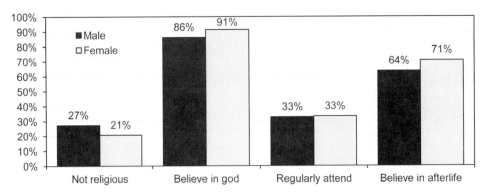

SOURCE: WVS

things like equality between the sexes, so they can set an example for the rest of society? Um, yeah, that's so ridiculous as to be humorous. Religions have not led the charge toward gender equality; they have been the primary opponents. Some have been pulled into the modern age, but typically not because they wanted to be.

My second point is all the more remarkable in light of the above: women are, amazingly, more religious than men. This is easily illustrated with data from both the General Social Survey and the World Values Survey. In both, women are more likely to report having a religious affiliation, believing in a god, attending religious services, and believing in an afterlife (see figures 16.1 and 16.2).

FIGURE 16.3. Attitudes toward Women by Religious Group

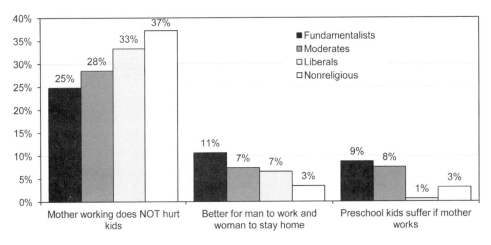

SOURCE: GSS, 2010

FIGURE **16.4. Attitudes toward Women by Importance of Religion**

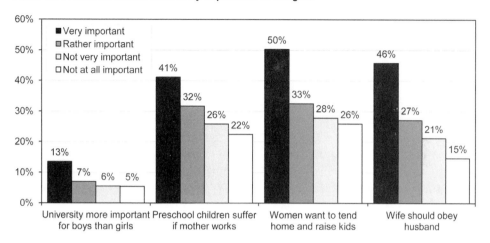

SOURCE: WVS

Unfortunately, I don't have a good explanation for you as to why women are more religious than men. This is currently being debated by social scientists, with explanations ranging from biological differences to differences in socialization. It's probably some combination of the two, but we don't really have a definitive answer on this question.

My third point is that religion does seem to make people, both men and women, more misogynistic. In both the General Social Survey and the World Values Survey, more religious people hold less egalitarian views toward women. They are less likely to be willing to vote for women, more likely to believe women should not work outside the home, less likely to think women should be educated, and more likely to think women should be focused primarily on raising kids; these relationships hold in the United States and internationally, as figures 16.3 and 16.4 indicate.

In short, the more religious the individual is, the more patriarchal he or she is likely to be. The less religious someone is, the more egalitarian he or she is likely to be. This holds despite the fact that men are more likely to be nonreligious. Women, if you want a feminist husband, marry an atheist!

It's not really all that hard to explain why highly religious people are more misogynistic than are less religious people: most extant religions today are patriarchal and that patriarchy is pervasive in their scriptures and teachings. Some anthropologists attribute the pervasiveness of patriarchy to food scarcity, which empowered men to the point that they were able to radically modify gender relations and begin to dominate women. Once patriarchy was established in those societies, religion was used to justify it. These groups then conquered other more egalitarian or matriarchal groups, leading to the pervasiveness of patriarchy and misogynistic religion around the world today.

Lots of religions don't allow women full equality when it comes to leadership positions—close to half in the United States alone. In some religions (e.g., Roman Catholicism), this discriminatory practice is literally based on the fact that Jesus had a penis. In those religions that do allow women to hold leadership positions, women are still treated poorly, with lower pay and less prestigious posts. Yet, women are more religious than men, which is completely and utterly baffling to me. Finally, more religious people tend to be more misogynistic, while nonreligious people are the most egalitarian in their gender views.

17

LOVE YOUR NEIGHBOR, EXCEPT WHEN HE'S. . .
RELIGION AND PREJUDICE

Just after I finished college I took a job teaching at a small therapeutic boarding school for adolescents with behavior problems. My primary job was to keep the kids up to speed on their studies so they didn't fall behind academically while in therapy. However, I also assisted with various other aspects of the boarding school's programs, like helping to cook and serve food and observing the kids while they engaged in exercise, and I even sat in on some of their therapy sessions, which were conducted by very competent, licensed therapists.

Working that closely with young people made it easy to get to know the kids pretty well, and I grew quite close to some of them. One of those students, Angie, was a very bright kid with a huge heart who had turned to drugs and alcohol to deal with her troubles at home. Her addictive behaviors and acting out aside, she really wanted to do the right thing. She and I bonded over our shared sense of humor and our common interests in movies and writing.

I've always been one to maintain professional boundaries in the interest of protecting my job security. While Angie and I were close, the relationship was fully within the boundaries of what would be expected between an adult educator and a student. I think my graduate advisor, Rhys Williams, said it best when describing his relationship with students, "I am friendly, but I'm not your friend." I was friendly with Angie, but not really her "friend." Given her troubled childhood, I don't think she was familiar with the distinction between "friendly" and "her friend." I sincerely cared about her well-being and wanted the best for her. That didn't mean I needed to know her intimate secrets, which I did not know. However, without any responsible adults to model appropriate adult-adolescent relationships, I think she misunderstood my interest in her well-being as suggesting I was her "friend." What's more, given my role in her life at the boarding school, she also held me in high esteem.

Religion largely destroyed my relationship with Angie.

Our relationship, which had developed over a period of a couple of months, was completely undermined when she learned what it was I believed. I was, at that time, still an active and faithful Mormon. Many Mormons believe, based on their scriptures, that there are only two religions: the church of god and the church of the devil (1 Nephi 14:9–12). That verse goes on to state that if you don't belong to god's church, then you must, by definition, belong to the church of the devil. While some Mormons today downplay the obvious implications of this verse, if interpreted literally it's not that hard to discern the implication: *if you're not a Mormon, you are a follower of Satan.* While Mormon beliefs concerning the afterlife are complicated, Mormons also believe that anyone given the chance to accept Mormonism in this life who does not will basically be punished in the afterlife. They won't go to a place of eternal torment and punishment, but it's definitely not as nice as the place reserved for good Mormons. While being Mormon doesn't guarantee that you get the *big rewards*, it is a requirement.

I don't recall how Angie found out about these beliefs; it may have been one of the counselors or it may have been her parents who told her. Regardless, when she did find out about them, she boldly confronted me about them. I recall her saying something like, "So, as a Mormon, you believe that, because I'm not a Mormon, I follow Satan and will basically go to hell?" After I pedantically corrected her on the fact that she wouldn't go to "hell," just a lesser degree of glory, I basically agreed with her summation of my religion's teachings.

Tearing up, Angie managed to say, "So, just because I'm not a Mormon you think I'm not as good of a person as you are." Before I could respond, she ran away, sobbing.

The worst part about this story is that, even if she had not run away, I wouldn't have had a response. She was right. Although I would not have admitted it, I thought less of her—because she was not a Mormon.

Have you ever heard someone say, "I'm not a racist, but. . ." The next thing that comes out of their mouth, of course, is typically something racist.

According to one passage in the Bible, god isn't a racist, "Then Peter began to speak: 'I now realize how true it is that God does not show favoritism but accepts men from every nation who fear him and do what is right'" (Acts 10:34–35; New International Version [NIV]). It kind of goes without saying that this quote runs counter to the bulk of the Old Testament, which is largely a book about genocide and ethnic favoritism. But the point I want to make is that, even if god isn't a racist, it turns out his most ardent followers often are. And it's not just racial minorities they hate. No. They hate sexual, religious, and even political minorities.

It has long been known that there is a positive relationship between religiosity and hate: the more religious someone is, the more likely they are to hate people who do not share their worldview. Admittedly there is some nuance in this relationship, which I explore briefly later in this chapter. But, in reality, the data on this topic generally paint a clear picture. Religious fundamentalists not only hate people who are not like they are, particularly religious and sexual minorities, but also members of other races. Their hate is rooted in their religious beliefs. Religious fundamentalists think in black and white terms: you are either with them, or against them. This was reflected in the scriptural passage from the Book of Mormon I cited earlier—you're either part of god's church, or you're not. You can't have one foot in and one foot out. This idea is reflected in the New Testament in Revelation 3:16, "So, because you are lukewarm—neither hot nor cold—I am about to spit you out of my mouth" (NIV).

But religious fundamentalists are not the only people who hate. Group memberships result in greater affinity toward members of the group just because they are members of the group. People who fall outside the group are not held in as high esteem simply because they do not belong to the in-group. And the more salient your group membership is to you, the greater your affinity toward your in-group and the greater your dislike of people in the out-group.

Now take a wild guess what religions are?

Groups!

Not surprisingly, previous research has established that religious identity reinforces in-group–out-group boundaries. Additionally, making religious identity salient increases prejudice toward out-groups.

If religion does anything well, it does a great job of reinforcing the importance of the group and membership in the religion. What that does is increase the salience or importance of group membership, which I just noted leads to greater prejudice. In other words, the more important your religion is to you, the more likely you are to hate people who don't belong to your religion. Religion, then, far from being a source for tolerance and acceptance, exacerbates divisiveness and hostility in pluralistic societies where religious identity is salient.

As I noted above, there is some nuance in this relationship. Not all highly religious people hate those outside their group. And the largely religious researchers working in the psychology of religion have done their utmost to point this out. One of the first scholars to realize there was a strong correlation between religiosity and prejudice was Gordon Allport, who was quite disturbed by this finding. Rather than accept that religion is divisive, he decided instead to see if he could parcel out some religious people who are tolerant. He considered such individuals to be more "mature" in their religiosity and called this type of religiosity "intrinsic," meaning these people pursue religion as the end, rather than as a means to an end. He contrasted these "intrinsically religious" individuals with "extrinsically religious" individuals who pursue religion as a means to an end or see religion as instrumental. He saw these religious people as being "immature" in their religiosity. To distinguish between these two groups, he created a survey. He was then able to show that those who score high on "intrinsic religiosity" aren't as prejudiced as those who score high on "extrinsic religiosity."

If you read the previous paragraph closely you should be scratching your head at this point. If the above approach seems problematic, that's because it is. You see, if you're religious, like Gordon Allport was, and you're not particularly prejudiced, then you are forced to commit the "No True Scotsman" logical fallacy (discussed in chapter 13). To recap, this fallacy basically works like this: let's pretend we have a person—we'll call him *"Gordon"*—who has a characteristic we'll call *"religion."* *Gordon* likes himself. *Gordon* likes having *religion*. And *Gordon* believes that having *religion* helps make him a better person. *Gordon*, in exploring the world, finds that some people who have *religion* are assholes. Rather than admit some people with *religion* can be assholes, *Gordon* says, "Well, no one who is 'mature' in their understanding of *religion* is an asshole. So they must be 'immature' in their understanding of *religion*." In other words, *Gordon* has made it impossible for anyone with his understanding of *religion* to be a bad person. This is, of course, illogical. There are "good" religious people and "bad" religious people, just like there are "good" and "bad" nonreligious people.

Returning to the research on this, psychologists have expended countless hours—definitely well into the millions by now—on this idea. While some psychologists of religion have seen through Gordon Allport's logical fallacy and rejected the idea, research in this area continues to get published despite research showing that "mature" religious people can be even more prejudiced than "immature" religious people, depending on the target group.

The above discussion returns me back to my point in this chapter: there is a generally positive relationship between religiosity and prejudice. While not every religious person will be prejudiced, and the degree of prejudice will vary by the individual and the target group, the general relationship holds.

Now let's examine some data.

The set of bars to the left in figure 17.1 show a clear relationship between religiosity and opposition to homosexual marriage in the United States. A majority of religious fundamentalists oppose it, but opposition against it drops below 50 percent for religious moderates and liberals. Nonreligious individuals are the most in favor

FIGURE 17.1. Percentage Who Oppose or Strongly Oppose Homosexual Marriage and Percentage Who Think Homosexual Sex Is Always Wrong by Religious Group

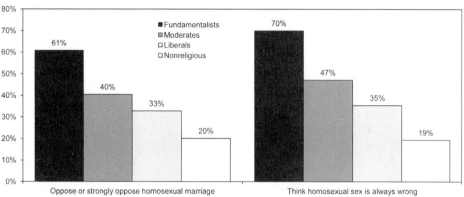

SOURCE: GSS, 2010

of homosexual marriage, with 80 percent supporting it. While some might argue that opposition to same-sex marriage is not a reflection of prejudice, there really is no other justification for such opposition. What's more, the bars to the right in figure 17.1 show a very similar pattern when asking a slightly different question—how people think about homosexual sex. The bars in figure 17.1 report the percentage of each religious group who think it is "always wrong." The relationship is virtually identical to opposition to same-sex marriage—fundamentalists are the most likely to say it is always wrong and the nonreligious are the least likely.

Figure 17.2 illustrates a similar pattern in the United States with four different variables. The variables here are variations of one question, "Suppose this admitted _____ wanted to make a speech in your community. Should he be allowed to speak or not?" The target groups are: atheists, communists, homosexuals, and racists. I chose, intentionally, an irreligious group, a political group, a sexual-orientation group, and an attitudinal group to show that the prejudice holds across targets. The nonreligious are the most willing to let atheists, communists, and homosexuals speak. However, they are also the most willing to allow a racist to speak. What this reflects is a remarkable degree of tolerance among the nonreligious. They are willing to let all viewpoints be heard. This is particularly amazing in light of the next figure, figure 17.3, which shows that the nonreligious are also the least racist.

The bars on the left reflect opposition to a close relative marrying a black person, while the bars on the right reflect opposition to a close relative marrying a Jew. In both cases, religious fundamentalists are the most opposed, while the nonreligious are the least opposed.

Figure 17.2. Percentage Who Would Not Allow Atheists, Communists, Homosexuals, or Racists to Speak in Their Local Community by Religious Group

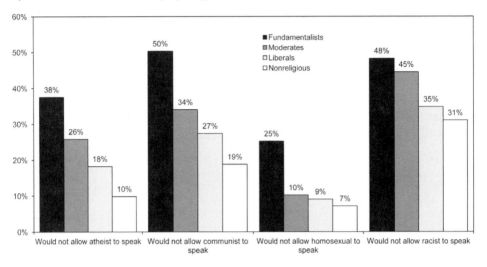

source: GSS, 2010

The figures make it quite clear what the relationship is between religiosity and prejudice: nonreligious people are remarkably tolerant and exhibit quite low levels of prejudice. Religious fundamentalists are the reverse; they exhibit much higher levels of prejudice and lower levels of tolerance. Religious moderates and liberals fall between them. In short, the more religiously fundamentalist people are, the more likely they are to hate people who are not like them.

Unfortunately, there are not comparable questions in the World Values Survey, so I have not included a figure from that survey. However, there is research suggesting this relationship is not unique to the United States. Similar relationships have been found in Canada, Australia, and Europe. In other words, the relationship between religiosity and prejudice is not unique to the United States and is likely a universal characteristic of religion.

While I have focused on survey data in this chapter, there is additional, experimental data that supports the connection between religiosity and prejudice. Priming research, in which an individual is shown a word or object either very briefly or before engaging in some task to see how it influences the performance of the task, can also be used to illustrate this relationship. Some researchers using priming techniques found that priming individuals with Christian concepts increased their prejudice toward blacks. Specifically, priming people with Christian words—that is, flashing them in front of individuals for just a very brief period of time—increases

Figure 17.3. Percentage of Whites Who Oppose or Strongly Oppose a Close Relative Marrying a Black Person or a Jew by Religious Group

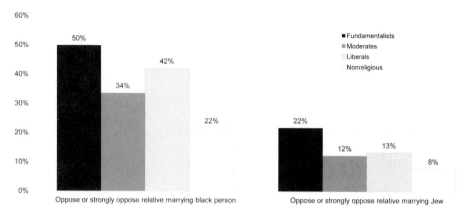

SOURCE: GSS, 1972–2010

racial prejudice. This line of research supports my earlier assertion that religion is generally a divisive force in society, not a unifying one.

—§—

Religions are groups. As a result, one of the ways religions influence their members is by increasing in-group solidarity and out-group prejudice. In short, religions can lead people to hate those who do not belong to the group. At times religions do this intentionally by emphasizing the importance of belonging to their group and highlighting the faults and flaws of those not in the group. The end result is both affinity toward members and hatred for those who are not members of the group. Since religious fundamentalists are the most likely to think about the world as being divided into two parts—black and white or good and evil—it is not surprising that religious fundamentalists are the most bigoted. They may claim they aren't racists, but research has found that religious people tend to be more prejudiced than nonreligious people around the world. Religion is unlikely to be able to bridge differences in a society because its very nature emphasizes in-groups versus out-groups, resulting in divisions in society. While we could debate whether or not god is a racist, there's no question that his followers tend to be.

18

THE SIGH OF THE OPPRESSED CREATURE
RELIGION AND MONEY

As a sociologist of religion, I regularly visit different churches. I don't go out of personal interest in converting, but rather to observe as part of my research. One of those visits in January 2008 was to Without Walls International Church (WWIC), a local megachurch in Tampa, where I live. The church was founded by husband and wife team Randy and Paula White, who have since divorced. When I attended, Randy was still leading the church, but Paula took over not long after when Randy resigned because of purported ill health.

During my visit to the church, there were three calls for donations. Yep, three! The service started with music, then Randy took the microphone and discussed his upcoming birthday celebration and asked for donations to fund it. He planned to rent an entire theater for those who wanted to attend and to go bowling afterward, all funded by the members of the church. After that call for donations, Randy spoke for a bit longer, then issued a general call for donations, before turning the microphone over to Jeff Fenholt, a former musician who looked as though he was still a drug addict, but who claimed he was clean and had a ministry aimed at helping drug addicts. He spoke for quite a while, butchered some songs (his voice hasn't aged well), then issued a call for donations for his ministry as well. To facilitate the third call for donations, Randy White gave Jeff a $5,000 check.

While the sanctuary at WWIC can hold about 4,000 people, the evening service I attended included just 250. If each of those in attendance gave a total of $20 during the earlier calls for donations, that would have covered the $5,000 check Randy gave to Jeff. I don't know if those in attendance did cover the check with their donations, but I don't think Randy was all that worried about a lack of money. At the time, the WWIC was holding three services every Sunday, with the evening service generally having the lowest attendance. He had no doubt brought in a lot more money earlier that day. Besides, the guy was loaded. He was living in a multimillion dollar home in one of the most exclusive neighborhoods in Tampa and bringing in tens of thousands of dollars in revenue every week.

Before the service ended, Randy took the microphone back and reminded the congregation about a new promise he had made them in conjunction with a book Paula had just published, *First Fruits: From Promise to Provision*. In the book, Paula selectively pulls quotes from the Bible to claim that Christians are supposed to donate their first month's salary to their church, in addition to their 10 percent tithing throughout the rest of the year. Randy reminded those in attendance that they would receive remarkable financial blessings if they donated their entire January salary or even their first paycheck to the church. As people filtered out of the service, ushers were handing out complimentary copies of the book to remind people of the promises that awaited them if they donated.

Whenever I attend these services, I study not only the service, but also the people in attendance. The 250 people at WWIC that night were not wealthy or even upper middle class. They were largely working class individuals, based on their clothing and the cars they drove. What were they doing giving their money to Randy, a multimillionaire?

I learned two very interesting lessons during my visit to WWIC. First, Randy and Paula were making a ton of money! If even a small portion of their members donated every week, they were bringing in thousands of dollars, and if they were successful at convincing their members to donate their first month's salary, that's hundreds of thousands more they could bring in, in just a single month (all tax free for the church, by the way, though Randy and Paula would have had to pay income taxes). So, the first lesson is: if you want to make a lot of money and don't mind selling people empty promises, start a church.

The second lesson derives from two questions that should be asked more often than they are: Why do people attend these services? And why do they donate money to such bald-faced crooks? The answer to this question helps explain some of the relationship between religion and social class. Religion functions as a compensatory mechanism for the poor, providing them hope for a better future. It "compensates" for their shitty life now by providing them with hope for a better life in the future (i.e., the future that doesn't actually exist, called the "afterlife"). The poor certainly need comforting; their lot in life isn't great, considering they are more likely to be sick, have more stressful and dangerous jobs, have more mental health issues, and die younger than the middle class or the rich. I could quote scripture showing where poverty is argued to be favored by god (e.g., Matthew 19:19–21; Mark 10:25;

Matthew 5:5), but I'd rather quote a somewhat well-known social theorist who understood this relationship between religion and social class over 150 years ago,

> Religion is the sigh of the oppressed creature, the heart of a heartless world, and the soul of soulless conditions. It is the opium of the people. The abolition of religion as the illusory happiness of the people is the demand for their real happiness. To call on them to give up their illusions about their condition is to call on them to give up a condition that requires illusions. The criticism of religion is, therefore, in embryo, the criticism of that vale of tears of which religion is the halo.

This quote from Karl Marx is more famous for the often misquoted line, "Religion is the opiate of the masses," but I think the better line is the one just before it, "Religion is the sigh of the oppressed creature, the heart of a heartless world, and the soul of soulless conditions." What Marx is saying here is that religion, of course, is an invention of humankind, but also that it serves a very specific function—it provides comfort to those who are oppressed and downtrodden. While Marx would refer to these individuals as the proletariat, I'll broaden that to modern understandings of social class. Religion is a salve for poverty; it leads those who are suffering the hardships of capitalism to believe there is a future state where all will be well: heaven. While the opium allusion is a good mental picture in its own right, I think more people can relate to the line that religion is the "sigh" of the "oppressed." If you're like most people, you've probably experienced disappointments, frustrations, and potentially even oppression. In those moments, don't you sigh and basically wish there was some way to just make it all better? Maybe you could call on some really powerful friend who always has your back to see if he'll help you—a god, maybe. That sigh of resignation and hope for deliverance from your suffering is religion. Religion helps the poor cope with being poor.

Okay, so that makes sense—religion alleviates the suffering of the poor by convincing them their suffering is temporary. But what about the rich? There are some rich people who are religious, aren't there? Well, yes, there are, though poor people are more likely to be religious these days. But religion does something different for the rich—it justifies their lot in life. In a sense, it serves a similar function as for the poor: with the poor, religion justifies their status by saying this is god's will and all will be well in the next life; with the rich it justifies their status by saying this is god's will as well. However, the rich get to tack on justifications like, "God is blessing me," or "I must be really righteous," which are also ideas that can be justified in scripture (e.g., Deuteronomy 7:13, 28:12). What's more, liberal religionists are the least likely to favor government action to reduce income differentials between the poor and the rich (see figure 18.1), while the nonreligious, probably because of their better education and despite their proclivity toward libertarianism, tend to

FIGURE 18.1. Percentage Who Favor or Oppose Government Involvement in Reducing Income Differences by Religious Group

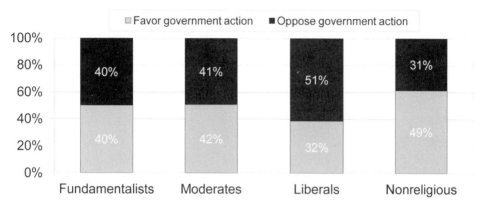

SOURCE: GSS, 2010

favor government intervention to help the poor. Religion is, then, quite instrumental; it helps the poor feel better about their suffering and the rich feel better about their fortunes, which were likely earned through the suffering of the poor.

Up to this point, this chapter has largely focused on class differences rather than differences by religiosity. The reason I started with the functions of religion for different social classes is because I think it is actually a more interesting idea than simply looking at income and class differences by religiosity. However, such class differences do exist, and other scholars have noted these as well. Religious fundamentalists and the highly religious make the least amount of money, both in the United States and internationally (see figures 18.2 and 18.3). The nonreligious make slightly less, on average, than the liberally religious in the United States, and internationally those who consider religion not very important have roughly the same social class as those who consider religion not at all important (WVS).

The primary relationship here, however, is just with religious fundamentalists. As several other scholars have found in their research, religious fundamentalists do make less money than other religious groups, and it is because of their religion. Not only do their religious beliefs discourage them from pursuing higher education, but their religious beliefs also discourage women from working outside the home. Combined, these two factors substantially reduce the earning power of male religious fundamentalists and remove female religious fundamentalists from the paid labor market entirely. As a result, religious fundamentalists make the least amount of money. On top of their lower salaries, the highly religious also give a percentage

Figure 18.2. Average Annual Income by Religious Group

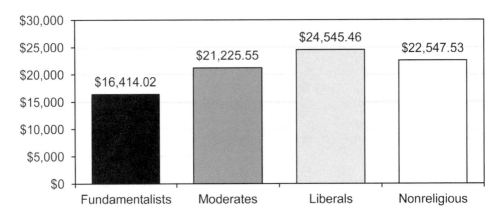

SOURCE: GSS, 2010

NOTE: THESE FIGURES INCLUDE EVERYONE IN THE GSS, INCLUDING THOSE WHO DON'T HAVE JOBS, ARE RETIRED, OR ARE STAY-AT-HOME PARENTS/SPOUSES.

of their income to religious organizations, which reduces their discretionary funds to spend on nonessential items.

What about the nonreligious? Well, the nonreligious don't make the most money. They are pretty close to the highest, but not quite. Their higher incomes are likely the result of the exact opposite of what ails religious fundamentalists. The nonreligious tend to have higher educational attainment (as noted in chapter six on education), which increases wages. Nonreligious women also tend to work, which increases household incomes. Finally, the nonreligious get to keep their money. The idea that you can sleep in on Sunday and save a percentage of your income is true. Being nonreligious is a guaranteed raise of whatever you were giving to your church; in the United States that can range anywhere from 1 percent to 10 percent, or even higher. That's not a bad reward for saving time, avoiding guilt, and hopefully getting more sleep.

Religion isn't the primary factor involved in making the poor, poor, nor in making the rich, rich. Religion does reduce the educational attainment of religious fundamentalists and discourages fundamentalist wives from working outside the home, reducing their income to the lowest of all the groups just examined. For these individuals, religion is a sigh away. The wealthy use religion to justify their social

Figure 18.3. Percentage in Social Classes by Importance of Religion

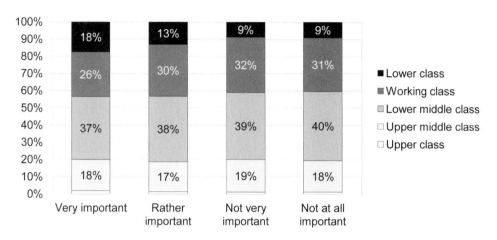

SOURCE: WVS

status, and they are less than generous in their attitudes toward government welfare for the poor. The nonreligious are not the wealthiest, but they do get to keep more of the money they make as they don't donate it to a religion to enrich a pastor. Finally, if anyone is going to get rich as a result of religion, it's not the people in the pews but those behind the pulpits.

19

WE'RE NOT HERE TO SERVE THE EARTH. . .
RELIGION AND ENVIRONMENTALISM

There are twenty-eight chapters in this book and each one begins with a story, except this one. Even when I was a devout Mormon I didn't litter, tried to minimize my environmental impact, and had a great deal of respect for the environment. In chapters where I don't have a good personal story, I've drawn on stories I've found elsewhere. However, religions don't have a horrible track record when it comes to pollution. Unlike, say, computer manufacturing, the products religions sell don't require toxic chemicals to manufacture (false promises and hot air, alas, are not toxic). Unable to find any good stories about religions or religious people acting in pro- or antienvironmental ways exclusively because of their religious beliefs, I'm simply going to provide you with some quotes. See if you can find a common characteristic among these quotes, other than their antienvironmental rhetoric:

> *Quote 1*: "I am today raising a flag of opposition to this alarmism about global warming and urging all believers to refuse to be duped by these 'earthism' worshippers."
> —Jerry Falwell on global warming and environmentalism

> *Quote 2*: "Indeed, if anything in this controversy might deserve to be called heretical—indeed blasphemous—it is the notion that God so designed His world that a minuscule change in atmospheric chemistry . . . would bring about catastrophic warming that would threaten human civilization and indeed all life on earth. There are strong theological and scientific reasons to deny catastrophic, manmade global warming, and powerful ethical and economic reasons to reject the energy policies promoted to fight it."
> —E. Calvin Beisner on global warming

Quote 3: "Energy, this idea that man is here to serve the Earth, as opposed to husband its resources and be good stewards of the Earth. And I think that is a phony ideal. I don't believe that that's what we're here to do—that man is here to use the resources and use them wisely, to care for the Earth, to be a steward of the Earth, but we're not here to serve the Earth. The Earth is not the objective. Man is the objective. I think a lot of radical environmentalists have it upside-down."

—Rick Santorum on the environment

Quote 4: "Oh dear heart, there ain't anything green that's gonna take care of your car. There's nothing wrong with drilling for natural gas, it's not going to hurt your environment. There's some possibilities that if they put too much water into a fracket [sic] they might pollute the wells but so far they haven't had any evidence that I know of about that. There is nothing green that will do it. Ethanol is a joke. Wind farms are a joke. Solar is a joke. There's no way that the great energy needs of this huge country can be met by wind, solar, or whatever else you got that's green. It just won't happen. I mean that's just the reality of things. So what have we got? I like nuclear but now, nuclear's having a problem over there in Japan, but I think we could make safe nuclear, we've got to do it. I hope one day we could get to 'solar fusion' which is the power of the sun. But to have everybody in the world have abundant supplies of energy would be marvelous but, so far they haven't got something. We need a crash program, what are we gonna do?"

—Pat Robertson on drilling for natural gas

What all of the people I quoted have in common is that they are conservative Christians. In fact, they are all fundamentalists. (Shocker, I know.) Now, before you think, "Oh, that's not fair. You can't just selectively quote a few fundamentalist Christians and suggest that they are all opposed to environmentalism," let me stop you right there. You're right. That wouldn't be fair or very good scholarship. I already apologized for my lack of a story, but let me make up for it with statistics.

Religious fundamentalists are generally much less worried about the environment than are other religious people and the nonreligious for two reasons. First, many religious fundamentalists—particularly Christians—believe the Bible suggests that they should have "dominion" over the earth (Genesis 1:26). They interpret that to mean that the earth exists for humans, and that gives them license to do what they want with it (see Rick Santorum's quote above). Second, most Christians

Figure 19.1. Percentage Claiming to Know Causes of Environmental Problems by Religious Group

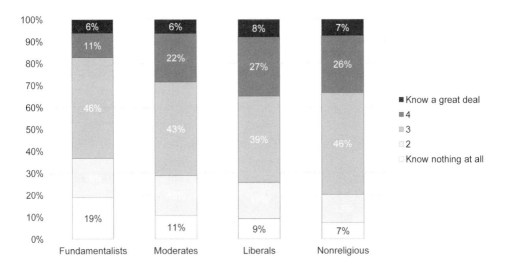

SOURCE: GSS, 2010

believe that there is an end to mortality and that Jesus Christ is going to return. When he does, the state of the planet won't be a real concern. Thus, the more millenniallist the religion, the less concerned they are with the environment. Combine these two ideas and you get substantially higher antienvironmental attitudes.

Fundamentalists' views on the environment are a little tricky to observe in statistics. As the following figures will show, religious people appear to be at least moderately concerned about the environment, sometimes as much as or even more so in some cases than the nonreligious. But when it comes to doing something to help the environment, religious fundamentalists and highly religious individuals are less likely to be involved and are more likely to suggest environmental concerns are exaggerated. They are also more likely to reject global warming and favor economic growth over the environment (though I do not have data on this for the United States). Finally, highly religious individuals are less likely to report knowing the causes and/or solutions to environmental issues (figure 19.1).

Figure 19.2 illustrates that religious fundamentalists are less likely to consider environmental issues a serious concern in the United States and that they favor putting the economy before the environment.

FIGURE 19.2. Percentage Who Agree or Strongly Agree on Various Environmental Issues by Religious Group

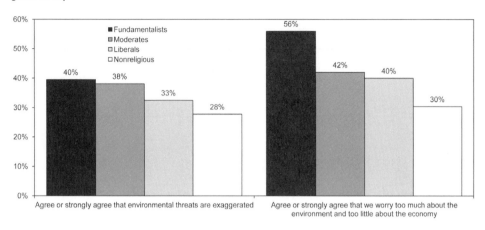

SOURCE: GSS, 2010

Outside the United States, religious individuals appear to be somewhat concerned about the environment. Religious individuals are slightly more likely to have signed a petition, contributed to environmental groups, and reduced their water consumption, but less likely to have chosen environmentally friendly products or recycled, as is shown in figure 19.3.

FIGURE 19.3. Percentage Who Have Done Specific Environmental Acts by Importance of Religion

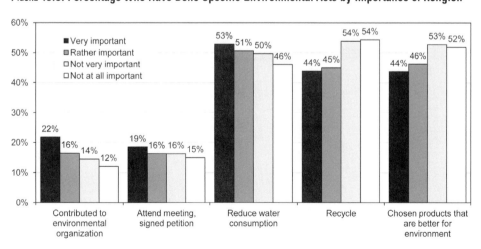

SOURCE: WVS

FIGURE 19.4. Views on the Environment by Importance of Religion

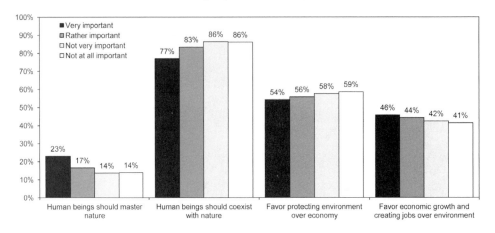

SOURCE: WVS

However, like in the United States, they favor the economy over the environment and are more likely to believe humans should master nature rather than coexist with it, as is illustrated in figure 19.4.

It does warrant mentioning that there was a short period in the United States when some evangelical Christians started to reflect pro-environmental attitudes and even began to accept global warming and the science behind it. However, with the rise of the Tea Party, the aligning of the GOP with evangelicals, and the economic recession, it appears evangelical environmentalism was short-lived.

Despite the fairly clear relationship between religion and the environment, this does appear to be one of the situations where religious rhetoric appears to be more smoke than fire—they are just about as likely to engage in pro-environment actions as are less religious and liberally religious individuals. And, of course, the data may indicate that nonreligious individuals, despite their slightly higher concerns for the environment, do not appear to be acting in accordance with those concerns as much as one might think.

What can we conclude about religion and the environment? Religious fundamentalists and highly religious individuals show somewhat less concern with the environment, particularly when it comes to climate change. They are also more likely to favor the economy over the environment. Intriguingly, there are not large differences between the highly religious and the nonreligious when it comes to expressing general concerns about things like pollution, and the differences in their actions toward the environment are not all that large. The reason fundamentalists and highly religious individuals are somewhat more antienvironment is accurately captured by Rick Santorum's statement that "we're not hear to serve the Earth." Some religious people put humans before environmental health and personal salvation over planets. If the earth is fleeting, what's a bit of flooding, a few extra hurricanes, and oxygen deprived rivers? Jesus will be here soon and none of that will matter.

20

I'D LIKE TO BUY THE WORLD A JOINT
RELIGION AND POLITICS

I've never smoked marijuana. I've come close twice. The first time was when I was in high school. I went to a UB40 concert in Park City with a friend. As a naive kid from rural Utah who had never smoked pot or even seen anyone smoking it, I was oblivious to the fact that everyone around us was getting high. The air was fetid, but I didn't realize why. As we left the concert, I recall looking up on the hillside where we had been sitting and seeing a haze of smoke wafting over the entire area. I pointed out the haze, and my friend told me everyone was smoking pot. I may have gotten a contact high that night, but I don't recall feeling all that different.

The second time I came close to smoking a joint was just recently. I was at a friend's home with several other friends when someone broke out a couple of joints. Most of those present partook; I chose not to. My religious upbringing has made me something of a teetotaler. I rarely drink alcohol—I generally don't like the taste or the accompanying buzz. I don't smoke, tobacco or marijuana, though I find the smell of pipe tobacco quite appealing. When my friends offered me the joint, I declined. I would be willing to try marijuana if there was no legal risk to myself. I'm not willing to take the risk of losing my job, especially now that I have a son who is dependent on me.

Here's the weird thing: today, despite never having smoked marijuana, I'm an advocate of legalization. What gives?

—§—

Well, apparently I'm like a lot of other nonreligious people in the United States, as I'll illustrate. I've already covered some political issues in other chapters, like abortion, same-sex marriage, and welfare. In this chapter I take a look at political preferences, political activity, and some positions on social issues.

FIGURE 20.1. Political Preferences by Religious Group

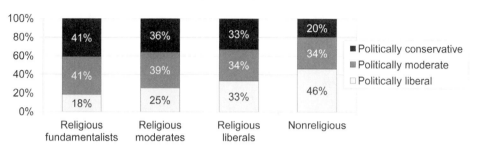

SOURCE: GSS, 2010

It probably won't surprise readers to learn that the nonreligious in the United States lean politically liberal (see figure 20.1). Well, lean is a bit of an understatement—almost half of the nonreligious consider themselves political liberals, more so than any of the other four groups, including religious liberals, who are the second most politically liberal, with one-third identifying as such.

But what may surprise readers is just how nonpartisan the nonreligious in the United States are. Over 50 percent of the nonreligious consider themselves politically independent, 10 percent more than the next closest group, religious moderates (see figure 20.2). The nonreligious are also particularly unlikely to identify as Republicans, with just 9 percent identifying as such. Given the recent alliance between Republicans and conservative Christians, this isn't all that surprising.

Although I've already covered a lot of the major social issues in American politics, I've examined a few more for this chapter to see how things fall out based on

FIGURE 20.2. Political Party Affiliation by Religious Group

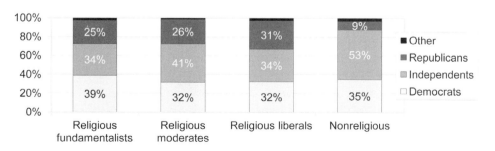

SOURCE: GSS, 2010

FIGURE 20.3. Political Preferences by Religious Group

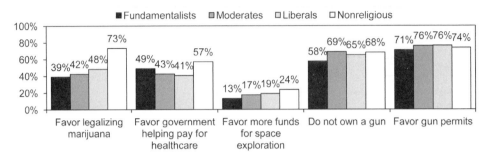

SOURCE: GSS, 2010

the various religious groups. Figure 20.3 presents the results of five questions on four topics: legalizing marijuana, universal healthcare, space exploration, and gun control.

The first set of bars suggest that the nonreligious are strongly in favor of legalizing marijuana; almost three out of every four of the nonreligious favor legalizing marijuana, just like me. This may not be so they can smoke marijuana; the nonreligious tend to be quite libertarian, and drug legalization is one of the manifestations of that position. However, Add Health data (not shown) suggest that young people who consider religion unimportant or who are not at all religious have smoked marijuana more times overall than have their more religious counterparts (though there is no difference in how many times they have smoked marijuana in the last thirty days). So, maybe they do want to legalize marijuana so they can smoke it without fear of legal prosecution.

The nonreligious are also the most in favor of universal healthcare and are more likely to want more money spent on space exploration than is any other religious group. Religious fundamentalists are the most likely to report owning a gun and the least likely to favor gun permits, though these differences with the nonreligious aren't nearly as large as their differences over pot legalization.

Political leanings of the nonreligious are similar outside the United States (see figure 20.4). The most religious are also the most right-leaning (i.e., conservative) and least left-leaning (i.e., progressive), while those who report that religion is not at all important to them are the least right-leaning and most left-leaning.

I don't include party affiliation based on importance of religion from the WVS because it's not feasible to do so. For those who aren't familiar with politics in countries other than the United States, most have multiple political parties, not just two, and they change regularly. Presenting the results would be far too cumbersome here.

FIGURE 20.4. Political Preference by Importance of Religion

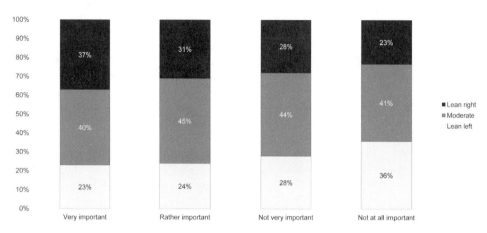

SOURCE: WVS

There also aren't identical questions to those I pulled from the GSS on other political issues, like the legalization of marijuana and gun control, in part because these issues aren't as disputed in lots of other countries (some of which have already legalized or decriminalized marijuana and have stricter gun control laws than the United States). There are, however, a couple of questions that help illustrate the differences in political views by importance of religion. For example, there is a question in the WVS asking about soft drug use and the nonreligious are the most accepting of it (what exactly is meant by "soft drug use" isn't all that clear). The most religious are also the most opposed to immigration, and the least religious are the most likely to belong to a labor union and report the greatest interest in politics.

What the data indicate is that highly religious individuals and religious fundamentalists tend to be more conservative while the nonreligious and less religious tend to be more progressive, with the other two groups falling in between those positions. The obvious question is: why? The answer is actually quite interesting. It turns out nonreligious individuals are more open to new experiences, more likely to embrace new technology, are less dogmatic, and are more accepting of ambiguity, while religious fundamentalists and the highly religious tend to dislike ambiguity, are more persistent in their judgments, are more habitual in their responses, and are more averse to threats.

What does this have to do with politics? I'll use the legalization of marijuana to illustrate the relationship. Marijuana is, for many, a new experience and, ethically, marijuana use is somewhat ambiguous. Marijuana has been shown to be medically beneficial in a number of contexts, but it may have some negative effects on health and functioning as well. Religious fundamentalists reject it because it is an "illicit drug," keeping things black and white (i.e., all illicit drugs are bad); the nonreligious embrace it because they don't think in black and white. While not all of the nonreligious are smoking pot, some data suggest they are more likely to have smoked pot and they definitely want to have the right to buy it.

Politically, where do our groups stand? Fundamentalists lean right and the nonreligious lean pretty far left, while the religious moderates and liberals are more balanced in their politics. Political proclivities are likely tied to respective psychologies. The nonreligious are more open to change and, as a result, are more progressive. Religious fundamentalists are threatened by change and tend to be more conservative. Not surprisingly, the positions of these groups on various social issues, like legalizing marijuana, tend to align with their political preferences. The majority of religious fundamentalists oppose legalizing marijuana, while the nonreligious would like to buy the world a joint (or at least make it legal to buy a joint). If the nonreligious did buy everyone a joint, I bet we'd be more likely to stand hand in hand and sing in perfect harmony—well, maybe not perfect harmony.

21

WHERE WOULD JESUS VOLUNTEER?
RELIGION AND CHARITABLE ACTS

There is a student-led volunteer group on my campus called People Exploring Active Community Experiences (PEACE). The students organize volunteering opportunities, including international and domestic volunteering trips. The participants on these trips pay to participate. Since most of the students who volunteer are under twenty-one, and almost all of them are under twenty-five, the university requires that a faculty or staff person go with the students to drive. Shortly after I arrived at the university a global e-mail went out asking for faculty and staff volunteers for these trips. As I have more time than money, I figured I'd donate some of my time to helping others. I signed up, and shortly afterward was asked if I would accompany a group of students to Fort Lauderdale, Florida, on a volunteering trip. I said yes, not realizing what adventures awaited me.

Since the students pay to go on these trips, the student organizers try to find the cheapest travel and accommodations possible. In Fort Lauderdale the student organizers arranged for us to stay in a hostel. I've traveled a fair amount, but had never stayed in a hostel before. Since I like adventures and wouldn't be sleeping in a car (which I have done and really dislike), I didn't see a problem with staying in a hostel.

There were eleven people on the trip—ten students and myself. There were eight female students and two males. Six of the females shared a room while the two males roomed with two females in a room not far from mine. As the "advisor," I volunteered to sleep in a different room. The room I was assigned had three other people in it, one of whom was amiable; the other two didn't really say much. The amiable guy, Steven, had come to Florida to captain and maintain a yacht for a wealthy individual. He was staying in the hostel to save money as he was only in town for a couple of weeks before he was going to take the boat to the Bahamas, where his wealthy employer was going to be staying for a few months. He and I chatted a bit as I moved my stuff into our room. Since the students and I arrived in the evening and were not going to begin our volunteering until the next day, we really didn't have much planned except a group dinner that night. I leisurely organized my stuff in the room then went to the bathroom.

Just as I was coming out of the bathroom there was a frantic knock on the door of our room. Steven opened the door to find the owner of the hostel looking very upset. She yelled at him to grab all the towels he could find and follow her. He did as he was told and hurried to the room next to ours. I didn't think anything too serious was going on, so I didn't follow along, but Steven told me what had happened a short while later.

In the room next to ours were two men. One was an older ship captain who was Korean-American and was between sailings. He was a little strange and liked to booze it up, but otherwise seemed fine. I'll call him "The Captain." The other guy was known throughout the hostel as being, well, rather hostile. He was young, fairly stout, belligerent, and bellicose and was not well-liked, but he paid his bill, so the owner let him stay, even though she had a hard time finding people who would share a room with him. I'll call him "The Drunk." Earlier in the afternoon, The Drunk had gone out shopping and came back with a case of beer, which he offered to share with The Captain. They turned on the TV in their room and drank beer all afternoon.

It's not clear what happened next, but someone must have said something the other person didn't like, as a fight ensued. The Drunk, decades younger and physically stronger than The Captain, laid into the older man pretty good. However, as the two tussled, The Drunk got a hand just a bit too close to The Captain's mouth. Largely defenseless against the younger and stronger man, The Captain took advantage of the proximity of the fingers, slipped one in his mouth, and bit down. Apparently his jaw hadn't weakened with age; he bit off one of The Drunk's fingers!

When Steven entered the room, it was covered with blood. It looked like someone had taken a pint can of red paint and a paintbrush and had whipped the paint all around the room—it was on the walls, the floor, the ceiling, the furniture, and, most importantly, it was all over The Captain. The Captain was unconscious and covered in blood when the owner of the hostel and Steven entered the room. The owner of the hostel initially thought he might be dead, but he wasn't. He had been beaten by The Drunk until he was unconscious—for biting his finger off! It turns out none of the blood was The Captain's; it was all The Drunk's. It had splattered all over the room from his finger, er, finger joint while he beat The Captain senseless. Once The Captain passed out, The Drunk ran out of the room, grabbed a taxi, and made his way to the hospital. His commotion drew the attention of the hostel owner, who walked in on what looked like a massacre.

The hostel owner and Steven called an ambulance, and of course police came, as The Captain wanted to press assault charges against The Drunk. The students and I saw the paramedics arrive, followed shortly thereafter by police. It was quite the scene. Oh, and they never found The Drunk's finger. . . The Captain swallowed it!

—§—

You're probably wondering what this story has to do with volunteering. That's a good question. It isn't directly related to it, but it is indirectly related to a key point I want to make in this chapter that is reflected in the title. The group of students and I stayed in a dive of a hostel where a man had his finger bitten off in a fight. That probably wouldn't happen at a Marriott or even a Days Inn. We stayed at the hostel because we were trying to save money since we were paying to volunteer at a nearby charity that helps people with physical and mental disabilities; we were basically the not-quite-poor helping the poor.

We were not volunteering by helping other college students on our college campus. And we wouldn't consider leading a group of students at our university in a book club or organizing a choir of college students to fall under the auspices of volunteering; that's really just spending time with people pursuing shared interests. But many religious people who report volunteering regularly spend a substantial portion of their time volunteering in their church. They consider teaching Sunday School or ushering at their church volunteering, even though they are really just hanging out with people like themselves.

This is illustrated to some degree in figure 21.1, which presents data from the Portraits of American Life Study (PALS). The PALS study has better data on volunteering and religion than the General Social Survey, and its data on volunteering are more recent than that in the GSS, so I used it in this chapter instead of GSS data. The figure shows the percentage of people in various religious groups who volunteer more than one hour in a month (dark bar) and the percentage of their volunteering that is *not* with a religious organization (light bar).

While there are some minor differences in the percentages who volunteer an hour or more per month, they are not substantial enough to be mathematically meaningful. In other words, the nonreligious are just as likely to volunteer as are the religious. The light gray bars indicate the percentage of the volunteering that is *not* done for or with a religious organization. Just to be clear, some of the volunteering for religions is like what I've mentioned—leading the choir at church or teaching Sunday School. But it also includes volunteering that is simply organized by a religion, like working at a soup kitchen or building homes for the poor. Black

Figure 21.1. Percentage Volunteering More Than One Hour per Month and Percentage of Volunteering Done with Religious Organizations by Religious Affiliation

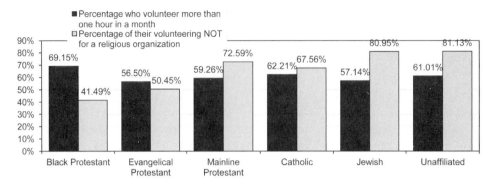

SOURCE: PALS, 2006

Protestants do most of their volunteering, 59 percent, with religious organizations. Jews and the nonreligious do 81 percent of their volunteering outside of religious organizations. The three other groups fall somewhere in between. Also, since the group designations are different from the four I've used throughout this book, I should note that Evangelical Protestants are the closest to fundamentalists, while mainline Protestants and Jews are typically categorized as liberally religious.

Not that I put much weight in Jesus or his teachings, but I do think this raises an interesting question: Where do you think Jesus would volunteer? Would he spend his time with the converted, in their air conditioned churches, passing out pamphlets at the door or teaching little kids dogmatic songs of praise? Or would he spend his time with thieves, adulterers, criminals, battered and bruised ship captains, and amputees? Yes, some of the volunteering done with religious organizations could be in the church's soup kitchen or in some other context in which the members of the religion are interacting with people who are not members of the church. However, a substantial portion of the volunteering done by religious people is volunteering within their own congregation. In short, religion doesn't increase volunteering in the United States, but it does guide where people volunteer—they spend more time volunteering in churches, while the nonreligious spend more time volunteering outside churches.

Outside the United States, volunteering relates to religion differently. There are only minor differences in the places where the religious and nonreligious choose to volunteer. According to WVS data, those who consider religion very important and those who do not consider religion at all important are just as likely to report volunteering with human rights campaigns, educational and cultural organizations, unions, political action groups, youth groups, sports groups, women's groups, peace groups, and health groups (no figure).

A number of past studies have suggested that nonreligious people in the United States are less charitable and spend less time volunteering, but recent data seem to contradict earlier findings and international data show no notable differences. Even so, I'm willing to give religion a small pat on the back when it comes to volunteering. Religions are actually quite good at getting people to volunteer because they present volunteer opportunities to the members. People who are not members of religious congregations do not regularly have opportunities to volunteer presented to them. Unless they are connected to some other group that regularly invites them to volunteer, the nonreligious will have to be proactive in seeking volunteer opportunities.

Religious people do volunteer, but so do nonreligious people. What's more, religious Americans spend a large portion of their volunteer time working with or even within their religious congregation, which is probably not where you would have found Jesus. Inside the United States, roughly the same percentage of religious people report volunteering as do the nonreligious; the same holds in the United Kingdom and in most other developed and largely secular countries. Religion may have historically inspired volunteering, but it appears that in the modern, secular world, religion is no longer required to either organize or motivate people to volunteer.

22

I KILL. YOU KILL. WE ALL KILL.
RELIGION AND VIOLENCE

Aqsa Parvez just wanted to be like her friends. And in Mississauga, Ontario, in 2007, that meant getting a part-time job so she could have some spending money, going out, having a little privacy, talking on the phone, and wearing fashionable clothing. Her father, Muhammad Parvez, a fifty-seven-year-old immigrant from Pakistan, didn't approve (nor did the rest of her family). As Aqsa pushed for greater freedom, her father responded by decreasing her autonomy. By the summer of 2007, Aqsa no longer had a door on her bedroom, was restricted in talking on the phone, was required to come directly home from school, and was not allowed to go out on weekends. Additionally, Aqsa's parents and family wanted her to wear the hijab and dress in a more traditional style, which Aqsa openly opposed.

Aqsa knew trouble was brewing. She told counselors at school that she was afraid of her father and what he might do to her. In late November 2007, Aqsa moved out of her parents' home and moved in with a friend where she had greater freedom to embrace modern Canadian cultural mores.

Aqsa's brother, Waqas, who was ten years her senior, stopped by Aqsa's bus stop on the morning of December 10, 2007, and picked Aqsa up, returning her to her parents' house, likely under the guise of collecting some of her belongings. As soon as Aqsa entered the house, her father and brother put their plan into action. Aqsa's brother, Waqas, strangled his sister until she lost consciousness, probably aided by their father. Just thirty-six minutes after Waqas picked her up from the bus stop, Muhammad, the father, covering for his son, called the police to report that he had killed his daughter.

When paramedics arrived, Aqsa was not dead, but the damage her brother had inflicted by strangling her was too great and she died later that evening. Religion killed Aqsa.

—§—

Some of those reading this will likely say that what killed Aqsa was culture, not religion. Those people would be wrong for three reasons. First, as any good sociologist will tell you, religion is part of culture. In order to assert that it was culture that killed Aqsa but not religion, those making this claim would have to clearly and definitively illustrate that the Parvez's were not at all inspired by their religion to kill Aqsa. They would have to delineate an aspect of Pakistani culture that is separate and distinct from religion and illustrate without question that it was that aspect of Pakistani culture that motivated the killing of Aqsa. The best anthropologists in the world would find such an undertaking daunting, if not impossible. Religion is part of culture, a large, very influential part of culture. Separating the two is virtually impossible. Anyone who claims that people kill in the name of culture but deny the connection with religion does not understand the relationship between religion and culture.

The second reason why I can say it was religion (and perhaps other aspects of culture) that killed Aqsa is because that is what both Muhammad and Waqas themselves say motivated their actions. Muhammad was infuriated by his daughter's refusal to wear the hijab and her rejection of his interpretation of the behavioral dictates of Islam for young women. Muhammad and Waqas have never said, "We killed Aqsa in the name of Pakistani culture." They believed they were doing what Allah wanted them to do. This is violence in the name of religion. In fact, Muhammad's wife said he would have killed Aqsa regardless of where they were living, Pakistan or Canada. Yes, the hijab is not, strictly speaking, a requirement of Islam. However, Muhammad believed that the hijab must be worn because of his interpretation of Islam, not his interpretation of Pakistani culture (his interpretation of Islam is no doubt influenced by Pakistani culture). Both Muhammad and Waqas believed they were acting according to the dictates of Islam when they killed Aqsa. That they believed they were acting in the name of Islam is not in doubt, even if their interpretation of their religion can be called into question.

If religion is part of culture and if Muhammad and Waqas believed they were acting in accordance with the dictates of Islam, then Aqsa was killed in the name of Islam. Someone could still claim that she was killed in the name of culture, but doing so is really a subterfuge; it is an attempt at misdirection to absolve religion from the blame. Religion killed Aqsa, not *other* aspects of Pakistani culture.

Some may still object to my presentation of this tragic event. Like many Canadian Muslim leaders suggested in the aftermath of this murder, some may say that this had nothing to do with Islam. They will blame this on personal failings of Muhammad or Waqas. Or they will blame this on domestic violence. Or they might say, and this is key to their defense of Islam, that Muhammad and Waqas had misinterpreted Islam. These individuals claim that Islam opposes violence, which means Muhammad and Waqas could not have been acting in the name of Islam. While it's pretty questionable whether Islam opposes violence, if their interpretation of Islam says that it does, that's fine. They can have that interpretation of Islam, but can't other Muslims have a different interpretation? Or does having a different interpretation mean that you can't be a Muslim?

This response is the same logical fallacy that I first described in chapter 13—the "No True Scotsman" fallacy—and is the third reason why you'd be wrong if you don't think religion killed Aqsa. Those who employ this argument want to believe that their religion is good because, well, it's their religion. And since they believe they are good, they can't accept that their religion might actually inspire horrible acts, like strangling your sister (with your father's help). These people assert that Islam does not allow those types of acts. And since Islam opposes violence, because that is how they interpret Islam, anyone who engages in violence cannot be acting in the name of Islam. See the problem with the logic?

Apologists use this parlor trick of logic regularly to defend Islam. The most common culprit they blame in lieu of Islam is "culture," reflecting their remarkable ignorance of the fact that religion is part of culture (which means they are really blaming religion but are unaware of that fact). For instance, when rape victims were flogged in Saudi Arabia, apologists for Islam blamed Saudi "culture," while the Justice Ministry of Saudi Arabia claimed the ruling followed "the book of God and the teachings of the Prophet Muhammad." When women in Afghanistan were beheaded for simply being accused of adultery, apologists claimed it was not Islam that motivated that brutality but Afghan "culture." When women were stoned to death in Iran, again it was not Islam but Iranian "culture." Do you see the pattern? The defenders of Islam always blame the evils committed in the name of Islam on something other than Islam, often "culture."

I would love nothing more than to be able to say, definitively, that Islam, Christianity, Judaism, Buddhism, Hinduism, and every other religion only teach love, peace, and happiness. And I would love for the relatively moral—though illogical—defenders of these religions to be right, that the problem is culture and not religion. But they are wrong. They are wrong because: (1) religion is part of culture; (2) those committing the horrific acts believe they are doing it in the name of their religion; and (3) because they have defined their religions in such a way that they can only ever be a source of good, never evil, and thus they are denying reality. Their defense of religion is illogical and misguided.

I don't mean to pick on Islam. All religions are guilty of this. The example above just works well to set up what I'm about to assert: religion can inspire people to do

FIGURE 22.1. Approval of Violence toward Various Targets by Religious Group

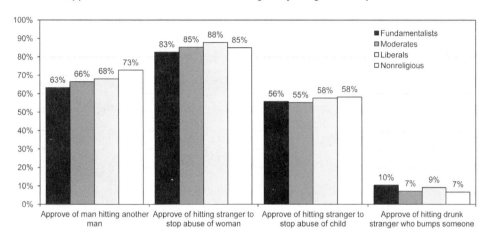

SOURCE: GSS, 1972–2010

bad things as well as good things. I know some religious people will balk at that. But remember, if you are balking, and I know some of you are, it's because you don't want to believe religion can inspire people to do horrible things. You know what might make this easier to accept? Let's try this. Think about someone else's religion rather than your own. Here are a few horrible actions motivated by different religions:

- What motivated the 9/11 hijackers to fly those planes into buildings? Was it the combined cultural mores of the various countries where they grew up, or was it their Muslim beliefs?
- What motivated Indira Gandhi's Sikh bodyguards to assassinate the woman they were sworn to protect? Was it the cultural mores of the Punjab region of India, or their Sikh beliefs?
- What motivated Scott Roeder to shoot and kill George Tiller, a doctor who performed abortions? Was it the cultural mores of the United States, or was it his Christian beliefs?

If you said two of the above were motivated by religion, but one was not, and the one you don't think was motivated by religion happens to be your own religion, you are a dogmatist. You are irrational and unable to be persuaded by logic, reason, or evidence.

All three of the acts above were motivated by religion. Again, you can disagree

FIGURE 22.2. Approval of Police Violence by Religious Group

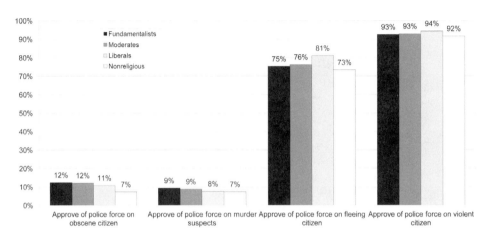

SOURCE: GSS, 1972–2010

with the way the individuals interpreted their religion. You may think that they were completely and utterly mistaken in how they interpreted their religion. You may think they were all evil assholes. But in all three of the above events, the perpetrators of violence were motivated by and believed they were acting in the name of their religion. Religion can inspire bad behavior.

Got it?

If you now understand that religion can inspire altruistic, moral behavior but also horrific acts of carnage and violence, then you've already gleaned my primary point in this chapter. The rest of the chapter addresses the following question: does religion increase the odds of people behaving violently or advocating violence?

The answer: maybe a little bit, but probably not really. This is another case where *religion doesn't seem to matter.*

Let's begin with data from the United States. Figure 22.1 indicates that fundamentalist individuals are least approving of violence in the specific situation of one man punching another one. That seems to suggest that religious people are less violent. The opposition of the religious to violence carries over to two hypothetical scenarios: fundamentalist individuals are less likely to agree that it's okay to hit a stranger if the stranger was observed beating up a woman or hitting a child, though these differences are quite small. However, if fundamentalists saw a stranger who was drunk bump into a man and his wife, then they are barely more likely to agree that it's okay to hit that person. What can we conclude from figure 22.1? Not

Figure 22.3. Attitudes toward Death Penalty and Law Enforcement Funding by Religious Group

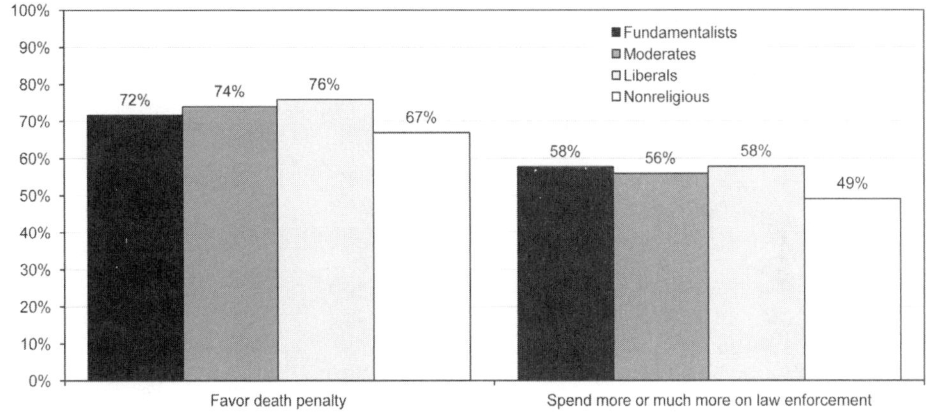

SOURCE: GSS, 1972–2010

much really given the negligible differences. These differences are so small that they actually just reflect chance fluctuations, with the exception of the first comparison. In short, there are not notable differences here.

Figure 22.2 further supports the idea that acceptance of violence doesn't really vary much by religiosity. This figure examines attitudes toward police using force. Religious individuals are slightly more likely to favor police using violence on citizens when citizens use obscene language, are murder suspects, try to escape custody, or attack the police. But, again, these differences are basically negligible. Religiosity doesn't seem to matter when it comes to approving of violence.

Figure 22.3 suggests religious individuals may be slightly more likely than nonreligious individuals to favor the death penalty and spending more on law enforcement, but the differences between the groups are, once again, small.

Unfortunately the World Values Survey does not have any questions that ask specifically about violence. However, I examined some variables that reflect an authoritarian mind-set, which is fairly common among religious fundamentalists and has been shown to be related to violence. Specifically, they tend to prefer highly structured political environments. This doesn't necessarily mean fundamentalists like to be bosses. They don't mind being in control, but if they aren't in control, they want someone with a lot of power to be in control. In short, they like structure, particularly structure that supports their worldview, which they want to be enforced, even if by violence. Figure 22.4 illustrates that highly religious individuals around the world are slightly more accepting of authoritarianism than are the nonreligious.

FIGURE 22.4. Attitudes toward Authoritarian Government and Beating Wife by Importance of Religion

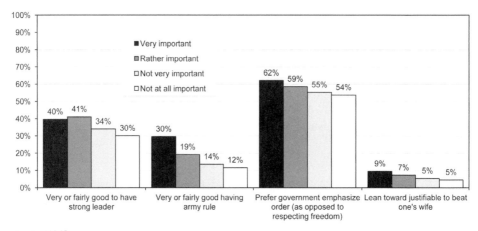

SOURCE: WVS

The more important religion is to someone, the more likely he or she is to say that governments need strong leaders, that governments should emphasize order over freedom, that having the army rule at times is a good thing, that crime should be severely punished, and that it is justifiable to beat one's wife. The differences here are slightly larger than in the United States, but they are also not particularly huge. More religious individuals may be slightly more likely to favor strict authority (at the cost of freedoms), severe punishments of criminals, and the right of a man to beat his wife, but not tremendously so.

Given that I'm not religious and generally oppose violence, if I had data that showed more religious or religiously fundamentalist individuals favored violence over the nonreligious, I would have presented them in this chapter. The best I could find is data that suggest small or negligible differences in attitudes toward violence. Yes, more religious individuals are more authoritarian, but that doesn't guarantee a greater acceptance of or proclivity toward violence. I included all of the figures just so I could assert that religion doesn't increase acceptance of violence, but neither does it decrease it. Religious people can be violent, but they can also be pacifists.

The fact that there aren't major differences in attitudes toward violence between the religious and the nonreligious may be why so many critics of religion do not use the data presented in this chapter and instead take a different approach. Many critics of religion have argued that millions have died in the name of religion, citing the Crusades, the Holocaust, and hundreds of other wars over the years, not to mention inquisitions and conquests. That's all true of course. Millions have died in the name of religion.

Religious apologists have responded by noting that millions have died in the name of secular ideologies, whether during the Great Leap Forward in China, as a result of Five-Year Plans in the Soviet Union, or in various other communist countries openly antagonistic toward religion. Critics of religion have tried to spin these deaths, claiming that these people died in the name of political ideology, not in the name of atheism. While that may be true, the people doing the killing—or at least responsible for ordering these deaths—were atheists. Their atheism did not stop them from killing or from allowing millions of people to be killed. One could argue here that, based on the criteria I laid out at the beginning of this chapter for why Islam bears responsibility for the death of Aqsa, atheism is not responsible. After all, although atheism was part of the culture and atheists were doing the killing, the killing was not done in the name of atheism but in the name of an atheistic ideology. That's true. But that's parsing things pretty fine for me, because, in the end, atheists were responsible for the deaths. I'm okay with laying those bodies on the doorstep of atheism. However, this still tells us little about the differences in attitude toward violence between the religious and nonreligious.

Inevitably those squabbling over who is more violent—the religious or the nonreligious—want to tally the bodies. Seriously? Let's consider that approach for a second. If I kill one person, and someone kills fifty, okay, I could see the point of counting bodies. I'm a murderer but you're a serial killer; that's different. But, hypothetically, if my ideology killed 15 million and yours killed 17 million, am I really going to assert that 2 million fewer deaths makes my ideology better than yours? The better assertion is that both religious and nonreligious ideologies are in need of improvement if the goal is fewer deaths.

Religion can inspire great acts of selflessness, but it can also inspire horrible acts of violence, often out of the same selflessness. When someone does something horrible in the name of religion, please don't blame it on "culture"! Religious and nonreligious people have similar attitudes toward violence, and neither can claim moral superiority when it comes to atrocities committed in the name of their ideologies. Humans are violent, whether they are religious or not.

23

THE HAPPINESS DELUSION
RELIGION AND MENTAL WELL-BEING

My wife, Debi, suffers from major depressive disorder (aka clinical depression). She has been on medication for her depression since she was eleven years old and has been in therapy much of that time. With antidepressant medication she functions perfectly well; if you met her you would not know she is clinically depressed. No one really knows the exact cause of depression. Her mother was clinically depressed, as was one of her brothers. Current theories on depression suggest a combination of biology, psychology, and sociology. That seems vague enough to be all-encompassing and compelling, if not all that satisfying.

But here's the point I want to make. I met Debi in 1999. I was twenty-three at the time; she was twenty-five. I had just returned from two years in Costa Rica as a Mormon missionary. I was a devout Mormon, attending services weekly and participating in other meetings about as often. I firmly believed in the teachings of the religion. Debi was less devout, but also attended services fairly regularly and believed most of what the religion taught. In 1999, Debi was clinically depressed.

In the summer of 2002, Debi and I decided we no longer wanted to be Mormons and left the religion. In 2002, Debi was clinically depressed. By 2004, Debi and I both considered ourselves skeptics and atheists. In 2004, Debi was clinically depressed. It's now 2012 and Debi and I are both still skeptics and atheists, and we have a child who is also an atheist. In 2012, Debi is still clinically depressed.

Do you see a pattern here? Debi was no less depressed when she was religious and no more depressed when she gave up religion and became an atheist. Religion did not cure my wife's depression. Atheism did not cure my wife's depression. Religion and nonreligion do not make people happy.

—§—

Scientists have an okay understanding of what makes people happy and a lot of what makes people happy is really outside of the individual's control. About 40 percent of happiness is personality-based. While the malleability of personality is debated in psychology, many psychologists would say that personality is largely fixed. Other factors that influence happiness include income, social characteristics, how we spend our time, attitudes and beliefs, relationships, and our environment. The happiest people are either really young or old, female, moderately well-educated, and healthy (probably the biggest contributor), live in countries that are developed yet do not have wide disparities in wealth, have a job that is close to home but with good hours, are not caring for elderly relatives, are involved in the community, exercise regularly, have a positive outlook on life, are trusting of others in a relationship, have sex a lot, have friends, and live in a stable, democratic country in a safe neighborhood, but not in a large city.

But what about the relationship between religion and happiness? People have studied this, right? Lots of research claims that being religious will make you happy, but this is a relationship where the details matter. People who regularly attend church report greater happiness. But there are some problems with this simple relationship. People who attend church are also healthy enough to attend and spend time with people. They also are able to take time off from work to attend, are more likely to be female, are moderately well-educated, are involved in the community, and are not unable to attend due to caring for a relative. In short, the ability to attend church includes many of the characteristics that predict happiness. So, using church attendance as a factor in predicting happiness is really not a very good approach unless you look at church attendance in addition to everything else. Let me put it in simpler terms: if you have two people who are healthy, are spending time with people, are involved in their community, are well-educated, are not taking care of a sick relative, have good jobs in stable countries, and live in safe neighborhoods, but one attends religious services regularly and the other doesn't, will there be a difference in happiness? Probably not.

What if you compare people by their type of religion, like we've been doing? Are fundamentalists happier than moderates? Are liberals happier than the nonreligious? Figure 23.1 shows the results from a self-reported measure of happiness from the 2010 GSS. Respondents were asked how happy they are and given three possible response options: very happy, pretty happy, or not too happy. There are slight differences in happiness, but the differences are not mathematically meaningful. The nonreligious report the lowest percentage who are "very happy" but also report the lowest percentage who are "not too happy." They have the largest percentage who are "pretty happy," but all the differences are quite small.

FIGURE 23.1. Happiness by Religious Group

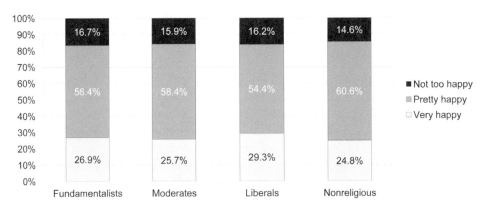

SOURCE: GSS, 2010

Outside the United States, the difference is more pronounced, but only for one group—the most religious appear to be the happiest, while there are no notable differences among the remaining three groups, as shown in figure 23.2.

While I have offered an explanation for why religious attendance might be correlated with higher levels of self-reported happiness, that doesn't really explain the findings in figure 23.2. In that figure, those who report religion is very important to them have the highest percentage reporting being very happy, though most of the difference is between "very happy" and "quite happy." The percentage difference is quite large—about 10 percent more. Does this mean religious people are happier? Yes, it does, but only in certain contexts. Recent research has found that religion does increase happiness in less developed countries but not in highly developed countries—which is why this shows up in the WVS and not the GSS. In highly developed countries, there aren't any significant differences in happiness between the religious and the nonreligious.

Why, then, is there a relationship in less developed countries? There are a couple of possibilities. First, it could be that nonreligious people in less developed countries are a disliked minority and are therefore subject to prejudice and discrimination. This may result in lower levels of happiness.

Another possibility is that the religious in these countries use their religion to overcome the reality of their less-than-ideal living conditions. There is a small body of research that has found that people suffering from depression are, in fact, more realistic in their perceptions of themselves and more accurate in their recollections of the past than people who are not suffering from depression. Interestingly,

Figure 23.2. Self-Reported Happiness by Importance of Religion

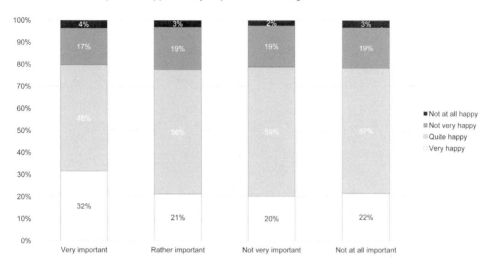

SOURCE: WVS

the evidence for the relationship between these two traits does not suggest causality. Does depression make someone more realistic or does being more realistic make someone depressed?

While the evidence for the correlation between these two traits is not overwhelming and the causal nature of the relationship is unclear, I wonder if this relationship may help explain the correlation between religiosity and happiness. Here's what I'm thinking: highly religious people believe things that are not supported by scientific evidence—they believe things for which there is no evidence. That is suggestive of a disconnect from reality; they are, quite literally, deluded. What's more, these "delusions" are generally geared toward rewarding those who believe in them—they offer support, comfort, and hope. If religious people are less realistic in their perception of day-to-day life, this may help explain why they report being happier. If realistic people are more depressed, shouldn't it stand to reason that deluded people may be happier? In other words, the greater reported levels of happiness of the religious may be a result of their disconnect from reality. Alas, I have no empirical evidence to support this idea at this point. Also, just to reiterate, differences in happiness between the highly religious and the less religious/nonreligious or between fundamentalists and nonfundamentalists are context specific— they vary from country to country.

What can we conclude about the relationship between religion and happiness? Religious people, depending on how you measure religiosity, can sometimes appear to be happier than nonreligious people, but it may not be the case that religion itself contributes anything to happiness. If you measure religiosity by frequency of attendance, there is a pretty good chance that it is the other characteristics that come with attending (e.g., having friends, being involved in the community, etc.) that increase happiness, not attending religious services in and of itself. However, there does occasionally appear to be something of a relationship between importance of religion or even type of religion and happiness, depending on the country and context, with the most religious and the most fundamentalist reporting slightly higher levels of happiness. It's possible this is due to the propensity for the highly religious to be disconnected from reality—a "happiness delusion"—but that warrants future investigation. It could also be that the nonreligious are subject to prejudice and discrimination, making their lives more difficult and reducing their happiness. For now, the evidence seems to suggest that religion contributes very little to people's happiness. If you want to be happy, you're better off finding a healthy, stable relationship, getting a good, reliable job, joining a community group, exercising, eating right, having lots of sex, and moving to a stable, democratic country with lower levels of inequality. Oh, and get lucky by being born with a positive disposition—that will help, too!

24

SLEEP IN ON SUNDAY
RELIGION AND HEALTH

My junior and senior years in college I worked in a couple of psychology research labs at the University of Utah. I was planning on going on to graduate school and thought the experience would help prepare me for what was to come. While my current research is closer to the work I did in Donald Hartmann's lab, I also spent a great deal of time working in Frances J. Friedrich's lab conducting priming experiments. One of the other student research assistants working in the lab at that time was a young woman with a fascinating history as relates to religion, Kenya. I'm not going to go into her history, but want to describe an incident that transpired between the two of us.

I was still a devout Mormon when I was working in Dr. Friedrich's lab in 1999. As such, I was a teetotaler—no alcohol, coffee, or tea. I was, however, very fond of meat—lots of meat. I didn't consider food a meal unless it included a serving of meat. Kenya was just the opposite; she was a coffeeholic and a vegetarian. If she didn't have coffee, she got severe headaches and she never ate meat. Ever the evangelist for my religious beliefs, I took it upon myself to convince Kenya that her coffee addiction was, in fact, bad for her health. This was in 1999, before I knew much about science, before I was a skeptic, and even before Wikipedia existed. It was the age of sketchy, unreliable Web sites created by anyone with the ability to type content into a third-rate HTML editor and post it on the Internet. I found a couple of sites that claimed all sorts of health risks related to coffee, printed them out, and gave them to Kenya. She was, amazingly, willing to consider what the sites said. She read the material and decided that the headaches were not worth it. She quit drinking coffee.

She then turned the tables on me. She went online and found a couple of equally sketchy sites that claimed eating meat was very unhealthy. She printed the information on those sites out and brought them to me. I wasn't very skeptical. I read the material she gave me and was gullible enough to accept it, despite the stunning lack of scientific evidence behind the claims. I became a vegetarian in 1999 in the interest of my health.

Skip forward to 2012. Today, I drink decaffeinated coffee—several cups every morning. Why? A cup of coffee with zero-calorie sweetener has about 2 calories in it; add a tablespoon or two of milk and you're looking at maybe 40 calories per cup. Compare that with a cup of orange juice at 110 calories. Three cups of coffee with milk has the calorie equivalent of a single cup of orange juice. In the interest of my waistline, that was a simple decision—drink coffee rather than orange juice. I do drink caffeinated coffee about once a week—Saturday evenings to help me stay awake so I can write into the early hours of Sunday morning without distraction. I'm not worried that drinking coffee is bad for me; current scientific research suggests coffee is either benign or offers slight health benefits, despite what I was taught when I was a Mormon.

I also eat some meat, at most one or two small servings per day, just like the U.S. Department of Agriculture's Center for Nutrition Policy and Promotion recommends. I was a vegetarian for about ten years after Kenya presented me with that information, but I eventually decided that a diet with small servings of meat—mostly chicken, since my wife dislikes fish—was even healthier than an ovo-lacto vegetarian diet.

I also exercise regularly, as the USDA recommends, and gauge how much I can eat each day based on my weight. I was fairly active in high school, playing soccer and dancing ballet. I ate pretty much whatever I wanted and didn't worry about weight. I'm six feet tall, and in high school I weighed about 155 pounds. The most unhealthy I've ever been was actually on my Mormon mission. Despite walking miles every day, I ate far more than I needed and my weight ballooned to 180 pounds. I had to buy new pants to fit my ever-expanding waist. After my mission I began dancing again and dropped about 20 pounds. Today, I'm back to my high school weight—155 pounds.

What does all of this have to do with religion and health? I followed the guidelines of my religion because I believed they were inspired recommendations for healthy living. Religions are not the experts on health and being religious doesn't guarantee that you'll be healthy. If you want the best recommendations for being healthy, look to science, not religion.

Despite science having a monopoly on knowledge about healthy behaviors and practices, it's pretty common to hear or read media reports talking about the health benefits of religion. I see them regularly. Whenever I do, I get really, really pissed. Why? Because they are always misleading.

Yes, being religious can correlate with better health. Mormons and Seventh-day Adventists are somewhat healthier and live longer than members of other religions, and there are a lot of studies suggesting very, very, very tiny benefits to self-reported health from being religious. But what most of these studies don't do is paint an accurate picture of what is going on.

Here's how simple this is to understand: if you take two people, Bruce and Jeff, who are identical in every way—same height, weight, food consumption, level of physical activity, level of social activity, number of friends, and genetics (they're twins)—but one of them, Bruce, is religious and the other one, Jeff, is not, do you think there will be a difference in their health? The answer, of course, is no.

What matters when it comes to religion and health is healthy behaviors, not religion. If a religion discourages its members from smoking cigarettes, guess what? Members of that religion will gain a significant health advantage. Is the advantage due to the religion, or is it due to the members not smoking cigarettes? Don't get me wrong. Props to the religion for discouraging smoking. But the religion can, at best, claim indirect responsibility for improving the health of its members if it discourages smoking, because it is the act of not smoking that matters for health, not being a member of the religion. Returning to our hypothetical twins, if both Bruce and Jeff take up smoking, but Bruce is still religious, will their health suddenly differ? Will Bruce's religiosity compensate for his smoking? Will Bruce's lungs be washed clean by the waters of baptism? By partaking of the sacrament? By bathing in the Ganges? By confession? By incense? Of course not. No scholar would dare claim as much.

Health benefits that derive from religion are almost entirely indirect. For instance, religions often provide a sense of community and a social network, which is beneficial for social health and indirectly beneficial for physical and mental health. Religion, of course, is not required to make friends, so you can get this same health benefit outside religion. Some religions discourage smoking, but, as noted, the benefit is from not smoking rather than from religion. There are plenty of nonreligious people who do not smoke and get the same health benefits. Many religions discourage alcoholism, but some actually serve alcohol as part of the service. Alcoholism is bad for your health, but religions can't claim credit for the health benefits stemming from not being an alcoholic. Many nonreligious people drink alcohol responsibly or do not drink alcohol at all, deriving the same benefits. Some religions have started encouraging members to exercise, somewhat ironically, since the members hear these exhortations as they laze in the pews. If religions were serious about health, as my wife is fond of saying, they would replace pews with exercise bikes and treadmills. Even an hour of physical activity per week would go a long way toward

Figure 24.1. Self-Reported Health by Religious Group

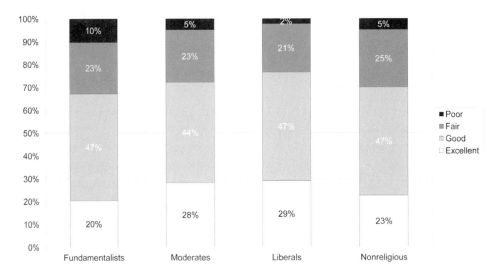

SOURCE: GSS, 2010

improving the physical health of Americans and people around the world. And, of course, nonreligious people exercise, too, many of them on Sunday mornings while the religious are sitting in the pews.

Let's look at the data. Figure 24.1 presents the results of a question asking Americans about their general health. They have four options: excellent, good, fair, or poor. The figure shows what percentage reported each of the responses by the four religious groups.

Liberal religionists have the best health overall. Fundamentalists have the worst health. However, all of the difference in these percentages disappear when you control for education and income. In other words, fundamentalists are less healthy because they are less educated and have less income; liberal religionists are healthier because they have more education and more money (see figure 24.3). Moderates and the nonreligious fall in between the other two groups. Also note that the differences here are quite small.

Figure 24.2 repeats this comparison with a five-point question from the WVS. In that question, respondents could rate their health as very good, good, fair, poor, or very poor. So few people report "very poor" that I didn't put the percentage in, but they are there (about 1 percent for all four groups). Otherwise, there are only

FIGURE 24.2. Self-Reported Health by Importance of Religion

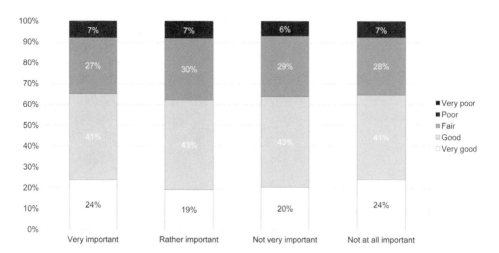

SOURCE: GSS, 2010

marginal differences, and they are actually the opposite of what the GSS data suggested about the United States. The most and least religious are the most likely to report very good health, while the other two groups report slightly worse health.

In both data sets, the relationship between religion and health is quite small. Yes, there are some minor fluctuations, but they don't mean much and the trends are different in the GSS and the WVS. To illustrate this, watch what happens when I replace religious group with highest degree earned in the GSS and thereby examine health differences by educational attainment, as shown in figure 24.3.

Almost 40 percent of individuals who have a graduate degree have excellent health, while just 10 percent of those with less than a high school diploma do, and even those with a high school diploma are only half as likely to have excellent health as are those with a graduate degree. It doesn't require a PhD in sociology to conclude that going to college is better for your health than going to church. There are lots of things you can do to improve your health that don't require religion, including exercising, eating right, having friends, not smoking, making a lot of money, having health insurance, living in a developed country, being married, not being obese, and even getting the recommended amount of sleep. The next time someone prods you to get up Sunday morning to go to church, tell them you're taking care of your health by sleeping in.

Figure 24.3. Self-Reported Health by Highest Degree Earned

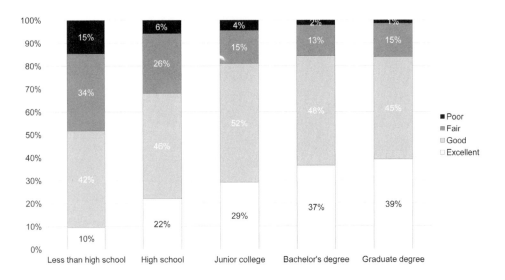

SOURCE: GSS, 2010

To date, no studies suggest *substantial* health benefits resulting from religion. Religion has been included in many of the biggest, most well-funded studies on health, but most of these find either no influence or a negligible contribution from religion on health. Even so, scholars continue to examine religion's influence on health (mostly because they have an agenda). Most studies that find a mathematical relationship between being religious and having positive health conclude that religion explains a grand total of roughly 1 percent of the differences in health of respondents. In practical terms, what does that mean? Nothing, really. Using our identical twins from earlier, does this mean that Bruce will live a year longer? No. Does this mean he'll have fewer health problems? Probably not. All it means is that scholars are, occasionally, able to find a mathematical relationship between religiosity and health, but it's largely confined to a mathematical relationship.

This relationship is so small that I regularly point out the meaninglessness of it in academic conferences when scholars report a difference in health by religion. At one conference in the summer of 2011 I noted how small this effect was during a session. After the session, a physician came up to me to express his concern about my dismissal of the benefits of religion on health. In the course of our discussion I asked him, as a physician, if he recommends that his nonreligious patients become religious for the health benefit. His response, "No. That would be ridiculous. The benefit is too small." My point exactly. If being religious improved peoples' health by, say, 10 percent, I might consider it a worthwhile sacrifice to make for my health. I don't always like riding my exercise bike, but it's a sacrifice I'm willing to make for my health. If religion offered the same health benefits as did exercise, I'd suffer through droll sermons and inane rituals with everyone else. But a 1 percent difference in self-reported health? I'll get more benefit from staying in bed.

The media regularly tout the health benefits of religion, and occasionally scientists find a mathematical relationship between religion and health. However, almost all of the health benefits associated with religion are indirect—healthy behaviors are what matter, not religion. Nonreligious people are just as healthy as religious people, all else being equal. If you want good health, follow the latest recommendations of scientists, not the dictates of archaic religious dogma.

25

WHO'S BETTER AT DYING?
RELIGION AND COPING

People die. I'm going to die.

I'm really not that old, but I'm old enough to have experienced the deaths of loved ones. All of my grandparents are dead (as are my wife's, though they died before I met her). Two of my uncles have died, one by suicide at around fifty and another from cancer at around sixty. One of my wife's brothers died in 2005; he was forty-two. The person to whom I was closest who has died was my brother Mark. He was the closest of my siblings to me in age, just two years older than I am. He died in 2010 at thirty-six after a long decline in health due to a variety of problems. Mark and I were typical siblings—we fought a lot, largely because of our competitive natures—but we also did a lot together, and I have many fond memories of time spent with my brother.

Losing those close to us forces us to deal with a serious aspect of the human condition—death. Intriguingly, I've been both religious and nonreligious when people close to me have died. I was a devout Mormon when my uncle Dave committed suicide in the early 1990s. Dave had been a very successful businessman for a long time; he had created a fortune, but had lost most of his money. He took the loss very hard and was suffering from clinical depression. I worked with Dave the day he committed suicide. He was more quiet than usual, but I didn't suspect what he was contemplating. It was a traumatic experience for me, though I'm sure it was much worse for his wife and children. I remember not only feeling the loss associated with his death, but also wondering whether he was going to be punished by god for taking his own life. Dave was my father's only brother and they had been quite close. I remember listening to my father's talk at his funeral and watching as my father wrestled with this very issue. My father concluded that Dave was not going to be punished for committing suicide because he was mentally ill. My father did not believe god would hold Dave responsible for his actions. My father's words helped me cope with the loss of my uncle by leading me to believe that he was in a "better place" (i.e., heaven) and that I would see him again.

When my brother died in 2010, I was the only member of my family who was not religious. In planning the funeral it was decided that all of the siblings and my parents would speak. All of my siblings reminisced about Mark's life, but they also talked about where they believed he was; they found solace in the idea that Mark was still alive, in a noncorporeal form, and that they would be reunited with him in the future. Their tool for coping with death was their belief in an afterlife. As I don't believe in an afterlife, I couldn't draw upon that to cope with Mark's death.

How, then, did I cope with my brother's death? There are several ways. First, I accepted then and I accept now that people die. Whether or not I like death doesn't change that it is a requisite part of life. Second, in Mark's case, I was relieved that he was no longer suffering. He had been sick and his health had been declining for a very long time. In death, there is no suffering. There is nothing. I would rather have nothingness than suffering. Third, I did my best to celebrate and remember Mark. That is all that remains of him now—the memories of those who knew him. I spent a fair amount of time writing down memories of my brother to keep him with me. Fourth, I have come to realize that the reason why the loss of loved ones to death is so hard on us is because we are social animals and we incorporate our loved ones into our selves. Knowing that I would never have another chance to interact with my brother helped brace me for the realization that the part of me that was Mark was likely going to slowly disappear over time. I would never again need to rehearse conversations with my mental representation of Mark or consider how he might respond to what I said or did. Mark was gone, and a little bit of me died with him.

I don't know that I had an easier time coping with the death of my brother than did the rest of my family. Maybe I didn't. But there was one thing I did not have to consider: his eternal fate. Adding questions of eternal fate to death seems to make coping harder, not easier.

A growing body of evidence seems to support the idea that the nonreligious have an easier time coping with death than do the religious, at least with their own mortality. Religious people appear to be more afraid of death than are nonreligious people. Nonreligious people are less likely to use aggressive means to extend their lives and exhibit less anxiety about dying than do religious people. That seems remarkably counterintuitive since the nonreligious are much less likely to believe in an afterlife, which is supposed to help people cope with death. But factor in that religious people are contemplating their eternal fate and it begins to make more

FIGURE 25.1. Frequency of Thinking about Death by Importance of Religion

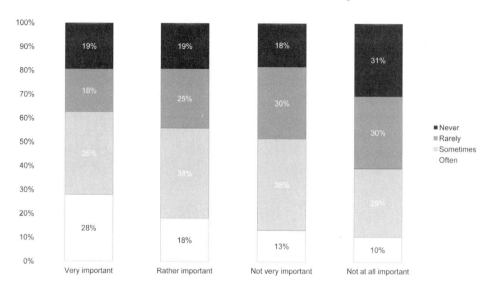

SOURCE: WVS

sense. Even if they have done everything their religion says they are supposed to do, there is always a bit of uncertainty about where they might end up. As a result, religious people appear to have a greater fear of dying than do nonreligious people. This is reflected in figure 25.1, which shows that religious people think about death more than do nonreligious people.

This raises an interesting question which, unfortunately, I cannot answer with the data at hand. Does being religious lead to an increased fear of death or does substantial fear of death lead people to be religious? We don't know the answer to that question yet, but I tend to think that it is the latter, and there are a number of social scientists who agree with me, arguing that the fear of death is the primary motivation for people to seek religion. There may, in fact, be innate differences in fear of death, which increases the appeal of religion for those who fear it more. But that is an empirical question for which we do not have an answer.

A related line of research has begun to examine religion's role in helping people deal with trauma, like the loss of a loved one. This function of religion is often re-ferred to as "coping" and there is some data suggesting that religion can help people cope with trauma. The basic idea is that religion offers explanations, justifications, or rationalizations for why people die and can offer hope of reunions with those who have died. Thus, religion can turn a traumatic, life-altering event into one filled with reassurances and hope of better things to come. Justifications like this can include ideas like it was god's will that someone died, that there was a higher purpose in the death, or that death is simply part of a cycle of rebirths.

However, religion does not guarantee positive coping outcomes. There are good and bad types of religious coping. Some people blame god. They become angry and wonder why they are being punished. For these people, religion ends up making the bereavement process much more difficult. Religion can also complicate things when the fate of the deceased is uncertain, as was the case with my uncle. Thus, while religion can help people cope with trauma and loss, it can also hinder coping and make things worse.

What's the take-home message here? Even in an area where religion is widely viewed to be a major help to people, it can be problematic. Religion can help people deal with the death of loved ones, but it can also hinder healthy adjustment to the loss of a loved one. What's more, some data suggest that nonreligious people are not as afraid of death as are religious people and that they are able to cope with death—at least their own deaths—quite well. Religion is not required for coping with thoughts of death and, in fact, it may be the case that thoughts of death are what drive people to religion. Nonreligious people do appear to be better at dying than religious people.

26

THE END IS NEAR-ISH
DECLINING RELIGIOSITY

I mentioned in chapter 21 that I regularly volunteer with a student group on my campus, PEACE. The student coordinators involved with PEACE are well organized. On a minimal budget, they put together more than a dozen volunteer trips a year. The students who participate in these trips are volunteers, but, more impressively, they pay for the opportunity to volunteer. Admittedly the volunteering is not grueling; usually there is a little time for sightseeing and education on each trip. But it is volunteering. And given that the students have to apply to participate and pay to volunteer, they tend to be very good students, which makes my job particularly easy.

And what is my job? Each trip requires a faculty or staff advisor, over the age of twenty-five, who is primarily responsible for driving. This "advisor" volunteers with everyone else and does virtually none of the planning—the student coordinators do all of that. I'm just the chauffeur. I'm also there in case there is a serious issue and the student coordinators need some help. I've really enjoyed the volunteering I've done with PEACE, and apparently the students like having me around as they keep asking me to be an advisor. It was on a recent trip—to Oklahoma to volunteer with the Cherokee Nation in spring 2012—that I saw what I want to recount as my example for this chapter.

When the students approached me about volunteering with the Cherokee Nation, I was very excited. I grew up in Utah and periodically drove through reservations in Utah, but I had never spent any appreciable amount of time working directly with Native Americans. I've read a small amount of Native American history and am aware of how horribly European-Americans treated Native Americans. As a sociologist, I talk about this treatment in my classes. I also talk about the poverty and social issues many Native Americans face. I thought this volunteer opportunity would give me the chance to observe some of that poverty firsthand, work to alleviate some of it, and allow me to give back to a group of people who were horribly abused by settlers of European descent. Obviously I wouldn't be righting significant wrongs, but it would be something.

I was quite excited by the opportunity, until I found out exactly what we were going to be doing. When you volunteer with the Cherokee Nation, a volunteer coordinator working for the Cherokee Nation assigns you wherever he or she wants to. The volunteer coordinator arranged for us to volunteer at Emmanuel Baptist Church. Ugh! To say I was conflicted about this assignment substantially understates the internal conflict I experienced once I found out what we were going to be doing. However, I only found out a couple weeks before we were to leave, and if I opted out at that point, the students would have been unlikely to find a replacement, which would have meant they couldn't go. I didn't think that would be fair to them. What's more, I came up with a rationalization for volunteering at a church. We were told that most of the members of this church were elderly Cherokee. Because of their age and limited incomes, they really didn't have the money or skills to maintain their church. I could have said, "Well, good. That's one less church infecting people with superstition and supernatural beliefs." But another thought also occurred to me, "The people attending that church are not the people I expect to read my book or give up fundamentalist religion. They are going to die religious. And it is highly likely that their small church gives them some comfort and hope in their old age. If this church is how they derive their comfort and camaraderie, what is it to me that I am working on a church? It could just as well be a community center or retirement home."

Whether my reasoning was sound on this point is certainly open for debate, but it's not the primary point I want to make with this story. That relates to our planned schedule. We flew in on a Saturday. The student coordinators had put together an itinerary for us so we knew which days we were going to be volunteering and at what times. On the itinerary they had scheduled us to begin volunteering the next day. . . Sunday! Some secular readers may have missed the significance of this. Think about it for a second. The student coordinators thought we were going to be volunteering. . . at a Baptist Church. . . on a Sunday.

Yeah. Not going to happen. What were we going to do, paint around them while they sang hymns?

As soon as the students gave me the itinerary, I saw the problem. I, personally, have no problem volunteering on a Sunday. But I knew we weren't going to be volunteering on Sunday. The members of the church would be at the church worshiping. However, and this is the key point I want to make here, the student coordinators, both of whom are religious, didn't think twice about volunteering on Sunday. The students in our group, including several very religious ones, didn't realize we were not going to be volunteering on Sunday until the volunteer coordinator, who met us when we arrived on Saturday, said, "Okay. Now that you're settled, I'll see you Monday morning." The students looked puzzled and were about to ask her for clarification when I piped up and stated the obvious, "I should have said something before now since I realized it when I saw the itinerary. We can't volunteer at a church on Sunday; the members will be using it."

What's my point with this lengthy, though not-quite-complete, story? My point is that young people today no longer see Sunday as a holy day. They are so naively secular that they see no issue with volunteering at a church—on a Sunday! That holds for highly religious young people as well as the nonreligious ones. As a sociologist of religion, watching these students realize that they couldn't volunteer at a church on Sunday was priceless. They are secularizing and don't even know it.

I'm not, however, quite done. The very next day I saw something equally illustrative of secularization. Unable to volunteer, I urged the students—yes, me, a rather strident secular humanist and atheist—to attend the worship service at the church where we would be volunteering. I suggested to the students that it would be a nice opportunity to meet those who would be benefiting from our week of service, and it was. The members were very welcoming. But we had an entire day to kill, so we decided that, after the service, we'd go do something more along the lines of what they (and I) typically do on a Sunday—go hiking in a nature preserve. We were in Claremore, Oklahoma, a very small town outside Tulsa, which is semirural and has some nice parks and scenic walks.

Claremore is also, like most of Oklahoma, very religious. But that doesn't mean what it used to mean. On the way from the church to the nature preserve we passed a Walmart. I wasn't surprised that Walmart was open. But knowing I was in the Bible Belt, I thought many people would still feel that you should respect the Sabbath and not go shopping. Um, yeah. Not so much—the parking lot was full!

What's the big deal? It used to be the case in the United States and in many predominately Christian countries that stores were closed on Sundays and people spent the day engaged primarily in religious activities. There are still some states that limit alcohol sales on Sundays and one county in the United States, Bergen County, New Jersey, that does not allow stores to be open on Sundays. The transition to stores being open on Sundays in Utah largely occurred during my lifetime (I was born in 1976). I remember how big of a deal it was when a major grocery store in Utah, Smith's, decided to open on Sundays; the decision by Smith's management played out in the news for weeks. Back then, people wondered if anyone would show up to make it worth the store's efforts. Now, when I visit family in Utah, Smith's is always busy on Sundays. And in conservative and highly religious Claremore, Oklahoma, people flock to Walmart on Sunday—after going to church, of course.

—§—

I could have told lots of stories to begin this chapter. Countless individuals have left the religions in which they were raised and suffered horribly as a result, like Damon Fowler, whose parents kicked him out when he stood up for the law and opposed prayer at his high school graduation. Those are compelling stories, but they don't quite illustrate what I want to illustrate in this chapter. My point with the two observations I've made is that Americans are more secular today than they realize. The young people with whom I was volunteering didn't think of Sunday as the Sabbath; it was just one more day to volunteer. That subtle shift away from religion is an example of "secularization," as is the widespread acceptance of shopping on Sundays.

At an individual level, secularization refers to the idea that, over time, people rely less on the supernatural and religion and more on science, reason, logic, and modern technology. Secularization can also happen at the institutional level, as organizations like universities and hospitals distance themselves from religions and begin to govern themselves based on modern, nonreligious ideas. Precisely why this happens isn't 100 percent clear, but the idea that it does has been around for a long time—over 100 years. There are several popular theories behind what drives secularization, but for simplicity I'll focus on just one.

With the development of new technology, people no longer turn to the supernatural for explanations or aid. An example may help illustrate this idea. Some readers will be more knowledgeable about cars than others, but even if you don't know how a car works, answer the following question for me, "Are cars powered by pixies? Fairy dust? Prayers?" The answer to this question is so obvious today that even asking it sounds ridiculous. You may not know exactly how an internal combustion engine, hybrid electric, or fully electric car works. Frankly, you don't need to know how it works. But you do know that no pixies, fairies, or prayers are required.

And what do you do if the car breaks down? Do you sacrifice a chicken? Cast a spell? Many people don't know how to fix a car, but this doesn't lead people to think that sacrificing a chicken will do the trick. Even if you don't know how to fix your car, you know that some people do—mechanics. And the fact that you know that they know how your car works is an illustration of secularization. Even if individuals don't have a perfect understanding of how technology works, they know that it's modern science and engineering speeding them around town, not gremlins and garden gnomes.

When examining individual-level secularization, sociologists look at all the ways people can be religious. If people attend religious services less frequently, are

FIGURE 26.1. The Rise of Nonreligion in the United States

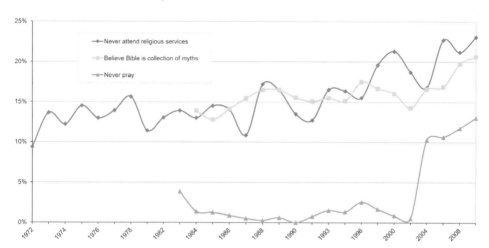

SOURCE: GSS, 1972–2010

less likely to identify as a member of a religion, pray less frequently, donate less money to churches, have less respect for churches, have less respect for the Sabbath, and so on, than they used to, they are exhibiting secularization. If we go with those measures, then the United States is definitely secularizing.

Using GSS data from 1972 to 2010, we can see evidence of this secularization. Figure 26.1 shows three variables over that time period—the percentage of Americans who never attend religious services, the percentage who believe the Bible is a collection of myths and not a literal history or the inspired word of God, and the percentage who never pray. In 1972, about 9 percent of people reported never attending religious services. By 2010, 23 percent of Americans reported they never attend religious services. In 1984, when the question about the Bible was first asked, close to 14 percent of Americans said they believed the Bible was a collection of myths. By 2010, close to 21 percent of Americans thought of the Bible that way. Finally, in 1983, when the question about prayer was first asked, about 4 percent of Americans said they never prayed. As of 2010, 13 percent of Americans never pray.

It has been widely reported in recent years that the fastest growing "religious" affiliation in the United States is actually those with no religion. GSS data support that conclusion. In 1990, 7 percent of adult Americans reported no religious affiliation. In 2010, close to 18 percent of American adults reported no religious

FIGURE 26.2. Percentage Nonreligious by Age

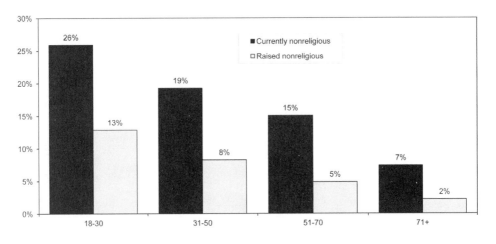

SOURCE: GSS, 2010

affiliation. Figure 26.2 shows the percentage of adult Americans with no religious affiliation by age in 2010.

I broke these responses down by age to illustrate a point I made earlier about secularization. While the total percentage of Americans in the United States today with no religious affiliation is about 18 percent, that number differs pretty substantially by age. For the youngest American adults, those between 18 and 30, more than 1 in 4 report no religious affiliation. Americans over 70 are the most likely to report a religious affiliation, with just 7 percent saying they have no religious affiliation. Also shown in figure 26.2 is the percentage in each of these age groups who were raised with no religious affiliation—18–30-year-olds were six times as likely to be raised without a religious affiliation as were those over 70. There is also a very good chance that many of those between 18 and 30 years old will raise their children without a religious affiliation as well.

Whenever these age differences in religiosity are pointed out, my religious colleagues are quick to point out that some of the young will return to religion. That's true, some will. But most will not. Statistically this gets complicated as we are dealing with age, period, and cohort effects. In simpler terms, each successive cohort (people born during the same period) tends to be less religious than the previous one, but there is a slight return to religion as they age. Additionally, it appears to be the case that certain periods are more conducive to secularization than others. The 1990s, for some reason, was particularly conducive to this, but it is not entirely clear why. Regardless, the general direction of all these numbers is toward lower levels of religiosity, both over time and in younger generations. The end of religion is near-ish. Okay, it's probably not that near, but the general trend is toward declining religiosity.

Some scholars and apologists are also quick to point out these are small percentages and that the majority of Americans remain at least somewhat religious. That's not exactly true. I've shown just the extreme end of these variables. When you adjust for overreporting and response bias in surveys, only about 20–22 percent of Americans attend church weekly. That means there are more Americans who never attend religious services than who attend weekly. Similarly, just because someone says they have a religious affiliation doesn't mean they ever go, ever pray, or even believe any of the teachings of the religion. I know lots of "Catholics" who are Catholic in identity only; I go to Catholic services more often than a fair number of Catholics, and I've never been Catholic.

For those who think the numbers above are small, try translating them into people. In 2010 there were about 308 million Americans. If we assume the discussed percentages apply to children as well as adults, which may not be a perfectly sound assumption, then here's what we have: 70.1 million Americans never go to church; 64.7 million Americans think the Bible is a collection of myths and fables; 55.4 million Americans have no religious affiliation; 24.6 million young people are being raised with no religious affiliation; and 40 million Americans never pray. Tens of millions of Americans are already nonreligious, and hundreds of thousands are joining them every year.

Some readers will, no doubt, insist that many of these people still believe in god. Um, yeah, let's examine that claim. The numbers commonly presented in the media are actually quite misleading on this question. It's pretty common that the media report 90–95 percent of Americans believe in god, which is complete and utter bullshit! While only 3–4 percent of Americans are atheists (which is more than Mormons and Muslims combined), 6 percent are agnostics, and 11 percent are deists or believe in some higher power, but not the personal god of Christians. Another 5 percent believe in god sometimes, which is not that far removed from being an agnostic, and 17 percent believe in god but have their doubts, which is also pretty close to being an agnostic. When you take all of the above out, that leaves just 58 percent of Americans who say they "know god exists." That's miles from 90–95 percent. How do some people arrive at the 90–95 percent figure? Those who claim that percentage take anyone who could possibly be considered to believe in a god, even if they doubt it, only believe sometimes, or believe in a higher power, and claim that they all believe in god. That's a statistical technique commonly referred to as "lying"!

Others might point out that there are some supernatural beliefs that have remained pretty steady over the last forty years or so, like belief in an afterlife. That's true, but most questions that ask about belief in an afterlife provide absolutely no nuance on what people understand by this. The question typically offers just two options, "Yes, I believe in an afterlife" or "No, I don't." That doesn't do a very good job capturing those who doubt it or believe in a nonorthodox version of an afterlife, like reincarnation.

Despite all of the data I've presented thus far, there will, no doubt, be some who object to my characterization of Americans as secularizing. For them, I have one more trend that is pretty compelling—the decline in confidence in organized religion and clergy. In 1973, when the scholars running the GSS first asked about confidence in organized religion, about 36 percent of Americans reported having "a great deal" of confidence in organized religion and clergy. In 2010, that was down to 21 percent. Nearly 80 percent of Americans report having "only some" or "hardly any" confidence in organized religion or the clergy. Granted, confidence in all types of organizations is down, but just 1 in 5 Americans say they have a lot of confidence in organized religion and clergy. That is a sad state of affairs for an institution that bills itself as the source of morality, honesty, and trust.

The general trend in the United States over the last forty years is toward lower levels of religiosity. But what about in the rest of the world? Well, it depends on the country. In the developed world (e.g., Western Europe, Japan, Australia, New Zealand, etc.) most people are even less religious than in the United States. While developed countries continue to grow even more nonreligious, in many countries the rapid periods of secularization took place decades ago. As of 2010, religion was the least mentioned "important value" in Europe, rated lower than human rights, peace, respect for human life, democracy, individual freedom, the rule of law, equality, solidarity, tolerance, self-fulfillment, and respect for other cultures. Just 6 percent of Europeans indicated that religion was one of their three most important values. Figure 26.3 gives an example of declining religiosity in the United Kingdom.

In 1851, 60 percent of the British people attended services weekly. By 1998 it was down to just 7.5 percent, and today it is closer to 5 percent. Similar patterns are observable throughout the developed world.

The developing world is a different story. People there do tend to be more religious than in the developed world. That is, of course, evidence for secularization, as the theory of secularization suggests that it is increasing modernization, education, and technology that reduces reliance on religion. Some scholars have suggested that the higher fertility rates in less developed countries means the world is actually growing more religious. That may be true using some measures of religiosity, but I don't find those arguments compelling. The primary reason why I don't is because

FIGURE 26.3. Weekly Religious Service Attendance in the United Kingdom as Percentage of Population, 1851–1998

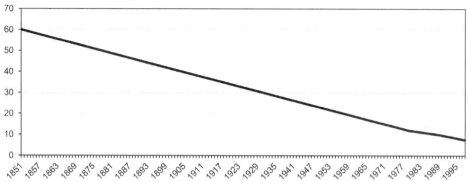

SOURCE: BRUCE, 2002; INTERPOLATED

many of these countries are reaching a level of development at which secularization begins to take hold. Additionally, in many of these countries, just like in the United States, what it means to be religious is changing.

This leads me to a recent observation. I spent eight days in the United Arab Emirates (UAE) in January 2012. The UAE is a Muslim country. While there are certainly indicators of high levels of religiosity, like no metro service Friday mornings when people are supposed to visit their local mosque (not very helpful for those who don't have cars), I also observed some rather interesting indicators of secularization. In several shopping malls and at a desert camp I found the most interesting thing—Christmas trees! I first noticed them in Dubai at Souk Madinat, a shopping mall owned by Emiratis. While you do not, strictly speaking, have to be Muslim in the UAE, almost all Emiratis are Muslim. Christmas, of course, is not a Muslim holy day; it's a Christian holy day. Why, then, would business owners in Dubai decorate their businesses with Christmas decorations? While I didn't get a chance to ask them, I'm fairly confident that the reason is because many of their customers are tourists and the business owners are trying to make the tourists feel more comfortable. I'm also guessing that the business owners have divorced Christmas trees from the Christian "Christmas" and instead see it, like many Americans now do, as a secular celebration of gift giving (and, more importantly for them, of gift buying). In their minds, they probably don't believe that they are decorating their stores with the symbols of another religion but rather with Western symbols of consumption. Perhaps I'm reading more secularization into these decorations than I should. But at the very least this indicates awareness of global differences and an acceptance and toleration of those differences; these business owners are unlikely to be religious fundamentalists. It also suggests, assuming they are aware of any religious connotation of the decorations, that they put "profits" before "prophets." Christmas trees no longer symbolize "Christ's birthday"; now they are universal symbols for shopping! That's as true in Dubai as it is in the Dakotas!

In summary, religiosity declines as technology advances and societies grow more modern and educated. Religiosity has to decline in the face of even a moderate understanding of the modern world, as people see the overwhelming evidence supporting the efficacy of science and technology because it helps them accomplish what they want to do. If you break a bone in Arkansas or Australia, whether or not you pray for help from the divine, you're going to go to a doctor to get a cast because you know doctors can help. If you live in a rural, undeveloped community in Africa or the Amazon, sacrificing a small animal at the urging of a shaman to cure malaria may be your only recourse. Wherever there is technology and education, secularization is soon to follow. Since both are spreading, it seems likely that the end of traditional religion is near-ish.

27

TAKING OFF THE TRAINING WHEELS
ALTERNATIVES TO RELIGION

As a Mormon, I had been taught my whole life that I was special in at least three ways. First, I belonged to the Mormon religion, which was the only true religion on the planet. Because I was born into the religion, that meant I was particularly valiant in the preexistence. Mormons believe that all humans are dual entities, comprised of a spirit and a body. Unlike many religions, Mormons believe in a period of existence prior to when we are born on Earth in which our spirits, with distinct personalities, resided in the presence of god. While there, we participated in a number of events, including a war between the forces of Jesus and the forces of Satan. The fact that we were born means we fought on the side of Jesus (except maybe blacks). And since being Mormon is the end-all be-all of Mormonism (obviously), being born into a Mormon family means you must have been very valiant in the preexistence. Since I was born into a Mormon family, I always found this particular doctrine attractive—it was a nice boost to my already very high ego.

The first way in which I felt special leads to the second way I did. Throughout the 1980s and 1990s when I was growing up (and still today), the leaders of the religion regularly talked about how great a generation the youth of the LDS Church were. They made all sorts of comments about how we were really devout in the preexistence. It was probably just to boost our egos, but it worked. I felt special because I was regularly told by the leaders of my religion that I was.

Finally, I also felt special because I believed there was a guy up in heaven who not only could hear my prayers, but actually wanted to hear my prayers, listened to them intently, and then carefully considered the best way to respond to my desires. I had an all-powerful buddy who wanted what was best for me. Granted, that sometimes included shitty stuff happening, like me getting robbed and assaulted on my mission, but that was clearly god's will. Regardless, god had my back and that made me feel special.

I note all of the above as background for something that occurred to me in the fall of 2002. I was living in Cincinnati, Ohio, attending graduate school. My wife and I had decided to leave the LDS Church several months prior and I was just beginning to adjust to life without an all-encompassing worldview. I had stopped by the Norwood post office on my way home from school one otherwise normal day. As I got out of my car, I looked around the parking lot and saw several other people—ordinary people—getting in and out of their cars.

And then it hit me! It was like a bolt of lightning had just shot through my brain and left me dumbstruck. It seems rather banal now, but here's the thought that went through my mind, "Ryan, you're *not* special. You're just like everyone else now."

Right then and there, my world and worldview changed. . . forever. There was no buddy in the sky who wanted to listen to me. There was no preexistence where I was a valiant general in god's army. I was, in that instant, just a regular guy living a regular life just like everyone else. Having spent the first twenty-five years of my life feeling like I was important, I remember this realization hitting me very hard. It hit me hard enough for me to stop in my tracks and ponder what I'd just realized. I stood there for a couple of minutes, just looking around as I processed this thought.

I also remember how I felt when this occurred. It wasn't exhilaration at the freedom that comes with moral autonomy. It wasn't joy at the thought of developing a new worldview. It was dread! I was afraid of being alone because there was no sky buddy looking out for me. I was afraid of what the future might bring because there was no longer a definitive endpoint, as Mormons believe, to mortality and this planet. I was afraid of what I might do or become as my moorings had just come loose. And I was afraid that I wouldn't be able to come up with a coherent worldview to replace the one I'd been handed when I was a child.

A part of me died that day. I can't say it was a good part of me, but it was a part of me. What followed was hard.

I don't know that what I've written in this book will influence anyone. But in case it does or has led some to reconsider where they stand, the goal of this chapter is to help people transition from the religion they have always felt was a safe place—like a bike with training wheels—to a worldview of their own making. It's time to take the training wheels off and ride free.

If you have grown a bit more critical in your thinking about organized religion as a result of this book, good. I've succeeded. My goal is to get you to be critical about religion. That doesn't mean I aim to get rid of religion altogether or encourage everyone to leave religion, but I do want everyone to question religion, especially the claims religions and clergy make about how beneficial religion is for people.

Although there are a number of atheists who would like to see the demise of religion, I'm of the opinion that not all religion is created equal. As I've repeatedly noted throughout this book, people who are liberally religious exhibit many of the same positive characteristics as those who are not religious. Even though I, personally, am not religious, I don't have a problem with liberal religionists. I see them largely as allies in the fight against bigotry, hatred, and violence, and they generally are more skeptical and scientific in their thinking than the moderately religious and the fundamentalists. Being liberally religious does, in many ways, offer the best of both worlds—the tolerance and critical thinking of the nonreligious but also a supportive community.

So, if you were a fundamentalist Christian when you started this book and want to retain religion, why not look up your local Methodist or Episcopalian church or, even better, the Unitarian Universalists. Of if you are a Muslim, Hindu, Buddhist, or Jew and are wondering what to do, there are likely more liberal interpretations of your religion to explore, and groups where individuals holding such views meet (e.g., Reform Jews). Give them a try. The people are nice—nicer, as this book demonstrates, than those with whom you may currently associate—and the doctrine, while not really defensible from an empirical standpoint, is rather benign. Liberal religion is, today, *the least offensive way to be religious.*

Of course, I don't feel the same way about fundamentalists. Those people are fucking scary! They pretty much hate everyone who isn't like them, they denigrate education and science, many of them want to oppress and control women, homosexuals, and nonbelievers, they are more likely to beat their kids and wives, and they do all of this despite the fact that strictly following their religious beliefs makes them less affluent, does not decrease their likelihood of committing crimes, and allows them to be manipulated by fiscally conservative rich Republican politicians. I'm obviously not being nice here or pulling any punches. The bottom line is: don't be a fundamentalist!

I don't hate fundamentalists; I know many and they are often reasonably kind (until they find out I'm an atheist). But thinking about the world the way they do is anachronistic; that way of thinking should have died out thousands of years ago. It can be hard giving up the beliefs you've long held, as well as a community of like-minded believers, but fundamentalists are not doing anyone any favors. They are fighting progress in a world that desperately needs progress if we want to maintain our remarkable standard of living without destroying our planet. Fundamentalism must die so humanity can live.

What about moderates? They're closer to "not so bad" than they are to "fucking scary." However, I would also encourage them to either give up religion or find nicer religions. We'll all be better off if they do.

The other alternative is the one I've chosen: nonreligion. Obviously I like this path, but it's not without its difficulties. The most obvious difficulty is that nonreligion is not "something" but rather the lack of something. Nonreligious people have one thing in common—they do not consider themselves part of organized religion. But that doesn't mean they all have the same worldview or beliefs or values. They don't, and that's what makes it so hard, as my own story indicated.

Because nonreligion does not consist of a set of shared beliefs or values (aside from not caring for religion), it is necessarily the case that nonreligious people are forced to come up with their own set of beliefs and values. For some, that may be an exciting prospect and the very impetus for becoming nonreligious. And, for some like me who have been provided beliefs and values their entire lives, that may be a scary prospect. While there are a lot of ways to resolve this problem, including spending lots of time considering different worldviews and philosophies (e.g., objectivism, skepticism, scientific naturalism, etc.), there is one rather popular worldview that is geared specifically toward nonreligious individuals: secular humanism. In fact, there is a very good chance that you are already a secular humanist and you don't even know it. Let's do a quick test to see if you are, in fact, a secular humanist. Read the following list and consider whether or not you agree with these statements:

- I use critical thinking, evidence, and reason to evaluate claims to knowledge.
- I use critical thinking, evidence, and reason to evaluate ethics and values.
- I am committed to a key set of values: happiness, creative actualization, reason in harmony with emotion, quality, and excellence.
- I emphasize moral growth (particularly for children), empathy, and responsibility.
- I advocate the right to privacy.
- I support the democratic way of life, tolerance, and fairness.
- I recognize the importance of personal morality, good will, and a positive attitude toward life.
- I accept responsibility for the well-being of society, guaranteeing various rights, including those of women and racial, ethnic, and sexual minorities, and supporting education, health care, gainful employment, and other social benefits.
- I support a green economy.
- I advocate population restraint, environmental protection, and the protection of other species.

- I recognize the need to engage actively in politics.
- I take progressive positions on the economy.
- I hold that humanity needs to move beyond egocentric individualism and chauvinistic nationalism to develop transnational planetary institutions to cope with global problems—such efforts include a strengthened World Court, an eventual World Parliament, and a Planetary Environmental Monitoring Agency that would set standards for controlling global warming and ecology.

If you agree with the above statements, you are already a humanist. And if you dislike religion, that makes you a secular humanist. If that describes you, welcome! This list summarizes a lengthier new humanist manifesto authored by Paul Kurtz, a long-time advocate of humanism and freethought. There are lots of resources available for those interested in secular humanism, but the primary point I want to make here is that, if you are considering leaving religion, which is perfectly fine to do, realize that you are not the first to choose that path, you are not alone, and there are others who have blazed this path and want to help you.

This leads to my final point in this chapter: you are not alone! Granted, your situation is likely unique and may include lots of complications, but there are literally hundreds of millions of nonreligious people on the planet. Yes, there are more people who are Christian and Muslim, but the nonreligious make up almost one-sixth of the world's population and that number is growing, literally by millions every year. Many people find it helpful during this period of transition to seek out a group of individuals on a similar path for support. If you live in or near a large city, it's highly likely there is at least one secular group nearby. Look one up and go visit it. Not only will the people there likely welcome you with enthusiasm, but they will also understand your situation, understand your struggles, and be willing to help you work through your transition from religious to nonreligious. You can choose to work your way out of religion on your own as well; I worked my way out without a community, though I had my wife and a few friends to help me on my way. Many find it helpful to know they are not alone. Just be aware that you don't have to do this alone; the first step toward secular humanism can be one you take with someone.

If you are considering this route, what lies in your future? Expect a turbulent period while you disentangle yourself from your past and develop a new worldview. It can be tough; there are no simple answers. Secular humanism is not entirely dissimilar to religions in that it provides a coherent worldview, but it includes a strong element of skepticism as part of that. That means you need to be skeptical of secular humanism as well, which means you'll be doing some thinking. There is some research on how long it takes people to make the transition from being religious to nonreligious, but not a definitive answer; for some it takes years while for others it happens quickly. There is no standard path or definitive guide; you'll have to find your own way, but that is part of the excitement.

There will, no doubt, be more than a few New Atheists who read this book who will likely be shaking their heads throughout this chapter. They'll be thinking things like, "All religion is superstition and all superstition is bad," or maybe, "Religion is always damaging and the world will be a better place without it." To my New Atheist friends I'm reminded of a line from *Star Wars: Episode III*. As Anakin embraces the dark side, he tells his Jedi Master, Obi Wan Kenobi, "If you're not with me, then you're my enemy." Obi Wan's response is the line I like, "Only a sith deals in absolutes." I'm not suggesting New Atheists who stridently oppose religion are sith, though they've been called worse. What I'm suggesting is that New Atheists need to tone it down a notch.

I've been very critical of religion throughout this book and obviously agree with the idea that religion is more of a hindrance in society than a help. But, as I noted above, not all religion is created equal. Fundamentalists are scary. If you want to criticize fundamentalist religion, be my guest. Use my book. I'll help you! But you really should stop lumping all religion together and claiming it is "all" bad. Not all religions are "bad" and not everything about religion is "bad." When you say things like "god is not great" or call god a "delusion," you come across as being the other side of the fundamentalist coin. No, I didn't call you fundamentalists, though you are adopting one of their characteristics. While the world is painted in shades of gray, fundamentalists have monochromatic vision—they only see black and white. New Atheists who paint religion monochromatically are acting like religious fundamentalists; they see all religion as black and nonreligion as white. If I thought that was a reasonable characterization of religion, I would have used just two groups throughout this book—the religious and the nonreligious. I didn't do that for a reason—religion is gray, too. I find this aspect of New Atheism particularly galling in light of the fact that many New Atheists consider themselves skeptics and scientifically minded. This book is filled with scientific data showing that liberally religious individuals are pretty similar in their views to the nonreligious; they are quite progressive. New Atheists, you are alienating potential allies when you paint religion with a single, broad brush. It's not very helpful.

If, for some reason, my New Atheist friends don't get that religions come in all shapes and sizes, let me try a slightly different approach. Many of the founding fathers in the United States and many Enlightenment thinkers around the world believed religion was a useful institution for the less educated masses, but unnecessary for themselves. This perspective is elitist and arrogant. But what if it is true?

Not everyone around the world has a PhD. In fact, very few people have the time to sit down and read a lengthy, complex book. The fact that I included charts in my own book means a large percentage of Americans won't understand what I've written, as 22 percent of American adults score below basic in their quantitative literacy; they can't interpret my simple bar charts! People who don't have the time or cognitive capacity to develop their morality may be better off simply being told what to do and how to think. This is an elitist position, but it is not without merit. As much as I'd love to believe every child born on this planet has the cognitive capacity to earn a PhD, experience has shown me that is not the case. I occasionally get functionally illiterate students in my college classes; they can write words, but they can't put them together into coherent sentences. They are high school graduates in the United States—which says something rather sad about our educational system here. Some of these students aren't motivated, but some of them are organically stupid. They are unlikely to ever have more cognitive capacity to reason about morality than is my two-year-old son, who simply needs to be reminded every now and then of what he is not supposed to do. My point: even if you insist that *all* religion is bad (how very sith-like of you), consider the possibility that some people may be cognitively better suited for the simplistic message of religion than the complex message of secular humanism. Let them believe in scary sky daddies to keep them in check so the rest of us can live in peace.

I have, throughout this book, shown that religious fundamentalists are scary. But I've also shown in the process that liberally religious people aren't so bad and, in fact, are quite like the nonreligious—they are tolerant, progressive, agreeable, educated, and even largely proscience. It is people with these characteristics I want to inherit the earth.

If this book has inspired you to reconsider your religious views, I encourage one of two options: join a liberal religion where you can retain a community of believers, or leave religion altogether. If you leave, there are communities of nonbelievers you can turn to for support. But you'll also need to deal with the fact that your worldview has changed; you'll need a new one. There may be better worldviews out there, but the one I think holds the most promise for the nonreligious is secular humanism. It values reason, logic, science, the environment, democracy, and most importantly, people. My dream is for all people to value people. Oh that we were all humanists!

28

THE FINAL JUDGMENT
WHO WILL INHERIT THE EARTH?

In the introduction of this book I recounted a story in which I condemned a woman to hell while a Mormon missionary because she had come to believe it was god's will for her to join the Mormon Church, but she was refusing to do so. I judged that woman worthy of eternal damnation.

You're probably expecting me to say that I learned from my past and that I'm now beyond judging people, but that's not true. I did learn from my past, but I still judge people. I just don't use the same criteria and I'm not nearly as punitive as I used to be. When I was Mormon, I judged people based on the standards laid out by my religion: Were they Mormon? Were they observant, orthodox Mormons? And if they were not Mormon, were they at least following the teachings of their religion or good people? In my Mormon judgment, my kind and loving Jewish relatives were in so many ways great people, but they were destined for an inferior afterlife to my own for not being Mormon, doubly so for drinking alcohol. One of my best friends in high school, a bright young man who was considerate of others and quite gracious was damned for eternity; he occasionally smoked pot, had sex, and worst of all, was a Presbyterian. Even my older brother was destined for a less than ideal afterlife despite being a Mormon; he smoked and drank alcohol.

Today, I judge people on different criteria: Are they kind or mean? Are they selfish or selfless? Are they considerate of others? And, more controversially, are they engaged in self-destructive behaviors, like smoking or eating too much? My judgments today are substantially less meaningful than they used to be, for me at least. While I used to worry about peoples' eternal salvation, today, when I find myself judging someone, the end result if I don't find that person to my liking is really just a determination to minimize my interactions with him or her. I don't consider such people inferior to me. I just don't want to spend much time with them.

Oh, and I do factor in religion. I try to be fair when judging people based on their religious beliefs. If they aren't particularly strident in their views, I'm generally okay with that. But religious fundamentalists score rather low in my estimation. Perhaps the clearest illustration of my judging people (or perhaps more accurately judging religion) involves the wills my wife and I drew up once we had our son. The addition of Toren to our family complicated our wills since there was the possibility, however remote, that we could both die and Toren might survive us as a minor. If that were the case, we wanted to make sure he would be taken care of in accordance with our values. So, what did we do? We contacted our one immediate family member who is also not religious, one of Toren's uncles, and asked him if he would be willing to be Toren's guardian and adoptive parent if both Debi and I were to die before Toren is an adult. He agreed. He is financially stable, bright, kind, and would make an excellent father for our son. We made that decision despite the fact that this uncle is single, knowing full well that the scientific research indicates that children raised in dual-parent households tend to have better outcomes in life.

There is no question that Toren's grandparents on both sides would lovingly care for him and may even wish to be his guardians if Debi and I were to die (thus the will to preclude a fight over this). Most of his other aunts and uncles would also gladly raise our son as their own. But, given our perspective on religion and what we went through disentangling ourselves from it, we wanted to give Toren what we believed would be a head start in life—being raised without religion. That meant finding a guardian for him who would raise him as a secular humanist, just like we would. We judged that would be in his best interest because most Mormons tend to be somewhere between religious fundamentalists and moderates. My wife and I believe that Mormonism is far too restrictive, wasted a great deal of our time, and added far too much unnecessary guilt to our lives. In light of findings about religion like those presented in this book, I think our decision was sound.

Now, you probably won't be all that surprised to hear that none of our religious brothers or sisters who have children (our combined siblings have a total of twenty-nine children) have asked that we care for their children if something were to happen to them. We accept that they, too, want what they believe is best for their children. They have, no doubt, judged that our lack of religion would be detrimental to their children and have therefore chosen not to have us raise their kids should that be necessary. I judge; they judge; we all judge.

I know the common recommendation is that it is wrong to judge people. I reject that idea. I reject it not only because I do judge people but also because it is actually beneficial to judge people. Yes, judging people can mean that we sometimes treat or think about people unfairly, and we may even miss out on great opportunities. I recognize that is an unfortunate consequence of judging others. But judging others can also help us avoid conflict, threats, violence, or even just awkward situations. And, like with my son, it can also help us achieve what we perceive to be in the best interest of ourselves, our loved ones, and even all of humanity. Thus, in this chapter I'm going to do some judging. But based on what criteria?

I haven't been all that objective in this book. And, you know what? So what?!? It's my book; it's my prerogative. The data I presented is publicly available; anyone can verify it. In that respect, I have been objective. But I have depicted things in a very specific way. I have biases, like everyone else, and those biases happen to align with most of the areas where the nonreligious outshine the religious. I favor empirical, scientific evidence as a basis for my decision making (chapter 2). I believe babies are born atheists and that children should be allowed to explore any and all beliefs and not be forced to join a religion (chapters 3 and 4). I think being educated and smart are good things (chapter 6). I'm in favor of science (chapter 7). I think exorcism is a sham and silly (chapter 8). I think women should have absolute control over their own fertility (chapter 9). I think people should marry or not marry when they want and that marriage should not be a gateway to sex (chapter 10). I don't think people should have lots of kids, especially if they cannot support them, and they should wait to have kids until they can support them (chapter 11). I believe authoritative parenting is ideal (chapter 12). I think most crime (as defined in Western societies) is bad (chapter 13). I'm in favor of thinking about moral issues in complex ways (chapter 14). I'm in favor of self-esteem, but dislike arrogance; I'm also keen on recognizing the limitations of my own knowledge and try to be humble, a characteristic I find appealing and value (chapter 15). I'm in favor of gender equality—true gender equality where women have all the rights and privileges of men and are treated equally (chapter 16). I'm opposed to racism, homophobia, sexism, and all forms of prejudice (chapter 17). I favor some degree of redistribution of wealth (chapter 18). I'm somewhat of an environmentalist; I worry about global warming and try to limit my impact on the environment (chapter 19). I'm politically progressive, but somewhat libertarian as well (chapter 20). I volunteer and donate to charities within my ability to do so (chapter 21). I really dislike war, murder, assault, and almost all violence (chapter 22). I favor happiness, though prefer contentedness as a more realistic realization of the pursuit of happiness (chapter 23). I think people should try to be as healthy as possible and that science holds the keys to revealing healthy behaviors (chapter 24). I also think people need coping mechanisms to deal with death and trauma (chapter 25). You've probably realized all of this, if you've made it this far in the book. But I figure I may as well just be honest about my position on these things.

TABLE 28.1. Religious Groups' Report Card

	Fundamentalists	Moderates	Liberals	Nonreligious
Education	D	C	A	A
Intelligence	C	B	A	A
Science acceptance	F	C	C	B
Belief in demons	F	D	B	A
Reproductive rights	F	D	B	A
Sexual repression	D	C	B	B
Healthy marriage attitudes	C	B	B	B
Pronatalism and fertility	D	C	B	A
Child rearing	C	B	B	B
Criminality	B	B	B	A
Morality	B	B	A	A
Humility	D	C	B	A
Gender equality	F	D	C	B
Prejudice	F	D	B	A
Social class and income	D	C	B	B
Environmentalism	D	C	B	B
Political views	D	D	D	B
Volunteering	C	B	B	B
Violence	B	B	B	B
Happiness	A	B	B	B
Health	B	B	B	B
Coping	B	B	B	A
GPA	1.545	2.227	2.955	3.455

This leads to my aims with this last chapter. You see, I'm about to do something that I probably shouldn't do, but that I feel an obligation to do: I'm going to grade the four religious groups I've examined throughout this book. In the classes I teach in college, I don't grade based on whether or not my students agree with me—that would violate my objectivity as their instructor. But in this book, I am going to grade based on my own personal biases—again, my book, my prerogative. So, here's the plan: on each of the above topics I have assigned letter grades to the different religious groups. These are shown in table 28.1. At the bottom of the table I convert the letter grades into an overall grade point average (GPA) for each of the groups.

It won't come as much of a surprise, but religious fundamentalists have basically flunked as good people with about a "D+" or "C-" average, based on my criteria of how moral, humane people should think and behave. If their overall GPA was their grade in college, they would be on the verge of being kicked out. Metaphorically, as this is a GPA for their lives, I think the same should apply: religious fundamentalists should be "kicked out" of everyday life. What do I mean by that?

After people read this book, they should view religious fundamentalists with sympathy and a bit of scorn. Religious fundamentalists are detriments to society and they should be treated as such. Now, don't get me wrong. I'm not suggesting that we round them up and lock them away—that would be awful and is unethical. I'm suggesting that you should think about religious fundamentalists as though they are misogynistic, racist, homophobic Luddites, because they are. It behooves those who are not religious fundamentalists to take the moral high road and not discriminate against such individuals, but you can pity them and, frankly, I think it is perfectly fine to tell them that you do. Tell them that you feel sorry for their choice to oppose the qualities of a progressive, modernized, advanced, democratic society. It's time that religious fundamentalists were considered socially deviant instead of the nonreligious.

Religious moderates are basically "C+" people, or about average. They are going to pass in life, but that's about it. These individuals blend in, since they aren't quite as detrimental to society nor as extreme in their views or behaviors as fundamentalists, but that doesn't mean they are doing much to help make the world a better place. Since it's rather difficult to ascertain whether or not someone is a religious moderate, it's probably best to reserve your scorn for religious fundamentalists and simply let these people be.

Religiously liberal individuals are "B" people, or above average at life. As a group these individuals are contributing members of society who are setting a standard for what is acceptable and what is not. They are typically tolerant, protective of minority rights, generally progressive, and in favor of modernization, modernity, and science. As I argued in the last chapter, this is really the only acceptable way for people to be religious in the twenty-first century.

The nonreligious are, in fact, the most successful in my grading scale of life with a "B+" or "A-" average. They have the highest overall GPA, but it is not a perfect 4.0. There are nonreligious individuals who oppose gender equality, are unconcerned about the human impact on the environment, and who reject science. That means there is room for improvement, despite their generally positive traits.

These groups are deserving of different fates. Religious fundamentalists are reversions to a period in human history when we were less developed and less rational. I dream of a future without them. The nonreligious are, quite literally, the future. In the truest sense of the idea, the "nonreligious" shall inherit the earth. They are the meek and they exhibit progressive characteristics. Progressive characteristics tend to be those that future generations adopt. More and more people are leaving religion, though current statistics on the religious makeup of humans suggests the nonreligious aren't taking over. . . yet! And since the nonreligious exhibit the characteristics that future generations will likely adopt, they are the figurative inheritors of the earth in that they are the progenitors of the values of the next generation.

While the nonreligious stand out in many respects as ideal citizens of the world right now, that is likely going to change over time. As more people become nonreligious, the nonreligious will gradually become like everyone else, because their characteristics will make statistically larger contributions to the average. Rather than standing out relative to the religious, it will be the religious who stand out relative to the nonreligious. What this means going forward is that the nonreligious are likely to stop exhibiting particularly progressive characteristics once they make up the majority of any given population.

It's also worth noting that the analyses conducted for this book were done with the nonreligious and not atheists for one primary reason—sample sizes. There really aren't great data sources with lots of atheists, who arguably represent one end of a nonreligious continuum. Research that has analyzed atheists typically finds that they fall farther along various continua than do the nonreligious: they are even better educated, smarter, more in favor of science, more rejecting of spirits and demons, about as egalitarian on gender issues, highly complex in their moral reasoning, extremely tolerant, and fairly well-to-do. Thus, using atheists rather than all the nonreligious would actually strengthen the arguments I have made in this book against religion rather than undermine them.

Do you remember the exercise I had you do at the beginning of the book, answering all those questions? Do you still have that piece of paper or note from the introduction? Pull that piece of paper out or pull up the note on your tablet and see what your answers were before you read this book. How did you do? Be honest. Did I, in fact, fulfill the goal of this book by teaching you some things about religion that you didn't know—but should?

Now, here's what I want you to do. Answer all of those questions again, based on the information I have provided. You have the facts. You have the answers. Here's the question: what will you do with the knowledge you now have?

I've made it clear what this information led me to do: I'm no longer religious. In my mind, the scientific research suggests to me a logical path—to reject religion. You need not do that. You could choose the best religious alternative to that: liberal religion. I can respect that choice; liberal religion has a fair amount to offer to those who feel a need to believe and belong.

What I hope to have done with this book, however, is undermine and destroy the appeal of religious fundamentalism. Religious fundamentalists exhibit characteristics that are harmful to society; religious moderates exhibit similar though less extreme characteristics. Our new, globalized, complex, multiethnic world demands a new worldview. Our new world needs tolerance. It needs technology. It needs science. It needs critical thinking. It needs education. It needs respect for the environment. It needs gender equality. It needs good parents. In my judgment, the data suggest those best suited to provide for our needs are the nonreligious; the second best are liberal religionists. The worst suited are religious fundamentalists.

If you're on the fundamentalist bandwagon, it's time to get off. Those of us who are no longer fundamentalists are waiting for you with open minds and outstretched arms. If you want to be part of the future, you can start by focusing on the now. We nonreligious will inherit the earth, but we won't share it with fundamentalists.

APPENDIX
METHODOLOGICAL NOTES

This appendix is a technical note for those interested in my methodology. I'm going to assume that most of the people who read this chapter are probably going to be questioning something I did somewhere in the book or my overall methodological approach to this book. If that's you, you're in the right place. If that's not you, well, you're done with the book, right? Congratulations! Feel free to pass it along to a friend you think might like it.

For those still reading, I'm going to assume that most are skeptical of my approach and are wondering if I have oversimplified things. Well, yes, I have *simplified* things to some degree. I have done so because I am writing for a lay audience, not a bunch of statisticians. I'm well aware of the importance of controlling for variables as well as the complexity of measuring religiosity. Perusing my more technical publications you'll see that I have used more complex statistical techniques elsewhere. I could have approached this book that way. But had I done that my audience would have dropped considerable. So I did simplify things. This appendix explains how and why.

One of the primary simplifications I employed throughout the book is my choice of independent variables from the General Social Survey and the World Values Survey. In the GSS, the variable I used is a slightly modified version of the variable "FUND," which was originally developed by Tom Smith. The variable is derived from respondents' self-reported religious denomination. Basically, the researchers at the National Opinion Research Center (NORC) categorized different religious denominations into three groups: "fundamentalist," "moderate," and "liberal." For the specifics on how denominations were categorized into these categories, see Tom Smith's report, which is cited in the notes for this chapter and included in the bibliography, or table A1. I modified the variable by pulling the nonreligious or "nones" out of the "liberal" group, as they really don't belong there. I use my modified version of "FUND" to draw conclusions about religious people throughout the book, contrasting individuals who identify with denominations that are considered fundamentalist, moderate, or liberal, and individuals who do not identify with a religion at all.

I'm aware of alternative schemes for classifying religious denominations and people. The alternative schemes are slight improvements over Smith's. But the differences are minimal. If you'd like to criticize the book based on the fact that I used a somewhat dated classification scheme from the GSS, feel free. But I would ask you to do one thing before you make a big deal out of this: rerun my analyses using one of the newer schemes. If you find a difference, feel free to level your criticism about outdated classification schemes. But if you don't find any differences, will you at least mention that fact if you write a review somewhere? You can say something like, "Dr. Cragun used an outdated classification scheme, but it doesn't really matter because when you replicate his analyses using newer schemes you find the same thing." If, however, you do find noteworthy differences, please let me know. I'll change my tables and analyses in future editions of the book and acknowledge your feedback personally in the future edition.

You may be asking yourself at this point, "If I'm aware of slightly improved classification schemes, why didn't I use them?" I have used them before. They're fine. But they are complicated to create. Using the modified variable I did, someone could go to the GSS Web site, download the data, and, with minimal effort, replicate what I've done to verify my analyses. Might the scheme I used be too simple as a result? Maybe. But I ran most of the analyses using the other schemes and it doesn't change the conclusions I have reached.

Criticisms can also be raised about the variable I used from the World Values Survey. The variable is named "a006"; apparently the researchers who manage the WVS aren't as creative in their naming conventions. The variable asks participants how important religion is in their life. Responses include: very important, rather important, not very important, and not at all important. I opted for this variable over other potential variables for several reasons. First, it was widely asked. In the WVS data set I used (1981–2008), 232,538 people answered that question, or 91.6 percent of the total number of respondents to the WVS. Other possible questions either didn't get at what I was trying to capture or were not as widely asked. It's not a perfect question, but it is satisfactory.

With both variables (i.e., FUND and a006), there are problems. For instance, with FUND, every member of a denomination is placed in the same category, regardless of individual variation within denominations, which we now know can be substantial. That is a problem. Using, say, a multidimensional, cross-cultural measure to classify people would be better. Without such a measure I am probably not

TABLE A1. Classification of Religious Denominations in the General Social Survey

CATHOLIC (*MODERATES*)

JEWISH (*LIBERALS*)

NONE (*NONRELIGIOUS*)

OTHER (*NOT CATEGORIZED*)

PROTESTANTS (*LIBERAL*)
Baptist (Northern)
Church of God, Saint & Christ
Congregationalist, 1st Congreg
Episcopal
Evangelical United Brethren
Friends
Hungarian Reformed
Latvian Lutheran
Methodist, Don't Know Which
Mind Science
Moravian
Polish National Church
Presbyterian
Presbyterian, Don't Know Which
Quaker
Reformed United Church of Christ
Religious Science
Spiritualist
Swedish Mission
Unitarian, Universalist
United Church of Canada
United Church of Christ
United Church of Christianity
United Methodist Church
United Presbyterian Church in the USA

PROTESTANTS (*MODERATES*)
African Methodist Episcopal Church
African Methodist Episcopal Church
African Methodist Episcopal Zion Church
American Baptist Churches in the USA
American Lutheran Church
American Reform
Brethren Church, Brethren
Christian Disciples
Christian; Central Christian
Disciples of Christ

PROTESTANTS (*MODERATES*) (cont'd)
Dutch Reform
First Christian Disciples of Christ
First Christian Disciples of Christ
First Reformed
Lutheran
Lutheran Church in America
Lutheran, Don't Know Which
Methodist
No Denomination/Nondenominational
Other Lutheran Churches
Presbyterian Church in the United States
Reformed
Zion Union
Zion Union Apostolic
Zion Union Apostolic-Reformed

PROTESTANTS (*FUNDAMENTALISTS*)
7th Day Adventist
Advent Christian
American Baptist Association
Amish
Apostolic Christian
Apostolic Faith
Assembly of God
Baptist
Baptist, Don't Know Which
Bible Missionary
Brethren, Plymouth
Calvary Bible
Charismatic
Christ Adelphians
Christ in Christian Union
Christian & Missionary Alliance
Christian Calvary Chapel
Christian Catholic
Christian Reform
Christian Scientist
Church of Christ, Evangelical
Church of Christ, Evangelical
Church of God in Christ
Church of God in Christ Holiness
Church of God (Except with Christ and
    Holiness)
Church of Prophecy

TABLE A1. (cont'd)

PROTESTANTS (*FUNDAMENTALISTS*) (cont'd)
Church of the Living God
Covenant
Eden Evangelist
Evangelical Congregational
Evangelical Covenant
Evangelical Free Church
Evangelical Methodist
Evangelical Reformed
Evangelical, Evangelist
Faith Gospel Tabernacle
Four Square Gospel
Free Methodist
Free Will Baptist
Full Gospel
Grace Brethren
Holiness (Nazarene)
Holiness Church of God
Holiness; Church of Holiness
Holy Roller
Individual Bible, Bible, Bible Fellowship
Jehovah's Witnesses
LDS
LDS-Jesus Christ; Church of Jesus LDS
LDS-Mormon
LDS-Reorganized
Lutheran Church–Missouri Synod
Mennonite
Mennonite Brethren
Mission Covenant
Missionary Baptist
Missionary Church
Mormon
National Baptist Convention of America
National Baptist Convention, USA, Inc.
Nazarene
Open Bible
Other Baptist Churches
Other Fundamentalist
Other Methodist Churches
Other Presbyterian Churches
Pentecostal
Pentecostal Apostolic
Pentecostal Assembly of God
Pentecostal Church of God

PROTESTANTS (*FUNDAMENTALISTS*) (cont'd)
Pentecostal Holiness, Holiness
    Pentecostal
Pilgrim Holiness
Salvation Army
Sanctified, Sanctification
Southern Baptist Convention
The Church of God of Prophecy
Triumph Church of God
United Brethren, United Brethren in Christ
United Holiness
Wesleyan
Wesleyan Methodist-Pilgrim
Wisconsin Evangelical Lutheran Synod
Witness Holiness
Worldwide Church of God

PROTESTANTS (*UNCATEGORIZED*)
Carmelite
Chapel of Faith
Christ Cathedral of Truth
Christ Church Unity
Christ in God
Church of the First Born
Church Universal and Triumphant
Community Church
Disciples of God
Eckankar
Federated Church
First Church
Grace Reformed
House of Prayer
Independent
New Testament Christian
Reformed Church of Christ
The Way ministry
United Church, Unity Church
Unity

Figure A1. Religious Beliefs and Behaviors by Type of Religiosity

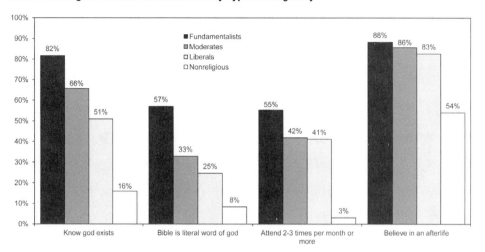

SOURCE: GSS, 2010

capturing the full variation between the theoretical categories (i.e., between fundamentalists and liberals). What that means, though, is that the differences I have found and reported throughout this book are probably smaller than the actual differences between these groups if good measures of religious fundamentalism and/ or multidimensional measures of religiosity were employed. Since such measures don't really exist in large, representative data sets, the variables I have used will have to do.

Additionally, I'm aware of the fact that someone can be a religious liberal and still be very religious in the sense that they strongly believe in the tenets of their denomination, regularly participate, and are heavily influenced by their religion. Thus, while FUND captures key differences in *how* people are religious, it does not accurately reflect the *degree* to which they are religious, even among a small minority of the nonreligious, who actually do attend religious services even though they don't report an affiliation. Thus, throughout this book, if I have, in places, interpreted the GSS data in such a fashion as to imply something along the lines that "more religious people" are X, Y, or Z, that is not 100 percent accurate. What the FUND variable actually says is, people who are more/less fundamentalist in their thinking about religion are X, Y, or Z. I have tried to be consistent in how I have conveyed this point throughout the book, but if there are places where that is not clear, hopefully this methodological appendix will help make that clear.

FIGURE A2. Religious Beliefs and Behaviors by Importance of Religion

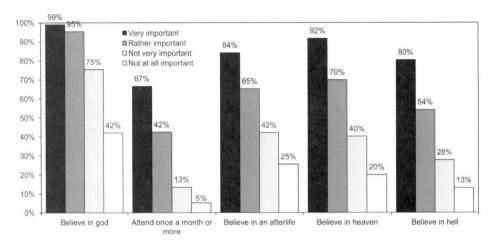

SOURCE: WVS

Despite my key variable being unidimensional, it is the case that religious fundamentalists are more religious in conventional ways than are religious moderates, liberals, and, not surprisingly, the nonreligious, as illustrated in figure A1.

Figure A1 shows that those categorized as fundamentalists using the FUND variable are more likely to believe in a personal god, more likely to hold a literalistic view of the Bible, more likely to attend religious services, and more likely to believe in an afterlife than are moderates, who are more likely than are liberals, who are much more likely than nones. This figure also illustrates the importance of modifying the FUND variable so that the nonreligious are a separate and distinct group since they are substantially different from liberals. In other words, FUND is a reasonable reflection of degree of religiosity, in addition to being a reflection of how people are religious (so long as the nonreligious are pulled out of the liberals).

The WVS variable I employed, a006, is actually quite different from the FUND variable. While FUND measures how people are religious, a006 measures how important religion is to them. Someone could report that religion is not at all important to them, but still regularly attend services and hold orthodox beliefs (it's unlikely, but possible). In other words, this, too, is not a perfect measure of religiosity. Throughout this book I have tried to be consistent in how I discuss the WVS data. When interpreting the findings I have tried to be clear that what the findings suggest is that people who consider religion more/less important score higher in X, Y, and Z. If I have not been clear or consistent in how I interpret the data, that is a failing on my part and I will make every effort to correct that in future editions of

TABLE A2. Year and Size of Total Sample of Participating Countries in the World Values Survey that Answered a006

COUNTRY	YEAR(S) PARTICIPATED	NUMBER OF PARTICIPANTS	COUNTRY	YEAR(S) PARTICIPATED	NUMBER OF PARTICIPANTS
Albania	2002	1,957	Ethiopia	2007	1,492
Algeria	2002	1,270	Finland	1996, 2005	1,989
Andorra	2005	1,000	France	2006	997
Argentina	1995, 1999, 2006	3,333	Georgia	1996, 2008	3,490
Armenia	1997	1,880	Germany	1997, 2006	4,027
Australia	1995, 2005	3,429	Ghana	2007	1,525
Azerbaijan	1997	1,974	Great Britain	2006	1,026
Bangladesh	1996, 2002	3,016	Guatemala	2005	999
Belarus	1990, 1996	2,854	Hong Kong	2005	1,218
Bosnia and Herzegovina	1998, 2001	2,376	Hungary	1998	649
Brazil	1991, 1997, 2006	4,423	India	1990, 1995, 2001, 2006	8,401
Bulgaria	1997, 2006	1,997	Indonesia	2001, 2006	2,999
Burkina Faso	2007	1,506	Iran	2000, 2007	5,148
Canada	2000, 2006	4,078	Iraq	2004, 2006	5,000
Chile	1990, 1996, 2000, 2005	4,650	Italy	2005	999
China	1990, 1995, 2001, 2007	4,737	Japan	1990, 1995, 2000, 2005	4,007
Colombia	1997, 1998	6,005	Jordan	2001, 2007	2,422
Croatia	1996	1,185	Kyrgyzstan	2003	1,036
Czech Republic	1990, 1998	2,036	Latvia	1996	1,148
Dominican Republic	1996	4,03	Lithuania	1997	981
Egypt	2000, 2008	6,050	Macedonia	1998, 2001	1,996
El Salvador	1999	1,248	Malaysia	2006	1,200
Estonia	1996	996	Mali	2007	1,497

TABLE A2. (cont'd)

COUNTRY	YEAR(S) PARTICIPATED	NUMBER OF PARTICIPANTS	COUNTRY	YEAR(S) PARTICIPATED	NUMBER OF PARTICIPANTS
Mexico	1990, 1996, 2000, 2005	6,922	Slovenia	1995, 2005	2,020
Moldova	1996, 2002, 2006	2,990	South Africa	1990, 1996, 2001, 2007	8,945
Morocco	2001, 2007	3,462	South Korea	1990, 1996, 2001, 2005	4,876
Netherlands	2006	1,010	Spain	1990, 1995, 2000, 2007	5,095
New Zealand	1998, 2004	2,054	Sweden	1996, 1999, 2006	2,994
Nigeria	1990, 1995, 2000	5,003	Switzerland	1989, 1996, 2007	3,778
Norway	1996, 2008	2,151	Taiwan	1994, 2006	1,995
Pakistan	1997, 2001	2,732	Tanzania	2001	1,070
Peru	1996, 2001, 2008	4,157	Thailand	2007	1,526
Philippines	1996, 2001	2,398	Trinidad and Tobago	2006	999
Poland	1989, 1997, 2005	2,723	Turkey	1990, 1996, 2001, 2007	7,661
Puerto Rico	1995, 2001	1,879	Uganda	2001	1,001
Romania	1998, 2005	2,960	Ukraine	1996, 2006	3,529
Russian Federation	1990, 1995, 2006	5,756	United States	1995, 1999, 2006	3,971
Rwanda	2007	1,504	Uruguay	1996, 2006	1,975
Saudi Arabia	2003	1,497	Venezuela	1996, 2000	2,394
Serbia	2006	1,201	Vietnam	2001, 2006	2,446
Serbia and Montenegro	1996, 2001	3,702	Zambia	2007	1,463
Singapore	2002	1,511	Zimbabwe	2001	1,001
Slovakia	1990, 1998	1,531			

this book. I do want to point out, however, that, like the fundamentalism measure above, people who report that religion is very important to them are more religious in all of the traditional ways, as shown in figure A2.

People who say religion is very important to them are more likely to attend religious services more frequently, to believe in god, to believe in an afterlife, to believe in heaven, and to believe in hell than those who say religion is rather important to them. Those who say religion is rather important to them are more likely to do these things than those who say religion is not very important to them. Those who say religion is not very important to them are more likely to do these things than those who say religion is not at all important to them. In short, I readily admit that the primary variables I employed throughout this book are not the perfect variables and they are simplistic. Nevertheless, they are pretty decent measures of religiosity.

To help address these concerns, in every chapter where I have argued there is a relationship based on simple statistical analyses using the outlined measures, I have done several things to strengthen those arguments. First, I have, where possible, shown that the relationships hold using two distinct variables—FUND and a006—in different locations, the United States and the world. Table A2 lists the countries that participated in the WVS, the years, and the number of participants. The fact that I am able to replicate the relationships in completely different data sets using different variables suggests the relationships I have presented in this book are robust. Second, in most cases I did actually run multivariate statistics that most experts would expect for publication in a peer-reviewed journal and the relationships held after holding constant obvious control variables such as gender, age, race, etc. I don't include them because many people would have no idea what they mean. And third, every chapter includes references to the leading research in the relevant area that finds the same basic relationships. Interested readers are welcome to examine those references in which more complicated statistical analyses are often performed.

Finally, as already mentioned, I invite readers to download the surveys I have used and replicate my analyses. I'm not perfect. I may have made a mistake in my analyses. If I have, I welcome corrections.

NOTES

Introduction

To add a little detail to the quote that opens the introduction, I noted that the woman was middle-aged and lower middle class. This happened during the first one or two months while I was in Costa Rica in the city of Cartago. My companion at the time, Elder Smith, was a bit taken aback by my bold assertion that she was going to hell and, after we left her home, he told me that it was okay to believe that she was going to hell, but that it was not really okay to say so directly to her. As a devout Mormon, I challenged him on this point by claiming that we were supposed to condemn those who rejected our message. I cited Doctrine & Covenants 76:32–38, specifically section 35, which states, "Having denied the Holy Spirit after having received it. . . . These are they who shall go away into the lake of fire and brimstone, with the devil and his angels." Today, most Mormons will claim that in order for someone to be a son or daughter of perdition and spend eternity with the devil you have to have absolute knowledge (like a personal visitation) of Jesus and then deny it, but that's not what the passage says. My companion countered by citing different passages in the Doctrine & Covenants, for example, 60:15, 75:20, and 24:15, which all state that you should condemn in secret by leaving the house of those who reject you and the message you carry, and then dust off your feet as a curse against them. We did dust off our feet a few times when people were particularly mean to us, but eventually we stopped doing that, too. Being that strident is more work than it's worth.

Relative to the quote at the beginning, I'm fully aware of the fact that Mormons do not believe in the same "hell" as do many other Christians. They believe, instead, in something called "outer darkness," which is kind of similar, but not really the same thing (R. T. Cragun and R. Phillips 2012; M. C. Thomas 1992).

On my mission I was trying to convince people that their religion was false and of the devil because the Book of Mormon says that there are only two churches—the church of Jesus Christ and the church of the devil (1 Nephi 14:10). Since I obviously belonged to the church of Jesus Christ, all other religions had to be part of the church of the devil.

The tools I used to convince people to join the LDS Church were developed by social scientists. I am referring, specifically, to the *Missionary Guide* (The Church of Jesus Christ of Latter-day Saints 1988). In that guide, missionaries were taught to use something called "the commitment pattern," which is a manipulative process that directly forces people to make or reject commitments, allowing missionaries to quickly discern how serious they are about what they are being taught. The book and tools were developed by social scientists and are effective for converting people to Mormonism as rapidly as possible.

There are better books for people to read if they are interested in the histories and doctrines of religion. A good one is Stephen Prothero's *Religious Literacy: What Every American Needs to Know—and Doesn't* (2007). While I disagree with his basic premise—that people need to know about religion—the focus is more on religious education than on the social science of religion.

By having people perform this exercise with such an extensive list of questions, I am hoping to accomplish what Redlawsk et al. (2010) suggested was possible with political views—to basically overwhelm those who hold conflicting views with so much information contradicting their views that they are eventually forced, through affective intelligence, to reconsider their views. The odds of me succeeding should increase relative to the percentage of the book people read.

One of the more recent studies that indicates atheists are more knowledgeable about religion than are the religious is a study by the Pew Forum on Religion & Public Life (2010).

Throughout this book I will refer to The Church of Jesus Christ of Latter-day Saints, which is the official name of the religion, as the "Mormon Church" and the "LDS Church." I'm fully aware of the official name, it's just long and tedious to write it out.

When I mentioned that I find some religions more objectionable than others and referred to Christians who kill doctors who perform abortions, I was thinking of George Tiller and the fundamentalist Christian who killed him (Bello 2009).

The religion I was thinking of when I mentioned that I find some religions much less objectionable because I agree with many of their positions was The Religious Society of Friends or Quakers, most of whom are pacifists and believe in equality for all and helping others (Friends General Conference 2012).

I state in this chapter that the existence of god is not a scientific question. I, of course, mean that in a very empirical way—there is no way to gather data to test the existence or nonexistence of a god, depending on how such an entity is defined. Some authors, like Richard Dawkins (2008) and Victor Stenger (2008), believe science can comment on things like the existence of god. But I think the general consensus among scientists is that supernatural entities, so long as they are defined in nonfalsifiable ways, are, by definition, nonfalsifiable. That means the question of their existence falls outside the domain of science and into the domains of philosophy and theology. While this can be an entertaining question to consider, it falls outside the scope of this book.

For those interested in the neurological basis of belief and the biology of religious behavior, you should look into the following books: *The Biology of Religious Behavior* (Feierman 2009) and *The Neuroscience of Religious Experience* (McNamara 2009).

Chapter 1—Buddhism Is In; Communism Is Out: Defining Religion
In case my attempts to be witty are too opaque for some readers, I will do my best to interpret what I was trying to suggest with my chapter titles. By calling chapter 1 "Buddhism Is In; Communism Is Out," I was referring to whether or not each of these systems of belief is considered religious. Buddhism, with its supernatural elements, is clearly a religion. Communism, since it lacks supernatural elements—most of the time—is not a religion. However, as is the case with many of my chapter titles, there is a double meaning. I was also subtly noting that it is currently "hip" to practice Buddhism, particularly among educated people in the West who find the meditative practices of Buddhism helpful in dealing with modern stressors. Likewise, communism is waning in the world today, with just a handful of communist governments retaining power throughout the world. Thus, Buddhism is doubly "in" while communism is doubly "out." See how witty I am?

In writing about Brian David Mitchell's actions, I drew upon a book by Tom Smart and Lee Benson (2006), *In Plain Sight: The Startling Truth Behind the Elizabeth Smart Investigation*, and a magazine article by John-Charles Duffy (2003).

The claim that Joseph Smith Jr. had an affair with Fanny Alger is discussed in detail in an article by Todd Compton (1996), called "Fanny Alger Smith Custer, Mormonism's First Plural Wife." The total number of women Joseph Smith married is debated. The most common estimate is thirty-three, but some have suggested as high as thirty-seven (Compton 1997).

Joseph Smith is held in very high esteem in Mormonism. While that assertion is unlikely to be disputed by most Mormons, I should note that this is, in fact, enshrined in Mormon scripture. See Doctrine & Covenants 135:3, which asserts that Joseph Smith has done more for the salvation of humanity than all but Jesus.

I do consider Joseph Smith's philandering as despicable. The most disturbing incident—of which there are many—is probably when he received a "revelation" that basically told his first and legal wife, Emma, to shut up about polygamy and his philandering or god would destroy her (see Doctrine & Covenants 132:54).

My reference in this chapter to Joseph Smith being a "religious genius" is to

Harold Bloom's (1993) *The American Religion*. While any reference to Smith as a "genius" is a bit unsettling to me, I will grant that he had a knack for manipulating people, which is, I guess, a certain form of genius—not a good form, mind you, just a form.

My definition of religion is primarily based on the work of Max Weber (1978), but it also derives from later modifications to his definition by sociologists of religion and is illustrated fairly well in William Swatos Jr.'s (1998) *Encyclopedia of Religion and Society*. My definition has been and continues to be debated, as is the definition I use of "supernatural." You are welcome to disagree with my definition of religion, as many social scientists do. However, it's my book, I needed a definition, and I like this one. So, it's the definition I use throughout the book. Deal with it.

The standard reference for religions being social constructions is Berger and Luckmann's (1967) classic book *The Social Construction of Reality*.

I argue in this chapter that Brian David Mitchell did not have followers. Some may object to this by claiming that his wife, Wanda Barzee, was a follower. That is, technically, true. However, Wanda was also mentally ill and, after being forced to take medication, was apologetic about what she did (B. Adams 2009). That seems like a fairly reasonable basis for excluding her.

In the case of Brian David Mitchell, an "expert" outsider, Daniel Peterson, a professor of Islamic Studies and Arabic at Brigham Young University, did analyze Mitchell's writings and did not consider them to be the writings of someone who was insane (Winslow 2010).

Some of the other definitions of religion that are common in the social sciences include things like "any worldview that examines existential questions" (Batson, Schoenrade, and Ventis 1993) and "areas of social life that examine the sacred" (Durkheim 2008). These definitions are, in my opinion, problematic because they are too broad. They would include things like secular humanism with the first definition and Chelsea FC for many of its fans with the second.

Some might debate whether Buddhism includes a supernatural element. Buddhists who accept samsara and nirvana certainly believe in the supernatural. While not all Buddhists hold those beliefs, many do, and they are quite central to many ideas in Buddhism.

I included the reference to Apple fans because there is an interesting study using MRI brain scans that illustrates Apple evangelists do, in fact, think about Apple the same way, say, Catholic monks think about a crucifix (Popken 2011).

The claim that communism is a religion isn't very common, particularly today, but some have made this claim (D. V. Benson 1967). And, as noted, this claim is usually connected to books illustrating some of the atrocities that have occurred under communist regimes (Courtois et al. 1999).

For examples of secular government claiming supernatural origins, consider ideas like "American exceptionalism" and "Manifest Destiny" that are discussed in Seymour Martin Lipset's (1997) *American Exceptionalism.*

For evidence that the imperial cult of Egypt considered the pharaoh divine, see Toby Wilkinson's (2001) *Early Dynastic Egypt.* The closest modern-day governments might come to having a leader considered to be divine is North Korea, where the country imbues its leader with supernatural characteristics. Japan used to consider its emperor divine, but no longer does so.

In discussing secular humanism, I draw heavily on the Humanist Manifestos, particularly Manifesto III, which can be found on the American Humanist Association's Web site (American Humanist Association 2003).

My definitions of agnosticism and atheism come from George Smith's (1979) *Atheism.* More modern work suggests similar definitions (Cliteur 2009, 2010; L. Lee 2012b).

For evidence that atheists rarely feel a sense of connection to a community, Stephen Bullivant's research is informative (Bullivant 2008). For a counter example, Luke Galen's research is informative (Galen and Kloet 2011).

Chapter 2—Without Data It May as Well Be Theology: Why Data Matter

Okay, the title for this chapter isn't that hard to decipher. I'm dissing theology because it is all about making shit up. Yeah, sure, theologians try to be logical and have to try to reconcile their ideas with shit made up in the past, but come on—it's all make believe. My favorite summary of theology is by H. L. Mencken, "Theology is the effort to explain the unknowable in terms of the not worth knowing" (Durant 2011). In the sciences, when you make stuff up, we call that fraud and censure you, essentially preventing you from ever working in the discipline again. Since this book is full of data backing up what I claim, I thought the title did a decent job setting up the purpose of the chapter: to illustrate how what I do is different from what theologians do.

The story about Walid Husayin was informed by two newspaper articles (Associated Press 2010; Donnison 2010).

The book by Glock and Stark was called *Christian Beliefs and Anti-Semitism* (1966) and it is, as far as I know, the first effort to examine the multidimensional nature of religiosity. There have been many efforts since then (Hill and R. W. Hood Jr 1999).

For a thorough treatment of what is and isn't a religious fundamentalist, I highly recommend Michael O. Emerson and David Hartman's article "The Rise of Religious Fundamentalism" (2006). For an illustration of the distinction between fundamentalist, moderate, and liberal religions, consider Roof and McKinney's (1987)

American Mainline Religion, as well as Tom Smith's (1987) methodological report *Classifying Protestant Denominations.*

For more information on the General Social Survey you can check out the Web site http://www3.norc.org/gss+website/. You can also contact the principal investigators—Tom W. Smith, Peter Marsden, Michael Hout, and Jibum Kim—or examine the data set yourself, as it is publicly available and free to download (T. W. Smith et al. 2010).

For more information on the World Values Survey you can check out the Web site http://www.worldvaluessurvey.org/. You can also examine the data set yourself as it is publicly available and free to download (World Values Survey Association 2009). I should note that I do use the combined waves of the World Values Survey, as not every country included in the survey was surveyed in every wave and the questions differed from wave to wave.

Chapter 3—All Babies Are Atheists: Why Belief in a Specific God Is Not Innate

I explain the title of this chapter in the chapter. It should be sufficient to say here that I chose the title, despite the lack of a double entendre, for shock value. The statement is, as I illustrate in the chapter, true, but it's still shocking.

I regularly bring this topic up in two of my classes: Introduction to Sociology to discuss culture and Sociology of Religion to discuss the point of this chapter. The student who said this was Joseph Ranalli.

Two studies illustrate that atheists are a hated minority: Edgell et al.'s (2006) "Atheists As 'Other': Moral Boundaries and Cultural Membership in American Society" and Gervais et al.'s (2011) "Do You Believe in Atheists? Trust and Anti-Atheist Prejudice."

Catholics and other religious groups that believe in original sin do, in fact, believe that babies are sinful, not because they have committed any sins, personally, but because Adam and Eve sinned and we're all being held responsible for that (U. S. Catholic Church 1995).

Once again I am drawing on others for my definition of atheism (G. H. Smith 1979; Cliteur 2009).

Njörðr is a Norse god and is associated with the sea, seafaring, wind, fishing, and wealth (Lindow 2002).

Chris Chiappari is the colleague who called these the "denominations of atheism."

Some might object to my assertion that belief in a god is not innate. However, note I how worded this. I said, very intentionally, that belief in a "specific god" is not innate. There is no biological proclivity toward believing in Njörðr, I'm sure we'd all agree. Some might suggest that young children have a biological proclivity to believe in something supernatural, which may be true but is debated (Feierman 2009), but belief in a specific god is not biological. That is learned, and there is no debate over that point.

For additional information on the Mormon conception of the Light of Christ, see C. Kent Dunford's (1992) article on this in the *Encyclopedia of Mormonism*.

Antisocial personality disorder is described in the DSM-IV (American Psychiatric Association 2000).

For more information about the Mangaia and their sexual practices, see a chapter on this topic in *Human Sexual Behavior* (D. S. Marshall 1971).

Chapter 4—The Religious Clone Wars: How Most People Become Religious
If you're not a science fiction fan, then maybe, maybe you can be excused for not getting the reference. The title for this chapter is obviously a play on the *Star Wars: Clone Wars* series on the Cartoon Network that takes place between the Star Wars movies *Episode II: Attack of the Clones* and *Episode III: Revenge of the Sith*. Since the aim of many religious parents is to produce religious "clones" of themselves despite the influence of the surrounding society, the title seemed fitting.

The story that begins this chapter is really tragic. Obviously Josh's religion was not responsible for the accident; it was an accident. But his religion is responsible for his death as the Jehovah's Witnesses do discourage blood transfusions (Watch Tower Bible and Tract Society of Pennsylvania 2006). The story is based on a news article in the *Telegraph* by Laura Roberts (2010).

I draw upon Long and Hadden (1985) for my general understanding of socialization, but I draw upon a variety of scholars for my information about religious socialization (Baker-Sperry 2001; R. L. Dudley and M. G. Dudley 1986; Hayes and Pittelkow 1993; T. F. Martin, J. M. White, and Perlman 2003; S. M. Myers 1996).

Arnett and Jensen (2002) were the scholars who observed that parental religiosity is the best predictor of adolescent religiosity, but not the best predictor of the religiosity of emerging adults. The influence of parents on their children through adolescence is supported by other research as well (C. Smith and Denton 2009). Acock and Bengtson (1978) illustrated that mothers are more influential when it comes to the religiosity of children than are fathers.

The evidence for an evolved acceptance of parental dictates is not particularly strong, but there is some research supporting this (Stayton, Hogan, and Ainsworth 1971). Richard Dawkins makes a compelling case for this in *The God Delusion* (2008), but this is an area where additional research is warranted.

I think it rather humorous to note that during most of the year parents use, "God is watching you," to control their kids' behavior, but in the run-up to Christmas, it changes to, "Santa is watching you." I guess it's not that big of a deal to replace one make-believe character with another.

Not that it needs a reference, but for those wondering if there is evidence that children typically want to please their parents, see John Bowlby's work (1953). The classic reference on children learning by imitating their parents is social learning theory by Albert Bandura (1976). Altemeyer and Hunsberger (1997) make a strong case for the idea that the emphasis placed on religion in one's family of upbringing typically gets passed on to children—the more religion is emphasized by one's parents, the more likely religion will be passed on to children and be highly emphasized. There are plenty of references to support the idea that humans are habitual in nature, but my favorite is Berger and Luckmann's classic book, *The Social Construction of Reality* (1967).

There is some debate as to whether or not "limbo" is an official doctrine of the Catholic Church, but the current Catechism says it is not (U. S. Catholic Church 1995).

I had to use the example of Microsoft to illustrate habitualization because this is such an underhanded tactic—and because I'm writing this book on a Linux machine using LibreOffice and Zotero. Your efforts at habitualization could not overcome my proclivities for freedom and customizability!

The idea that we accumulate "religious capital" was introduced into sociology by Laurence Iannaccone (1990). One of my favorite examples of religions trying to suck young people into churches by any means possible is a religion in Colorado that bought Xboxes and copies of *Halo* to hold local area network (LAN) parties in the basement of the church in order to attract young men (Richtel 2007). The assumption was that the young men would find the church appealing, spend time there, be exposed to religion, and eventually develop sufficient religious capital such that they would not want to throw it away. Religious capital can include personal relationships with other members of the congregation, but also includes a specific body of knowledge, habits, and ways of thinking and behaving.

For evidence that the nonreligious are more open to letting their children explore their religious options, see the work of Hunsberger and Altemeyer (2006) and Christel Manning (2010). Hunsberger and Altemeyer also illustrate that religious fundamentalists are much less open to letting their children explore options and would actively work to convert nonfundamentalist children to their worldview if given the chance.

One function of Mormon missions is actually to convince the missionaries of the "truthfulness" of Mormonism. This results from a rather interesting psychological finding—that public commitment to a belief or behavior increases dedication to those beliefs and behaviors, thereby reducing the likelihood that external attacks on those beliefs or behaviors will be successful (Halverson and Pallak 1978; Werner et al. 1995).

Richard Dawkins does argue in *The God Delusion* (2008) that he thinks religious indoctrination is a form of child abuse. I disagree—though there are certainly some instances when religious indoctrination is absolutely child abuse, like in instances when the life of the child is endangered as a result of the indoctrination. Otherwise, I think parents should be allowed to teach their kids pretty much whatever they want. There are some obvious exceptions. For instance, it's probably not a good thing if parents teach their children that pedophilia or necrophilia are okay.

I give a scenario in which nonreligious parents could potentially abuse their children by threatening to disown them if they believe in a god. I've only found one case where such a thing happened—Madalyn Murray O'Hair disowned her son William Murray when he became a Christian (Dracos 2003). So, I guess it's possible, but it seems like it is pretty rare.

Chapter 5—Why You Don't Know Why You're (Non)Religious: Why Social Networks Matter

The title of this chapter isn't actually a play on words so much as an effort to convince people that they don't always know why they do what they do. Much of our behavior, as was noted in the previous chapter, is habitual, and habits can form very early in our lives, before we are even consciously aware of them, as the story that begins this chapter illustrates.

While this chapter provides evidence that most people don't really know why they believe in the supernatural, I got the idea for this from Thomas Pataki (2009) from a chapter in an edited volume titled *50 Voices of Disbelief*. Another perspective on why many people are oblivious to the sources of their beliefs can be found in Peter Berger's work on religion (Berger 1990) in which he develops the idea of a "plausibility structure." A plausibility structure is the collection of sociocultural artifacts that prop up a given belief and can include parents, family, friends, pastors, books, beliefs, values, churches, etc. In short, we often believe because we live within a sociocultural milieu that props up our beliefs. Additional evidence for this comes from an unpublished manuscript based on some research I conducted in which I was examining conformity in religious settings. We found that people could be persuaded to conform in their religious beliefs (R. T. Cragun, Panageotou, and Harder 2009), just like people conform on factual information (Bond and P. B. Smith 1996). We are strongly influenced by our environment and those around us, even when it comes to religion.

The prior research on prevalence of religious doubts to which I refer in this chapter was conducted by Bruce Hunsberger and colleagues (B. Hunsberger et al. 1996; B. Hunsberger, Pratt, and Pancer 2002).

I suggest in this chapter that traumatic events can force a reconsideration of religious beliefs; I am drawing upon the findings of Hunsberger and Altemeyer (1997).

There are several studies that have tried to examine the influence of genetics on religiosity by examining twins (T. J. Bouchard Jr. et al. 1990; D'Onofrio et al. 1999; Waller et al. 1990). These studies typically find that genetics plays a subordinate role to socialization and social life, but how influential nature and nurture are is not exactly clear.

The research suggesting atheists are more liberal and intelligent (Kanazawa 2010) is somewhat controversial. The research finding that conservatives are opposed to change while liberals are more accepting of it, however, is pretty robust (Jost 2006).

The role of peers, family, and friends in religious exiting is just beginning to be investigated (L. Lee 2012a; R. T. Cragun, Ranalli, and Yeager 2011). The influence of peers, family, and friends on other aspects of social life is pervasive and can be seen in a variety of areas, like weight management (Fletcher, Bonell, and Sorhaindo 2011); criminal behavior (Hochstetler, Copes, and DeLisi 2002); political views (Glass, Bengtson, and Dunham 1986); and religious affiliation and views (Aho 1990; Stark and Glock 1970). See James Aho's *The Politics of Righteousness* (1990) on recruitment through social networks.

Chapter 6—Sunday FSchool: Why Religion and Education Don't Go Together

This chapter title shouldn't be that hard to get. I'm trying to point out a bit of irony. Religions refer to their religious education classes as "Sunday school." Yet, in fundamentalist religions in particular, "school" is really a misnomer. Those attending aren't really learning much, and most of what they are learning runs counter to what is taught in real schools that teach math, science, history, philosophy, etc. In other words, "Sunday school" is not really school at all and, instead, results in "Sunday fools."

The story that begins this chapter is based on an article in the *New York Times* by Dexter Filkins (2009).

My assertion that Jehovah's Witnesses discourage nonreligious education is based on an article on their official Web site (Watch Tower Bible and Tract Society of Pennsylvania 2008). Jehovah's Witnesses' educational attainment is detailed in *Religion in a Free Market* (Kosmin and Keysar 2006).

Obviously critical thinking doesn't guarantee that people will leave religions, but it does play a role. People who think more analytically are less likely to believe in god (Gervais and Norenzayan 2012), and those who rely more on intuition are more likely to believe in god (Shenhav, Rand, and Greene 2011).

Prior research does show compellingly that religious fundamentalists have lower educational attainment because parents discourage it (Darnell and Sherkat 1997). College students who experience increases in religiosity while in college show a significant decline in interest in continuing their education (A. W. Astin, H. S. Astin, and Lindholm 2010).

The causal relationship between intelligence and religiosity is tricky. Some research suggests intelligent people reject religion and less intelligent people find it more appealing (Nyborg 2009). This certainly seems to be the case with scientists, who are particularly likely to reject religion (Ecklund 2010), especially if they are very prestigious scientists (E. J. Larson and Witham 1998). The relationship between atheism and country-level intelligence (Lynn, Harvey, and Nyborg 2009) isn't particularly compelling evidence for this connection, but it helps build the case that there is a connection.

Current research on the effect of education on religiosity does show a complicated relationship. Those who retain their religiosity through college tend to be more active in their religion than religious individuals who don't attend college (Daniel Carson Johnson 1997), in large part because college increases civic engagement. But many religious individuals who attend college see a decline in orthodox religious belief as a result of their college education (Funk and Willits 1987).

Chapter 7—I'll Be a Monkey's Cousin: Religion and Science
The title for this chapter is my attempt to riff on the more famous phrase, "I'll be a monkey's uncle," which is an expression of surprise, particularly at the idea of evolution. The phrase is an odd one, since it suggests humans are the ancestors of monkeys, rather than the descendants of common ancestors with other primates. My phrase is a more accurate representation of the relationship between monkeys and humans—we are cousins on the evolutionary tree. Of course, the whole point of bringing this up is so I can talk about science—particularly evolution—and attitudes toward science by the various religious groups under examination.

My estimate of the pages of scripture I read relies upon Mormon editions of the relevant books: Book of Mormon = 531 pages; Doctrine & Covenants = 294 pages; Pearl of Great Price = 61 pages; and the Bible = 1,590 pages.

For an example of an ethicist suggesting that scientists need to be guided by religion, see *Unprecedented Choices* (Chapman 1999).

Stephen Jay Gould's assertion about nonoverlapping magisteria can be found in his book *Rocks of Ages* (2002). For a good example of fundamentalist religions continuing to argue over issues that scientists settled decades ago, Bob Allen's article in the *Baptist Standard* is useful (2011).

Chapter 8—All Demons Are from Hollywood: How Media Created the Possession Fad

The meaning behind this chapter title isn't necessarily obvious until you've read the chapter. Basically, the disturbingly widespread belief in demons in the United States today is largely thanks to the efforts of Hollywood movies, which regularly depict demonic possession in horror films, and to books about demonic possession. Thus, in a figurative sense, demons in the United States today are really "from" Hollywood.

There is an extensive literature on the characteristics of autism that is readily available to those interested (Rossignol and Frye 2011). My source for the story about Terrance Cottrell Jr. is a CBS News story (2003).

I searched for the word "deliverance" using Google Maps in fall 2011 (http://maps.google.com/maps?q=deliverance&hl=en&sll=27.950575,-82.457178&sspn=0.510105,1.056747&vpsrc=0&t=h&z=11) and found eight ministries geared toward performing "deliverances" just in Tampa. In the greater area surrounding Tampa there were close to 120 different groups that used "deliverance" in their name, though it's unlikely all of them performed exorcisms. I have examined a number of the Web sites of deliverance ministries and that's where I found the varying "expected donation" rates. Logos Christian Fellowship, in Leesburg, Florida (http://www.logoschristian.org/exapp.html), used to request a $50 donation (Fall 2011), but now simply states, "We do not charge for Deliverance but we do accept donations," and "Counseling is free but donations are expected."

My primary source for this chapter is the excellent and remarkably underread book, *American Exorcism*, by Michael Cuneo (2002). For a detailed examination of the claims in William Peter Blatty's book *The Exorcist*, the best source is a *Strange Magazine* article (2000) by Mark Opsasnick.

The Barna Group survey I cite for the data in this chapter was titled "Most American Christians Do Not Believe that Satan or the Holy Spirit Exist" (Barna Group 2009).

I performed a keyword search on imdb.com (http://www.imdb.com/find?s=kw&q=exorcism) on September 18, 2011, and found just over two hundred films with exorcism in the title or as a prominent element of the film.

For those who are wondering why I suggest that the Christian god is not above testing the faith of his followers, you need only consult the book of Job in the Old Testament for a straightforward illustration of how much of an ass Jehovah can be. He allows Satan to kill Job's whole family just to test his faith. That's pretty dickish. Giving him a new family doesn't really make up for that move in my mind.

Chapter 9—God Owns Your Uterus: Religion and the Right to Choose

This is another chapter title that is more an effort at shock value than a double entendre. The basic idea of the title is that patriarchal religions use a rather sinister technique to subordinate women: controlling them through reproduction. By telling women that they have no right to control their own reproduction, religions are basically handing ownership of a woman's uterus to god, whose proxy on earth is, of course, men.

The story that begins this chapter is one of the most disturbing stories in the book (Agence France-Presse 2009). It was widely publicized at the time and is, unfortunately, just one of many horrific acts by the Catholic Church in the last few decades.

There is an extensive body of research on the relationship between attitudes toward abortion and religion (Jelen and C. Wilcox 2003; Bolzendahl and Brooks 2005; Evans 2002).

I note in this chapter that there are some reasons why people oppose abortion that are not rooted in religion. Perhaps the clearest nonreligious rationale for doing so comes from Don Marquis, an American philosopher, who argues that aborting an embryo deprives it of the possibility of a valuable future (Marquis 1989). However, it is highly unlikely most of the nonreligious individuals who oppose abortion have thought about the issue as carefully as have philosophers like Don Marquis.

There is an extensive body of literature examining the benefits to women's health and autonomy deriving from accessible birth control (Chesler 2007; Holmes, Hoskins, and Gross 1980; Morgan and Niraula 1995; Robertson 1983; Shorter 1973; Sousan 1996; Blyth and Landau 2009).

In the National Survey of Family Growth I use in this chapter for information on having abortions, the "other" category is a "catch-all" category for smaller religious groups, like Jews, Hindus, and Buddhists.

It is possible that the data illustrated in figure 9.4 are not perfectly accurate due to response bias. A book written by a doctor who provides abortions (Wicklund and Kesselheim 2008) suggested conservative Protestants often do get abortions because they are more likely to get pregnant accidentally due to limited sex education and therefore have poor knowledge about contraception. But since these people belong to religions that oppose abortion, they may be less likely to report getting abortions.

The fact that most monotheistic deities are traditionally male is not a coincidence. These male gods are idealized notions of the role of men in society.

Chapter 10—Marry Now, Stay Forever: Why Religions Are "Pro-Family"

The title in this chapter is riffing on a phrase that is somewhat common in retail—"buy now, pay later." Of course, I could have used "marry now, pay later" for the title of this chapter as well, but that seemed just a little too cynical for me, even though it reflects part of the motivation for getting people to stay—they will be paying "later."

The relationship between age at first marriage and religion is strongly supported by research on countries around the world (Bourdais and Lapierre-Adamcyk 2004; Lehrer 2004; Garenne 2004; Kalmijn 2007). The relationship between age at first marriage and risk of divorce is also widely known by experts on demography and marriage and the family (Booth et al. 1986; Schoen 1975). There is some excellent research illustrating that family formation results in reduced likelihood to leave religion and/or greater likelihood of returning to religion if people had previously left (Stolzenberg, Blair-Loy, and Waite 1995).

It's rather easy to find examples of religious leaders attempting to muzzle members of the religion when they want to go public with accusations of sex abuse (Gershman and Cohen 2012; Goodstein 2012).

Just for fun, I use the names of friends in my hypothetical scenarios, though the scenarios in no way depict their actual lives. This is just me giving "shout-outs" to people for fun. In this chapter, "Brad" and "Amber" are Brad and Amber Anderson, two friends from Morgan, Utah, who are now married and have three great kids, Ethan, Spencer, and Benjamin.

There is a substantial body of research indicating that adolescents are quite similar to their parents religiously (R. T. Cragun and Autz 2011; C. Smith and Denton 2009).

My source for the primary evolutionary advantages of humans over other animals being our large brains and sociality is a book by Leakey and Lewin (1991). For evidence that we are at higher odds of being deviant if we are surrounded by deviants, see the work of Charles Tittle (1977). For evidence that having overweight friends increases the odds of you being overweight, see the work of Macdonald-Wallis et al. (2011). And for evidence that social networks are very important in religiosity, see the work of Stark and Bainbridge (Stark and Bainbridge 1980).

I am referring to research along the lines of that of Mark Regnerus (2007) when I note in this chapter that some scholars claim premarital sex is unhealthy. The preponderance of scholarly research suggests that premarital sex and adolescent sex is benign (Billy et al. 1988; McCarthy and Grodsky 2011; Legkauskas and Stankevičienė 2009; J. R. Kahn and London 1991; Teachman 2003).

Chapter 11—Multiply and Replenish the Pews: Why Religions Encourage Procreation

The chapter title is a play on the famous directive from god to Adam and Even in the Old Testament to "multiply and replenish the earth" (Genesis 1:28; King James Version). The real motivation for having lots of kids isn't to populate the earth but to keep the pews full so the money keeps flowing.

My summary of Vyckie Garrison's story largely derives from her version of it on her blog (http://www.patheos.com/blogs/nolongerquivering/vyckie-garrison-2/) as well as her radio interview with Dick Gordon (http://thestory.org/archive/the_story_092311_full_show.mp3/view). For more information on Quiverfull, you can see the movement's Web site (http://www.quiverfull.com/) or the Wikipedia page on Quiverfull (http://en.wikipedia.org/wiki/Quiverfull), or Kathryn Joyce's book (2010).

The relationship between religion and fertility is well established (Adsera 2006; Janssen and R. M. Hauser 1981; Mosher, L. B. Williams, and D. P. Johnson 1992; Heaton 1986). Hout et al. (2001) illustrated that high fertility helped conservative Protestantism grow in the post–1960s United States. The reference for the current number of Shakers is a news article by Leanne Ouimet (2009).

Eric Kauffmann (2008) is the scholar who proposed that the fertility of the religious will counter secularization.

Chapter 12—Spare the Rod? Not with God!: Parenting and Religion

I really like the title of this chapter because many religious people are actually quite proud of the fact that they hit their kids, and they turn to a biblical passage (Proverbs 13:24) to justify corporal punishment of children, "He who spares the rod hates his son, but he who loves him is careful to discipline him" (NIV). Thus, while I'm suggesting that some religions advocate corporal punishment of children, this is a situation where the religions won't deny it. I don't have to be subtly witty on this one; the religions do a sufficient job of impugning themselves.

I have changed the name of the scholar who shared this story to protect his identity. I did not use the name of a friend in this story, like I do in some of my hypothetical scenarios. The name comes from a book series I read while writing this, *A Song of Ice and Fire*, by George R. R. Martin. Bronn is a secondary but very likable character in several of the books.

As noted in an earlier chapter, I've only found one instance of an atheist disowning her child when he became religious, and that was the rather infamous Madalyn Murray O'Hair (Dracos 2003). I also cited research in chapter 4 on socialization supporting the idea that the nonreligious are more open to letting their children explore their options (Manning 2010; B. E. Hunsberger and Altemeyer 2006).

The relationship between corporal punishment being employed as a parenting tactic and religiosity is well established (Greven 1992; Giles-Sims, Straus, and Sugarman 1995; R. D. Day, Peterson, and McCracken 1998; Clifton P. Flynn 1994; Hamman 2000; Capps 1992), as is the relationship between religious fundamentalism and desiring obedience in children (Danso, B. Hunsberger, and Pratt 1997). The relationship between religious fundamentalism and authoritarian personality was clearly illustrated by the work of Bruce Hunsberger (Danso et al. 1997; Duck and B. Hunsberger 1999).

Diana Baumrind first published her research in the late 1970s examining the different styles of parenting and their corresponding outcomes (Baumrind 1978).

Chapter 13—There Are No Atheists in. . . Prison Cells?!?: Religion and Crime

You've probably heard the statement, "There are no atheists in foxholes." While that is, of course, not true—there are lots of them (Torpy 2012)—I thought I'd actually create a phrase to replace that one that is far closer to being accurate. As this chapter illustrates, there aren't many atheists in prison. The next time someone says that there are no atheists in foxholes, feel free to correct them by telling them that it would be more accurate to say that you're less likely to find an atheist in prison than you are in a foxhole.

I actually saw a TV show about the story I used to begin this chapter, which drew my attention to it. However, my primary source for my summary of the story was an article from ABC News (Avila 2010).

Johnson et al. (2000) suggest that attending church is correlated with lower rates of crime, but admit that importance of religion is not. Benjamin Beit-Hallahmi's book chapter examining morality among the irreligious is perhaps the best summary of the data on religiosity and crime rates (Beit-Hallahmi 2010). While not without its flaws, Gregory Paul's international comparisons do compellingly show that, among developed countries, more religious countries have higher crime rates than less religious countries (Paul 2010).

An excellent book by Pippa Norris and Ronald Inglehart, *Sacred and Secular* (2011), illustrates a compelling connection between provision of social services and secularization.

Hutterites did sue in order to not have their photographs taken for driver's licenses (CBC News 2009) and also sued to not have to pay income taxes (Esau 2005). Catholic officials have been caught trying to cover up sexual abuse by priests; finally they are starting to be convicted for doing so (Hoye 2012). And Brigham Young did send some of his followers to harass federal troops on their way to Utah (Fleek 2006).

Chapter 14—Moral Development—Win for Atheists; Moral Behavior—Draw

Despite my best efforts, I was unable to come up with a witty or even pithy title for this chapter that accurately conveyed the relationship between religiosity and morality. The truth of the matter is that the nonreligious do think about morality in more complex ways but that doesn't mean they behave in more moral ways. Sorry for the disappointment on this one. However, feel free to send me a witty title if you can think of one. If I use it in a revision of this book, I will acknowledge you!

For an excellent review on whether religion is required for someone to be ethical, see the work of Benjamin Beit-Hallahmi (2010). For a superb comparison of religious and nonreligious ethical systems, I highly recommend Paul Cliteur's book *The Secular Outlook* (2010).

There are some standard references on Kohlberg's work (Kohlberg 1973; Kohlberg and Hersh 1977), but also some recent modifications (Rest et al. 2000). There are also some individuals who believe Kohlberg's work is unfair to religions (Richards and Davison 1992); I don't find their objections to Kohlberg's work compelling.

While somewhat older, the research I found on consensual, nonprocreative sibling sex does indicate there aren't any real consequences (Finkelhor 1980). It is kind of weird to think that is true given the taboo against incest in our society, but I knew some siblings growing up who were alleged to have had consensual, experimental sex and they didn't seem particularly screwed up, er, messed up.

There is a broad array of research indicating that religious fundamentalists have less developed moral reasoning than do the nonreligious (Glover 1997; Haan, M. B. Smith, and J. Block 1968; Stevens, Blank, and Poushinsky 1977; Bar-Yam, Kohlberg, and Naame 1980). In fact, one of the key characteristics of religious fundamentalists is their reliance on black-and-white thinking, including in their moral decision making (Emerson and Hartman 2006).

There are some studies that suggest the nonreligious are less moral because they are more accepting of certain behaviors and activities that the religious find morally objectionable (C. Kirk Hadaway 1989; McAllister 1988). I drew upon those as the basis for what I suggested the religious found immoral. I discussed the differences in what the religious and nonreligious consider immoral in a book chapter published (or soon to be published) elsewhere (R. T. Cragun, Hammer, and Hwang forthcoming).

There are several books and a number of articles that present research on the minimal differences in moral behavior between the religious and nonreligious (M. Hauser 2006; Franzblau 1972; R. E. Smith, Wheeler, and Edward Diener 1975).

Chapter 15—If You're Humble and You Know It. . .: Religion and Arrogance
Phew! Back to multiple layers of meaning in the titles for chapters. This title is an obvious play on the song, "If You're Happy and You Know It." I've always liked that song. But there is another level to the title. You see, I'm suggesting that the assertion that the religious *know* they are humble is actually both hypocritical and arrogant. Anyone who goes around claiming he or she is humble, isn't humble. Humble people don't say they are humble; they are, in a very Zen-like fashion, just humble. Arrogant people claim they are humble. So, when religious people claim they are humble, what are they really saying?

The story that begins this chapter is based on chat logs I still have. I do, in fact, keep my chat logs. This is made even easier in Google Chat, where all your logs are stored in your Gmail account. This took place before I was using Gmail—hell, it took place just as Google was giving birth to Gmail. This was recorded over MSN Instant Messenger, back when I was using Hotmail. Oh Hotmail, how I loathe thee! Anyway, I exported all my chat logs every so often and was sure to save this one just in case it ever came in handy in the future. Turns out it did.

There is an extensive body of literature in a variety of fields noting the importance of having pride in one's self, which is also sometimes referred to as "self-esteem," though they are technically distinct (McBride Murry et al. 2005; M. Lewis et al. 2010; J. L. Tracy, Robins, and Schriber 2009; J. L. Tracy, Shariff, and Cheng 2010; J. D. Brown and M. A. Marshall 2001).

My definitions for the negative connotations of pride come from Merriam-Webster online.

My wife, who proofread this book, was actually the person who recommended that I add the note about my nickname, "Arro," no longer fitting. She thought I was arrogant when we first met, and somehow still put up with me. Now she doesn't think I'm arrogant. I do like to jokingly say that "I'm never wrong." But she and I both know that isn't true and, when people provide evidence that I am wrong, I'm relatively quick to change my mind. I'm not easily persuaded, but I can be persuaded. I also know that my expertise is limited to a very narrow range of the universe, and I don't claim expertise beyond that at all.

The paper that turned me on to this idea is a brilliant piece of scholarship by Rowatt et al. (2002) that should be required reading for, well, everyone!

There is a fair amount of evidence that religion works as a salve for those who feel lost, alone, and disconnected in the modern world (Holden 2002; R. T. Cragun and Lawson 2010). There is also an excellent recent study showing that people believe god holds the same opinions as they do, which makes god an even better justifier of our behavior (Epley et al. 2009).

The characteristics of the monotheist god I gave are based on the following scriptural passages: jealous—Exodus 20:4-5; supreme—Colossians 1:18; superior—Hebrews 1:4; all-knowing—Acts 15:18; all-powerful—Matthew 19:26; perfect—Psalm 18:30. Many others can be cited, but these characteristics are commonly believed by most theists.

Chapter 16—'Cause Jesus Has a Penis: Religion and Gender (In)equality

This is one of my favorite chapter titles. It's short, expresses my point, and yet has multiple layers of meaning. To begin with, the chapter is about gender and patriarchy, which is suggested by the reference to Jesus's penis, which is actually more important in religion than many people realize. So, the title is a bit ambiguous and requires you to think about what the topic might be. But the title is also based upon the Catholic justification for not allowing women to be priests or hold the priesthood—the fact that they cannot be in the "likeness" of Jesus because the essence of Jesus is his penis. I love pointing this out in my classes and noting that there are lots of other ways that people could represent Jesus, like having long hair (which is likely fictionalized, assuming Jesus existed), wearing a robe (probably more accurate), or wearing sandals (also probably more accurate). Also, the title makes people think about Jesus's penis, and who doesn't want to think about a perfect penis?

I created names for the people in the story that begins this chapter. I got the story from this Web site: http://www.exmormon.org/whylft76.htm. The story didn't have names, but to make it easier to tell, I added some. Astute readers, particularly fantasy fans, may realize the source of the names for this story—George R. R. Martin's series *A Song of Ice and Fire*.

There is an excellent book about the ordination of women in religions in the United States by Mark Chaves, *Ordaining Women* (1999), that I highly recommend. There are a number of excellent studies on discrimination against women in religions that allow them to be ordained (J. Adams 2007; Banerjee 2006; Fobes 2004).

There are many attempts to explain the gender disparity in religiosity (J. P. Bartkowski and Hempel 2009; J. E. Hoffmann and J. E. Bartkowski 2008). I don't think any have satisfactorily answered the question. Gerda Lerner introduced the idea of food scarcity as an explanation for patriarchal societies and religions (Lerner 1987).

Chapter 17—Love Your Neighbor, Except When He's. . .: Religion and Prejudice
This is another chapter title of which I'm quite proud. The obvious source is Mark 12:31, in which Jesus is giving the two great commandments, (1) love god and (2) love your neighbor as yourself. Jesus doesn't add the "except" portion, but the evidence indicates that there are exceptions. And that's the beauty of the title—Jesus's command to love your neighbor is unconditional, but the religious don't live up to that command. They put all sorts of conditions on it, like the neighbor not being gay or lesbian, or an atheist, or a communist, and so on. That the religious do not live up to Jesus's command would be ironic if it were not for the fact that it is so damaging to society.

I changed the name of the student in the story to protect her identity.

1 Nephi 14:9–12 is a passage from the Book of Mormon. It describes a conversation a prophet in the book, Nephi, had with an angel. Here is the passage, "And it came to pass that he said unto me: Look, and behold that great and abominable church, which is the mother of abominations, whose founder is the devil. And he said unto me: Behold there are save two churches only; the one is the church of the

Lamb of God, and the other is the church of the devil; wherefore, whoso belongeth not to the church of the Lamb of God belongeth to that great church, which is the mother of abominations; and she is the whore of all the earth. And it came to pass that I looked and beheld the whore of all the earth, and she sat upon many waters; and she had dominion over all the earth, among all nations, kindreds, tongues, and people. And it came to pass that I beheld the church of the Lamb of God, and its numbers were few, because of the wickedness and abominations of the whore who sat upon many waters; nevertheless, I beheld that the church of the Lamb, who were the saints of God, were also upon all the face of the earth; and their dominions upon the face of the earth were small, because of the wickedness of the great whore whom I saw." While many Mormons today try to minimize the obvious implications of this passage, it's pretty clear what it's saying—if you aren't with us, you're against us.

There are a variety of places where Mormon beliefs in the afterlife are detailed (R. T. Cragun and R. Phillips 2012; Dahl 1992). Mormon beliefs in the afterlife are quite forgiving compared to many other Christian religions. The basic idea is that everyone gets at least one chance to receive Mormonism. Once someone has had a clear opportunity to learn about Mormonism, if they reject it, they are punished by being sent to a version of heaven that sucks compared to the other, better versions of heaven. The "better version" of heaven, or "big reward" I reference in this chapter, is detailed in various publications as well (Ricks 1992).

Some might dispute my assertion that the Bible is filled with genocide and ethnic favoritism, but reading the Bible pretty compellingly supports my assertion. Here's just one example from 1 Samuel 15:2–3, which says, "This is what the LORD Almighty says: 'I will punish the Amalekites for what they did to Israel when they waylaid them as they came up from Egypt. Now go, attack the Amalekites and totally destroy all that belongs to them. Do not spare them; put to death men and women, children and infants, cattle and sheep, camels and donkeys" (NIV). Sounds like genocide to me.

There are hundreds, if not thousands, of articles examining the relationship between religiosity and prejudice (Laythe, Finkel, and Kirkpatrick 2001; Altemeyer 2003; Galen 2012). It is a well-studied phenomenon that membership in a group leads to favoritism toward other members of the group (Tajfel 1982). Research has established the effects of the group nature of religions on the attitudes of members (Jelen 1993) as well as what happens when you increase the salience of religious group membership (Greenberg et al. 1990).

Allport's early work (Allport 1966) attempting to dismiss the relationship between religiosity and prejudice or at least limit it to "immature" religionists began a line of research in the psychology of religion that is, unfortunately, ongoing. There are some critiques of this approach that seriously undermine it (Kirkpatrick and R. W. J. Hood 1990), but research on this continues (Carpenter and M. A. Marshall 2009). I'm reticent to admit it, but I've even published using this distinction, though it was an article that showed that "mature" religious people can actually be more prejudiced than the immature ones, showing the ridiculous nature of this distinction (Nielsen and R. T. Cragun 2010).

A note is in order for figure 18.3 in this chapter. Figure 18.3 is combined GSS data from 1972 to 2010. I used the combined GSS data set, as the question about marrying a Jew was not asked in 2010.

I noted in the chapter that research has found similar relationships around the world, specifically in Canada (Altemeyer 2003), Australia (M. Mason, Singleton, and Webber 2008), and Europe (Bagley 1970).

The priming research that illustrates increased prejudice when people are primed with religious terms is fascinating (M. K. Johnson, Rowatt, and LaBouff 2010). For a good summary of the literature illustrating the prejudice of religious people, Galen's (2012) review article is highly recommended.

Chapter 18—The Sigh of the Oppressed Creature: Religion and Money
Alas, no double entendre with this chapter title. And, frankly, I pretty much explained the title in the chapter—the "sigh of the oppressed creature" is that moment when the world has you on the edge of admitting defeat and you sigh in resignation of your fate, wishing there was a higher power that could make everything right. The point, of course, is that god and religion play a compensatory role for many people. Monty Python largely got it right in *Life of Brian,*

> *Some things in life are bad*
> *They can really make you mad*
> *Other things just make you swear and curse.*
> *When you're chewing on life's gristle*
> *Don't grumble, give a whistle*
> *And this'll help things turn out for the best. . .*
> *And. . . always look on the bright side of life. . .*
> *Always look on the light side of life. . .*

Since the entire movie is a mockery of Christianity, Eric Idle wasn't about to include "turn to god for comfort when life sucks," but the idea is basically the same—find a way to cope with life being a piece of shit.

Randy White, like so many public figures, didn't explain exactly why he was resigning, but claimed it was for health reasons (S. Day 2009). Jeff Fenholt's Wikipedia page is pretty comprehensive (Wikipedia contributors 2012b). Paula White's book (2006) is remarkably bad; bad, as in, I worry for humanity that someone gave the book five stars on Amazon.com.

I have written at length elsewhere about tax policy and religion (R. T. Cragun, Yeager, and Vega 2012), for those interested in what taxes religions don't have to pay. The short answer is pretty much all of them, with the exception of employment taxes for their employees and unrelated business income taxes, which are quite paltry.

The relationship between income and poorer quality of life is very well established. Poorer people have worse physical (J. M. Park, Fertig, and Allison 2011; Galea et al. 2011; Louie and Ward 2011) and mental health (J. M. Park et al. 2011; Najman et al. 2010), have more dangerous and stressful jobs (Orrenius and Zavodny 2009; Borooah, Dineen, and Lynch 2011), are more likely to divorce (T. C. Martin and Bumpass 1989; Amato and S. J. Rogers 1997), die at younger ages on average (Galea et al. 2011; Crimmins, J. K. Kim, and Seeman 2009; Muennig et al. 2005), and have children who are at a greater risk of dying young than do wealthier people (Olson et al. 2010).

The quote is from Karl Marx, of course (Marx 1977). Bonus trivia: my son, Toren, is named after Karl Marx. His full name is Toren *Marx* Cragun.

The rich used to be more religious than the poor in America, probably because religion was associated with being a good American (Dillingham 1965; Mueller and W. T. Johnson 1975; Roof and McKinney 1987). Today, however, there is an inverse relationship between wealth and religiosity—poorer people are more religious (Kosmin and Keysar 2006; Keister 2008).

The nonreligious do tend to be more independent, politically, than do the religious, as is shown in the chapter on politics in this book. Evidence for the libertarianism of atheists can also be seen in other research (B. E. Hunsberger and Altemeyer 2006).

Religiously fundamentalist parents actively discourage their children from pursuing higher education (Darnell and Sherkat 1997). Wives in homes led by religiously fundamentalist men are less likely to work outside the home, which reduces the earnings of such households (N. H. W. Civettini and Glass 2008).

In at least one study, sleep was found to have a greater positive impact on health than being religious (D. L. Cragun, R. T. Cragun, and Nathan 2012).

Chapter 19—We're Not Here to Serve the Earth. . .: Religion and Environmentalism

Not my best chapter title, but I do like it. I obviously stole this from Rick Santorum's quote, which suggests the earth is here for us to exploit. I opted for accuracy in representing the relationship between environmentalism and religion over wit.

The quotes from the religious fundamentalists that open this chapter aren't hard to find. Jerry Falwell's was reprinted on *Christianity Today*'s Web site (Banks 2007). E. Calvin Beisner, who founded the Cornwall Alliance for the Stewardship of Creation, wrote an entire article ridiculing environmentalism in the Baptist Press (Beisner 2011). Rick Santorum's quote made the big time by appearing on CBS News's Web site (Caldwell 2012). I found the quote from Pat Robertson on an environmentalist Web site (RCG 2011).

I'm not the first scholar to note the dominion element of Christianity and its relationship to religion; this idea was first floated in the 1960s (L. White 1967). Previous scholars have also found the same relationship between religiosity and attitudes toward the environment I illustrate in this chapter—fundamentalists are the least concerned; liberals and the nonreligious are the most concerned (Greeley 1993). Several sources support the idea that religious fundamentalists aren't particularly concerned about the environment because they don't think it will matter when Jesus returns (Goldberg 2007; Mooney 2006).

I was somewhat surprised to see the rise of evangelical environmentalists, and somewhat disheartened to see the rather quick demise of the movement (Redden 2011).

Chapter 20—I'd Like to Buy the World a Joint: Religion and Politics
The title here is a play on the somewhat famous song, "I'd Like to Buy the World a Coke" (aka "I'd Like to Teach the World to Sing (in Perfect Harmony)") (Wikipedia contributors 2012a). Buying everyone a joint would be better for the world than buying them a Coke—just imagine the happiness (and mellowness) that would result. However, my real point here is to illustrate that there are some prominent differences in political views by religiosity—the nonreligious are much more progressive than are religious fundamentalists and the highly religious.

I'm so in favor of legalizing marijuana that I wrote and published a persuasive essay on the topic (R. T. Cragun 2011). I discuss the pros and cons of marijuana when it comes to health and criminal behavior at length in this essay and provide numerous citations.

Some scholars have suggested that the rise of the nonreligious in the 1990s had to do with the alliance of the Republican Party with conservative Christians (Hout and Fischer 2002).

That the nonreligious are more open to new experiences and accepting of ambiguity while fundamentalists are the opposite is based on a variety of studies (Beit-Hallahmi 2006; Galen and Kloet 2011). For a lengthy summary of these differences and a list of the relevant studies, see my book chapter in the forthcoming *Handbook of Psychology* edited by David Wulff (R. T. Cragun et al. forthcoming).

Chapter 21—Where Would Jesus Volunteer?: Religion and Charitable Acts

While an obvious play on the "What Would Jesus Do?" phrase that became quite popular among Christians in the recent past, this title is really all about trying to guilt the religious into thinking about the service they do and where they spend most of their time. I do applaud the religious for all the service work they do, but think their time would be better spent working outside the confines of their own congregations.

The story at the beginning of this chapter really did happen. I changed the names to protect the identities of those involved.

Previous studies have reported similar results on amount of volunteering and where it is done (Uslaner 2002; Galen 2012); some prior studies have reported substantially higher rates of volunteering among the religious, though they don't always pull out volunteering in one's own congregation when doing so (Lam 2002; J. Z. Park and C. Smith 2000).

Chapter 22—I Kill. You Kill. We All Kill.: Religion and Violence

This title is another play on a song title, "I Scream, You Scream, We All Scream for Ice Cream." The point is pretty obvious—neither the religious nor the nonreligious can claim the moral high road when it comes to violence. People have died in the name of religion and people have died in the name of atheistic ideologies. Both groups need to carefully consider what they would like their legacy to be moving forward.

I drew upon several news stories in order to arrive at what I believe is a fairly accurate representation of Aqsa Parvez's story (CBC News 2010; *Globe and Mail* 2010; ctvtoronto.ca 2010). The quote from Aqsa's mother about Muhammad killing Aqsa regardless of where they were living is from these same stories.

That the hijab is not technically a requirement of Islam is illustrated by the cultural variations in covering found in the Muslim world. In some predominantly Muslim countries, women are not required to cover at all, while in others they must be covered from head to toe. This suggests the passage in the Quran motivating many Muslims to cover is subject to cultural interpretation.

Muslim leaders in Canada tried very hard to disassociate the death of Aqsa from Islam (Canadian Press 2007). Muslim leaders have also tried to blame culture in other instances, like the Saudi Arabian rape victim who was punished according to the Saudi government in accordance with Islam (Associated Press 2007; Islam-Today.net 2007).

I described the authoritarian mind-set in an earlier chapter as well, but should note that authoritarianism has been found in people around the world (Duck and B. Hunsberger 1999; Henry et al. 2005).

For a reasonable treatment of the body counts of the opposing ideologies, there is a nice skeptical podcast by Brian Dunning (2007) that references some of the people who have tried to tally deaths on this issue. He and I basically agree on this issue—body counts are pretty silly.

Chapter 23—The Happiness Delusion: Religion and Mental Well-Being

Back to the double entendres. I am riffing here on Richard Dawkins's book *The God Delusion*, but I'm also hinting at my explanation for why some people may have found that the religious might be slightly happier—they are less in touch with reality. Thus, their happiness is a result of their delusions.

There are many studies that examine the causes of depression, finding they are a combination of biology, psychology, and sociology (Kendler et al. 2006; Caspi et al. 2003). Looking at the other side of the spectrum, there is a lot of research examining the factors that influence happiness (Dolan, Peasgood, and M. White 2008; Steel, Schmidt, and Shultz 2008). As noted in the chapter, there is some debate as to the malleability of personality (Ashton and K. Lee 2008; Pogue-Geile and Rose 1985).

There are a number of studies that have suggested religiosity increases happiness (C. A. Lewis and Cruise 2006; Larrimore 2010). However, recent research on this by Diener et al. (2011) notes the connection between religion and happiness is mediated by societal development—in highly developed countries, there is no benefit from religion to happiness. This is supported by other research as well (Snoep 2008).

The research on depressive realism is controversial (Carson, Hollon, and Shelton 2010; Alloy and Abramson 1979; Dobson and Franche 1989), but I do think it may help explain the relationship between religion and happiness that has been found in the past and continues to be observed in less-developed countries.

Chapter 24—Sleep in on Sunday: Religion and Health

The title to this chapter is a suggestion based on recent research—getting enough sleep is better for your physical health than is being highly religious (D. L. Cragun et al. 2012).

I have changed the name of the person in this story to protect her identity.

The health benefits associated with the healthy lifestyles of Mormons and Seventh-day Adventists are fairly well documented (Enstrom and Breslow 2008; J. L. Lyon and Nelson 1979; Merrill and Thygerson 2001; Melby et al. 1989; Snowdon and R. L. Phillips 1985), though it is worth reiterating that these benefits derive from the lifestyles of the members, not from simply being members of the religion. There are lots of studies that claim small benefits to health associated with religion

(Benjamins and Buck 2008; Ferraro and Koch 1994; Hummer et al. 1999; Koenig, McCullough, and D. B. Larson 2001), though see Richard Sloan's book *Blind Faith* (2006) for a critique of many of these studies.

Bruce and Jeff in my hypothetical example are two colleagues and friends, Bruce Friesen and Jeff Skowronek. This is my inadequate effort to acknowledge all that the two of you have done for me since I've known you! And, no, they are not identical in every way, nor is one religious and the other not.

Things that are beneficial for your health that do not require religion include: exercise (Sudeck and Höner 2011; Archer et al. 2011; Gavin III, K. M. Fox, and Grandy 2011; Asikainen, Kukkonen-Harjula, and Miilunpalo 2004; Saltin et al. 2000), eating right (Santesso et al. 2012; Garza-Gisholt, Rivas-Ruiz, and Clark 2012; An and Simopoulos 2005), having friends (Preyde and Brassard 2011; Beck 2007; Egan et al. 2008; Briscoe and Aboud 2012; O. J. Mason and Holt 2012), not smoking (Kaczynski, Mannell, and Manske 2008; Max 2001), having a higher income (J. M. Park et al. 2011; Galea et al. 2011; Louie and Ward 2011), having health insurance (Buchmueller et al. 2005; Hadley 2003), living in a developed country (Bambra et al. 2010; Buxton, Hanney, and Jones 2004; Allegranzi et al. 2011), being married (Maselko et al. 2009; Jasilionis et al. 2012; Bourne 2009; Huijts and Kraaykamp 2011; Grundy and Tomassini 2010; Hosseinpoor et al. 2012), not being obese (Karnik and Kanekar 2012; Pelone et al. 2012; Kemp et al. 2012; Zamboni et al. 2005), and getting enough sleep (Geiger, Sabanayagam, and Shankar 2012; Luyster et al. 2012).

To give just one example of major studies not finding religion worthy of mention, the Behavioral Risk Factor Surveillance System (BRFSS) is a survey that has been used to gather data on hundreds of thousands of people in the United States. Most of the analyses of the data either fail to mention religion as an important variable or find it has little to no effect on health (D. W. Brown et al. 2003; Ahluwalia et al. 2003).

Chapter 25—Who's Better at Dying?: Religion and Coping

While not a double entendre, I am having a little fun with this chapter title. Since most people want to avoid death, arguing over who is better at dying is kind of odd. But, as it turns out, there are differences in how people think about and deal with death. Despite religions spending such a remarkable amount of time discussing death, religious people seem to have a harder time coping with it than do nonreligious people. Go figure. . .

The idea that we incorporate those close to us into our own self-identity was developed by Charles Horton Cooley (1983). He called this the "looking-glass self."

Phil Zuckerman found that nonreligious people in Europe were less afraid of death than were religious people (Zuckerman 2010), and other research has found that atheists want a "good death" (Smith-Stoner 2007). Recent research suggests nonreligious people are less likely to use life-extending medical treatment than are religious people (Phelps et al. 2009), suggesting less fear of the afterlife.

One of the more prominent theories in the sociology of religion—which I don't find compelling at all—starts with the assumption that the fear of death leads to a constant demand for religion (Stark and Finke 2000). The fact that there are hundreds of millions of nonreligious people flies in the face of this assumption, but reality has never seemed to be an important component in the thought processes of Rodney Stark. However, fear of death may in fact increase interest in religion (Chen 2010), but not uniformly, as nonreligious individuals do not appear to turn to religion for comfort when it comes to death, just religious individuals (Norenzayan and Hansen 2006).

There is a substantial body of research on the role of religion in coping (Pargament 2001). However, that line of research has started to realize that religion can hamper coping or even result in negative coping outcomes (Bjorck and Thurman 2007; N. Fox 2012).

Chapter 26—The End is Near-ish: Declining Religiosity

This is more of a play on words than a double entendre, but I thought it was fun. Devotees of monotheistic religions are fond of suggesting that the "end" of life as we know it is "near," based on scriptural suggestions that the world will at some point end (e.g., 1 Peter 4:7). Well, I think the end of something is kind of near—the end of widespread religiosity in developed countries. Now, I'm not going to go so far as to suggest that religion will completely disappear as people become more educated, but the "writing is on the wall" (to steal another religious metaphor; Daniel 5) for religion: it is declining quite rapidly.

In the story at the beginning of this chapter I mentioned that I had visited a Native American reservation and then noted that I volunteered at the Cherokee Nation. Just to be clear, the Cherokee Nation is not a reservation; it is organized and structured differently.

There is a growing body of research on blue laws and how they have changed over time (Laband and Heinbuch 1987). The decline of blue laws in the United States is just one more manifestation of the declining influence and authority of religion in everyday life (M. Chaves 1994).

There are lots of stories about people leaving religions (Zuckerman 2011), like Damon Fowler (Christina 2011). I didn't draw on those because I wanted to show how pervasive the decline of religion actually is, and the subtlety of that decline.

There is a lot of research that provides evidence for the occurrence of secularization in the United States and around the world (Abrams, Yaple, and Wiener 2010; Achterberg et al. 2009; Argue, D. R. Johnson, and L. K. White 1999; Bogomilova 2004; Bruce 2001, 2002; M. Chaves 1993; Mark Chaves 1989; Crockett and Voas 2006; De Graaf and Te Grotenhuis 2008; Dobbelaere 1987, 2002; A. Gill and Lundsgaarde 2004; R. Gill, C. K. Hadaway, and P. L. Marler 1998; C. Kirk Hadaway, Penny Long Marler, and Mark Chaves 1998; Halman and Draulans 2006; J. P. Hoffmann 1998; Lesthaeghe and Neels 2002; McAllister 1988; Norris and Inglehart 2011; Paul 2005; Rees 2010; Sasaki and Suzuki 1987; Voas 2007). The suggestion that secularization occurs at three levels comes from Karel Dobbelaere (2002). The connection between modernization and secularization is widespread in theories of secularization (Bruce 2002).

It's not uncommon for some social scientists who study religion to suggest that young people will return to religion (Hoge 1981; C. Kirk Hadaway and Roof 1979). There is some research on the influence of age, period, and cohort on religiosity (Schwadel 2010; R. T. Cragun 2007). Studies that have tried to examine American overreporting of church attendance have found that Americans, not surprisingly, overreport church attendance (C. Kirk Hadaway et al. 1998). One study estimated close to 600,000 people are becoming nonreligious in the United States every year (Kosmin et al. 2009).

The finding that Europeans rate religion lower in a hierarchy of values than pretty much everything else comes from the Eurobarometer survey from autumn 2010 (see page 32).

I should note that the Christmas tree came from Pagan religions in Germany and represented the idea that life would return after winter. Christianity syncretized this idea from Pagan religions. So, while it is viewed as a Christian symbol today, it wasn't originally.

Chapter 27—Taking Off the Training Wheels: Alternatives to Religion

For those who have never ridden a bicycle, the idea of taking off the training wheels indicates that you are ready to ride a bike like an adult—it suggests maturity. While there is greater risk associated with taking the training wheels off—you can now fall over—it also provides greater freedom and maneuverability. Religion functions like training wheels—it keeps you from falling, but also restricts your ability to do what you want. This is, in a sense, a pejorative descriptor of religion—that it is for immature individuals. I don't necessarily agree with that 100 percent. I think people can be religious and mature in their thinking about religious ideas. However, in order to be so, I think you have to have considered all your alternatives, including nonreligion and atheism.

The idea that blacks were less worthy in the preexistence was taught as Mormon doctrine for quite a while, but it is now disavowed by the religion (R. T. Cragun and R. Phillips 2012). The idea that young people born in the 1970s and 1980s were particularly valiant was taught by some leaders of the religion at that time (Haight 2003; E. T. Benson 1979).

The elements of secular humanism I include in this chapter come from Paul Kurtz's "Neo-Humanist Statement of Secular Principles and Values," which is available at http://paulkurtz.net/. If you're looking for a community of nonbelievers, try the American Atheists' Web site, which lists freethought groups around the United States: http://atheists.org/group-database.

There is limited research on how long the transition takes from religious to nonreligious (Zuckerman 2011; Pasquale 2010); for some it is quite fast but for others it takes years.

Some individuals who found religion useful to control the masses were Abraham Lincoln and Benjamin Franklin, despite being nonreligious themselves (Jacoby 2005; Cady 2010).

See the 2007 U.S. Department of Education report "The Condition of Education 2007" (http://nces.ed.gov/fastfacts/display.asp?id=69) for the reference that 22 percent of Americans score below basic in their quantitative literacy.

Chapter 28—The Final Judgment: Who Will Inherit the Earth?

The title for this chapter was pretty obvious to me. Like I noted in Chapter 26, many monotheistic religions believe there will be an endpoint for god's creation. Many also believe there will be a final judgment. This chapter is my version of that for this book—it's the conclusion of the book. However, I also literally "judge" the different ways of being religious/nonreligious as well by assigning them grades and tallying their overall GPA.

The current research on children's outcomes related to their parents does suggest two parents are better than one (McLanahan and Sandefur 1994; Pong, Dronkers, and Hampden-Thompson 2003), but the sex of those parents doesn't matter (Wainright, Russell, and Patterson 2004; Perrin 2002).

The idea that you shouldn't judge people is really rather misleading. The general assertion that you should not judge anyone is wrongheaded. Yes, prejudging entire groups of people, which is commonly called "stereotyping," is not a good thing as it taints the way you think about people whom you've never met. However, the ability to judge people is actually quite important (Taft 1955). It allows us to determine who we can or should trust and the risks associated with different people. We judge people all the time. The concern is that we never change our assessments of people based on further information we gain about them. That, too, is problematic. But judging people is something we do all the time, and it is in our best interest to do so.

For data on atheists, see the forthcoming *Handbook of Atheism* by Oxford University Press.

Appendix: Methodological Notes

My classification of denominations is based on Tom Smith's system (T. W. Smith 1987). His system was developed primarily to classify Protestants, but the groups I use include Protestants, Catholics, Jews, and the nonreligious. Other religious groups, like Muslims, Buddhists, and Hindus, are excluded from my analysis of religion in the United States due to small sample sizes for those groups.

There are a variety of alternative schemas for classifying religions (Roof and McKinney 1987; Kosmin and Keysar 2006). The most popular at the moment is Steensland et al.'s measure (Steensland et al. 2000). There is a growing understanding of the diversity of views within religious denominations (Harrison and Lazerwitz 1982).

BIBLIOGRAPHY

Abrams, Daniel M, Haley A Yaple, and Richard J Wiener. 2010. "A mathematical model of social group competition with application to the growth of religious non-affiliation." *1012.1375*. Retrieved March 26, 2011 (http://arxiv.org/abs/1012.1375).

Achterberg, Peter et al. 2009. "A Christian Cancellation of the Secularist Truce? Waning Christian Religiosity and Waxing Religious Deprivatization in the West." *Journal for the Scientific Study of Religion* 48(4):687–701.

Acock, Alan C., and Vern L. Bengtson. 1978. "On the Relative Influence of Mothers and Fathers: A Covariance Analysis of Political and Religious Socialization." *Journal of Marriage and the Family* 40(3):519–530.

Adams, Brooke. 2009. "Smart Kidnapping: Wanda Barzee's Return, A Mother's Forgiveness." *sltrib.com*. Retrieved July 22, 2012 (http://www.sltrib.com/news/ci_13890174).

Adams, Jimi. 2007. "Stained Glass Makes the Ceiling Visible Organizational Opposition to Women in Congregational Leadership." *Gender & Society* 21(1):80–105.

Adsera, Alicia. 2006. "Marital Fertility and Religion in Spain, 1985 and 1999." *Population Studies* 60(2):205–221.

Agence France-Presse. 2009. "Vatican defends excommunication for 'raped' nine-year-old girl's abortion." *theage.com.au*. Retrieved August 5, 2012 (http://www.theage.com.au/world/vatican-defends-excommunication-for-raped-nineyearold-girls-abortion-20090308-8s49.html).

Ahluwalia, Indu B., Deborah Holtzman, Karin A. Mack, and Ali Mokdad. 2003. "Health-Related Quality of Life among Women of Reproductive Age: Behavioral Risk Factor Surveillance System (BRFSS), 1998–2001." *Journal of Women's Health (15409996)* 12(1):5.

Aho, James Alfred. 1990. *The Politics of Righteousness: Idaho Christian Patriotism*. 1st ed. University of Washington Press.

Allegranzi, Bendetta et al. 2011. "Burden of endemic health-care-associated infection in developing countries: systematic review and meta-analysis." *Lancet* 377(9761):228–241.

Allen, Bob. 2011. "Debate over Adam and Eve continues." *Associated Baptist Press*. Retrieved March 25, 2012 (http://www.abpnews.com/content/view/6694/53/).

Alloy, Lauren B., and Lyn Y. Abramson. 1979. "Judgment of contingency in depressed and nondepressed students: Sadder but wiser?" *Journal of Experimental Psychology: General* 108(4):441–485.

Allport, Gordon W. 1966. "The Religious Context of Prejudice." *Journal for the Scientific Study of Religion* 5(3):447–457.

Altemeyer, Bob. 2003. "Why Do Religious Fundamentalists Tend to be Prejudiced?" *International Journal for the Psychology of Religion* 13(1):17–28.

Altemeyer, Bob, and Bruce Hunsberger. 1997. *Amazing Conversions: Why Some Turn to Faith & Others Abandon Religion*. First Printing. Prometheus Books.

Amato, Paul R., and Stacy J. Rogers. 1997. "A Longitudinal Study of Marital Problems and Subsequent Divorce." *Journal of Marriage & Family* 59(3):612–624.

American Humanist Association. 2003. "Humanist Manifesto III." *American Humanist Association*. Retrieved July 22, 2012 (http://www.americanhumanist. org/Humanism/Humanist_Manifesto_III).

American Psychiatric Association. 2000. *Diagnostic and Statistical Manual of Mental Disorders DSM-IV-TR Fourth Edition*. 4th ed. American Psychiatric Publishers.

An, International Conference on Nutrition, and Artemis P. Simopoulos. 2005. *Nutrition And Fitness Mental Health, Aging, And the Implementation of a Healthy Diet And Physical Activity Lifestyle: 5th International Conference on …* 1st ed. edited by Artemis P. Simopoulos. S Karger Pub.

Archer, Trevor, Anders Fredriksson, Erica Schütz, and Richard Kostrzewa. 2011. "Influence of Physical Exercise on Neuroimmunological Functioning and Health: Aging and Stress." *Neurotoxicity Research* 20(1):69–83.

Argue, A., D. R. Johnson, and L. K. White. 1999. "Age and Religiosity: Evidence From a Three-Wave Panel Analysis." *Journal for the Scientific Study of Religion* 38(3):423–435.

Arnett, Jeffrey Jensen, and Lene Arnett Jensen. 2002. "A Congregation of One Individualized Religious Beliefs among Emerging Adults." *Journal of Adolescent Research* 17(5):451–467.

Ashton, Michael C., and Kibeom Lee. 2008. "The HEXACO Model of Personality Structure and the Importance of the H Factor." *Social and Personality Psychology Compass* 2(5):1952–1962.

Asikainen, Tuula-Maria, Katriina Kukkonen-Harjula, and Seppo Miilunpalo. 2004.

"Exercise for Health for Early Postmenopausal Women: A Systematic Review of Randomised Controlled Trials." *Sports Medicine* 34(11):753–778.

Astin, Alexander W., Helen S. Astin, and Jennifer A. Lindholm. 2010. *Cultivating the Spirit: How College Can Enhance Students' Inner Lives.* 1st ed. Jossey-Bass.

Avila, Jim. 2010. "Former Texas Pastor Matt Baker Convicted in Wife's 2006 Murder." *ABC News.* Retrieved August 12, 2011 (http://abcnews.go.com/2020/texas-pastor-matt-baker-convicted-wifes-2006-murder/story?id=11092046&singlePage=true).

Bagley, Christopher. 1970. "Relation of Religion and Racial Prejudice in Europe." *Journal for the Scientific Study of Religion* 9(3):219–225.

Baker-Sperry, Lori. 2001. "Passing on the Faith: The Father's Role in Religious Transmission." *Sociological Focus* 34(2):185–198.

Bambra, C. et al. 2010. "Tackling the wider social determinants of health and health inequalities: evidence from systematic reviews." *Journal of Epidemiology & Community Health* 64(4):3.

Bandura, Albert. 1976. *Social Learning Theory.* 1st ed. Prentice Hall.

Banerjee, Neela. 2006. "Clergywomen Find Hard Path to Bigger Pulpit." *The New York Times,* August 26. Retrieved August 26, 2012 (http://www.nytimes.com/2006/08/26/us/26clergy.html).

Banks, Adelle M. 2007. "Dobson, Others Seek Ouster of NAE Vice President: Interim president Leith Anderson says he supports Richard Cizik's work on creation care." *Christianity Today.* Retrieved September 2, 2012 (http://www.christianitytoday.com/ct/2007/marchweb-only/109-53.0.html).

Bartkowski, John P., and Lynn M. Hempel. 2009. "Sex and Gender Traditionalism Among Conservative Protestants: Does the Difference Make a Difference?" *Journal for the Scientific Study of Religion* 48(4):805–816.

Bar-Yam, Miriam, Lawrence Kohlberg, and A. Naame. 1980. "Moral Reasoning of Students in Different Cultural, Social, and Educational Settings." *American Journal of Education* 88(3):345–62.

Batson, C. Daniel, Patricia Schoenrade, and W. Larry Ventis. 1993. *Religion and the Individual: A Social-Psychological Perspective.* Revised. Oxford University Press, USA.

Baumrind, Diana. 1978. "Parental Disciplinary Patterns and Social Competence in Children." *Youth & Society* 9(3):239–267.

Beck, Lisa. 2007. "Social status, social support, and stress: a comparative review of the health consequences of social control factors." *Health Psychology Review* 1(2):186–207.

Beisner, E. Calvin. 2011. "FIRST-PERSON: Revisiting 'climate change denialism'"

Baptist Press. Retrieved September 2, 2012 (http://www.bpnews.net/bpnews.asp?ID=35090).

Beit-Hallahmi, Benjamin. 2006. "Atheists: A Psychological Profile." Pp. 300–318 in *The Cambridge Companion to Atheism*, edited by Michael Martin. Cambridge University Press.

Beit-Hallahmi, Benjamin. 2010. "Morality and Immorality among the Irreligious." Pp. 113–148 in *Atheism and Secularity: Volume 1—Issues, Concepts, and Definitions*, vol. 1, edited by Phil Zuckerman. Santa Barbara, CA: Praeger.

Bello, Marisol. 2009. "Late-term abortion doctor killed at church." *USATODAY. com.* Retrieved July 14, 2011 (http://www.usatoday.com/news/nation/2009-05-31-abortion-kansas_N.htm).

Benjamins, Maureen R., and Anna Campbell Buck. 2008. "Religion: A Sociocultural Predictor of Health Behaviors in Mexico." *Journal of Aging Health* 20(3):290–305.

Benson, David V. 1967. *Christianity, Communism, and Survival.* Glendale, Calif.: G/L Regal Books.

Benson, Ezra Taft. 1979. "In His Steps." *BYU Speeches*, March 4.

Berger, Peter L. 1990. *The Sacred Canopy: Elements of a Sociological Theory of Religion.* Anchor.

Berger, Peter L., and Thomas Luckmann. 1967. *The Social Construction of Reality: A Treatise in the Sociology of Knowledge.* Anchor.

Billy, John O. G., Nancy S. Landale, William R. Grady, and Denise M. Zimmerle. 1988. "Effects of Sexual Activity on Adolescent Social and Psychological Development." *Social Psychology Quarterly* 51(3):190–212.

Bjorck, Jeffrey P., and John W. Thurman. 2007. "Negative Life Events, Patterns of Positive and Negative Religious Coping, and Psychological Functioning." *Journal for the Scientific Study of Religion* 46(2):159–167.

Bloom, Harold. 1993. *The American Religion: The Emergence of The Post-Christian Nation.* Simon & Schuster.

Blyth, Eric, and Ruth Landau. 2009. *Faith and Fertility: Attitudes towards Reproductive Practices in Different Religions from Ancient to Modern Times.* Jessica Kingsley Publishers.

Bogomilova, Nonka. 2004. "Reflections on the Contemporary Religious 'Revival': Religion, Secularization, Globalization." *Religion in Eastern Europe* 24(4):1–10.

Bolzendahl, Catherine, and Clem Brooks. 2005. "Polarization, Secularization, or Differences as Usual? The Denominational Cleavage in U.S. Social Attitudes Since the 1970s." *Sociological Quarterly* 46(1):47–78.

Bond, Rod, and Peter B. Smith. 1996. "Culture and conformity: A meta-analysis of studies using Asch's (1952b, 1956) line judgment task." *Psychological Bulletin* 119(1):111–137.

Booth, A, D R Johnson, L K White, and J N Edwards. 1986. "Divorce and marital instability over the life course." *Journal of family issues* 7(4):421–442.

Borooah, Vani K., Donal A. Dineen, and Nicola Lynch. 2011. "Health, employment and the Quality of Life in Ireland." *Irish Journal of Sociology* 19(2):144–169.

Bouchard, T J, Jr, D T Lykken, M McGue, N L Segal, and A Tellegen. 1990. "Sources of human psychological differences: the Minnesota Study of Twins Reared Apart." *Science (New York, N.Y.)* 250(4978):223–228.

Bourdais, Céline Le, and Évelyne Lapierre-Adamcyk. 2004. "Changes in Conjugal Life in Canada: Is Cohabitation Progressively Replacing Marriage?" *Journal of Marriage and Family* 66(4):929–942.

Bourne, Paul Andrew. 2009. "Self-rated health and health conditions of married and unmarried men in Jamaica." *North American Journal of Medical Sciences* 1(7):345–352.

Bowlby, John. 1953. *Child Care and the Growth of Love*. London, England: Penguin.

Briscoe, Ciara, and Frances Aboud. 2012. "Behaviour change communication targeting four health behaviours in developing countries: A review of change techniques." *Social Science & Medicine* 75(4):612–621.

Brown, David W. et al. 2003. "Associations between recommended levels of physical activity and health-related quality of life Findings from the 2001 Behavioral Risk Factor Surveillance System (BRFSS) survey." *Preventive Medicine* 37(5):520.

Brown, Jonathon D., and Margaret A. Marshall. 2001. "Self-Esteem and Emotion: Some Thoughts about Feelings." *Personality and Social Psychology Bulletin* 27(5):575–584.

Bruce, Steve. 2001. "Christianity in Britain, R.I.P." *Sociology of Religion* 62(2):191–203.

Bruce, Steve. 2002. *God Is Dead: Secularization in the West*. London: Blackwell Publishers.

Buchmueller, Thomas C., Kevin Grumbach, Richard Kronick, and James G. Kahn. 2005. "The Effect of Health Insurance on Medical Care Utilization and Implications for Insurance Expansion: A Review of the Literature." *Medical Care Research & Review* 62(1):3–30.

Bullivant, Stephen. 2008. "Research Note: Sociology and the Study of Atheism." *Journal of Contemporary Religion* 23(3):363.

Buxton, Martin, Steve Hanney, and Teri Jones. 2004. "Estimating the economic value to societies of the impact of health research: a critical review." *Bulletin of the World Health Organization* 82(10):733–739.

Cady, Daniel. 2010. "Freethinkers and Hell Raisers: The Brief History of American Atheism and Secularism." Pp. 229–250 in *Atheism and Secularity: Volume 1 - Issues, Concepts, and Definitions*, vol. 1, edited by Phil Zuckerman. Santa Barbara, CA: Praeger.

Caldwell, Leigh Ann. 2012. "Santorum: Obama's worldview upside-down." *CBS News*. Retrieved September 2, 2012 (http://www.cbsnews.com/8301-3460_162-57381029/santorum-obamas-worldview-upside-down/).

Capps, Donald. 1992. "Religion and Child Abuse: Perfect Together." *Journal for the Scientific Study of Religion* 31(1):1–14.

Carpenter, Thomas P., and Margaret A. Marshall. 2009. "An Examination of Religious Priming and Intrinsic Religious Motivation in the Moral Hypocrisy Paradigm." *Journal for the Scientific Study of Religion* 48(2):386–393.

Carson, Richard C., Steven D. Hollon, and Richard C. Shelton. 2010. "Depressive realism and clinical depression." *Behaviour Research and Therapy* 48(4):257–265.

Caspi, Avshalom et al. 2003. "Influence of life stress on depression: moderation by a polymorphism in the 5-HTT gene." *Science (New York, N.Y.)* 301(5631):386–389.

CBC News. 2010. "Father, son plead guilty to Aqsa Parvez murder." *CBC News*. Retrieved September 2, 2012 (http://www.cbc.ca/news/canada/toronto/story/2010/06/15/parvez-guilty-plea.html).

CBC News. 2009. "Hutterites need driver's licence photos: top court." *cbc.ca*. Retrieved August 5, 2012 (http://www.cbc.ca/news/canada/story/2009/07/24/hutterite-supreme-court024.html).

CBS News. 2003. "Minister Charged In Exorcism Death." *cbsnews.com*. Retrieved September 18, 2011 (http://www.cbsnews.com/stories/2003/08/25/national/main569963.shtml).

Chapman, Audrey R. 1999. *Unprecedented Choices: Religious Ethics at the Frontiers of Genetic Science*. Fortress Press.

Chaves, M. 1993. "Intraorganizational Power and Internal Secularization in Protestant Denominations." *American Journal of Sociology* 99(1):1–48.

Chaves, M. 1994. "Secularization as Declining Religious Authority." *Social Forces* 72(3):749–774.

Chaves, Mark. 1999. *Ordaining Women: Culture and Conflict in Religious Organizations*. Harvard University Press.

Chaves, Mark. 1989. "Secularization and Religious Revival: Evidence From U.S. Church Attendance Rates, 1972-1986." *Journal for the Scientific Study of Religion* 28:464–477.

Chen, Daniel L. 2010. "Club Goods and Group Identity: Evidence from Islamic Resurgence during the Indonesian Financial Crisis." *Journal of Political Economy* 118(2):300–354.

Chesler, Ellen. 2007. *Woman of Valor: Margaret Sanger and the Birth Control Movement in America*. Simon and Schuster.

Christina, Greta. 2011. "High School Student Stands Up Against Prayer at Public School and Is Ostracized, Demeaned and Threatened." *AlterNet*, May 25. Retrieved September 11, 2012 (http://www.alternet.org/story/151086/high_school_student_stands_up_against_prayer_at_public_school_and_is_ostracized%2C_demeaned_and_threatened).

Civettini, Nicole H. W., and Jennifer Glass. 2008. "The Impact of Religious Conservativism on Men's Work and Family Involvement." *Gender & Society* 22(2):172–193.

Clifton P. Flynn. 1994. "Regional Differences in Attitudes toward Corporal Punishment." *Journal of Marriage and Family* 56(2):314–324.

Cliteur, Paul. 2009. "The Definition of Atheism." *Journal of Religion and Society* 11. Retrieved (http://moses.creighton.edu/jrs/2009/2009-4.pdf).

Cliteur, Paul. 2010. *The Secular Outlook: In Defense of Moral and Political Secularism*. 1st ed. Wiley-Blackwell.

Compton, Todd M. 1996. "Fanny Alger Smith Custer, Mormonism's First Plural Wife?" *Journal of Mormon History* 22(1):174–207.

Compton, Todd M. 1997. *In Sacred Loneliness: The Plural Wives of Joseph Smith*. Signature Books.

Cooley, Charles Horton. 1983. *Human Nature and the Social Order*. Transaction Publishers.

Courtois, Stephane, Nicolas Werth, Jean-Louis Panne, Andrzej Paczkowski, and Karel Bartosek. 1999. *The Black Book of Communism: Crimes, Terror, Repression*. Harvard University Press.

Cragun, Deborah L., Ryan T. Cragun, and Brian Nathan. 2012. "Effects of Secularity on Physical, Mental, and Social Health." in *Annual Meeting & Scientific Sessions of the Society of Behavioral Medicine*. New Orleans, LA.

Cragun, Ryan T. 2007. "A Role Conflict Theory of Religious Change: An Explanation and Test." Dissertation, Cincinnati, OH: University of Cincinnati.

Cragun, Ryan T. 2011. "Why Marijuana Should Be Legalized." in *Issues: Understanding Controversy and Society*. ABC-CLIO.

Cragun, Ryan T., and Nicholas Autz. 2011. "Religious Social Distance: How Far Apart Are Teenagers and Their Parents?" in *Annual Meeting of the Association for the Sociology of Religion*. Las Vegas, NV.

Cragun, Ryan T., Joseph H. Hammer, and Karen Hwang. forthcoming. "Psychology of the Nonreligious." in *Handbook of the Psychology of Religion*, edited by David Wulff.

Cragun, Ryan T., and Ronald Lawson. 2010. "The Secular Transition: The Worldwide Growth of Mormons, Jehovah's Witnesses, and Seventh-day Adventists." *Sociology of Religion* 71(3):349–373.

Cragun, Ryan T., Steve Panageotou, and Brittany Harder. 2009. "Conforming Our Way to Heaven." in *Annual Meeting of the Society for the Scientific Study of Religion*. Denver, CO.

Cragun, Ryan T., and Rick Phillips. 2012. *Could I Vote for a Mormon for President? An Election-Year Guide to Mitt Romney's Religion*. Washington, DC: Strange Violin Editions.

Cragun, Ryan T., Joseph Ranalli, and Stephanie Yeager. 2011. "We Have 'None' In Common." in *Annual Meeting of the Society for the Scientific Study of Religion*. Milwaukee, WI.

Cragun, Ryan T., Stephanie Yeager, and Desmond Vega. 2012. "Research Report: How Secular Humanists (and Everyone Else) Subsidize Religion in the United States." *Free Inquiry*, 39–46.

Crimmins, Eileen M., Jung K. Kim, and Teresa E. Seeman. 2009. "Poverty and Biological Risk: The Earlier 'Aging' of the Poor." *Journals of Gerontology Series A: Biological Sciences & Medical Sciences* 64A(2):286–292.

Crockett, Alasdair, and David Voas. 2006. "Generations of Decline: Religious Change In Twentieth-Century Britain." *Journal for the Scientific Study of Religion*.

ctvtoronto.ca. 2010. "Father, son sentenced in murder of teen daughter." *CTVNews*. Retrieved September 2, 2012 (http://toronto.ctvnews.ca/father-son-sentenced-in-murder-of-teen-daughter-1.523211).

Cuneo, Michael W. 2002. *American Exorcism: Expelling Demons in the Land of Plenty*. Broadway.

Dahl, Larry E. 1992. "Degrees of Glory" edited by Daniel H. Ludlow. *Encyclopedia of Mormonism* 367–369.

Daniel Carson Johnson. 1997. "Formal Education vs. Religious Belief: Soliciting New Evidence with Multinomial Logit Modeling." *Journal for the Scientific Study of Religion* 36(2):231–246.

Danso, Henry, Bruce Hunsberger, and Michael Pratt. 1997. "The Role of Parental Religious Fundamentalism and Right-Wing Authoritarianism in Child-Rearing Goals and Practices." *Journal for the Scientific Study of Religion* 36(4):496–511.

Darnell, Alfred, and Darren E. Sherkat. 1997. "The Impact of Protestant

Fundamentalism on Educational Attainment." *American Sociological Review* 62(2):306–315.

Dawkins, Richard. 2008. *The God Delusion*. Mariner Books.

Day, Randal D., Gary W. Peterson, and Coleen McCracken. 1998. "Predicting Spanking of Younger and Older Children by Mothers and Fathers." *Journal of Marriage and Family* 60(1):79–94.

Day, Sherri. 2009. "Without Walls Pastor Randy White steps down as ex-wife Paula White steps in." *Tampa Bay Times*. Retrieved September 2, 2012 (http://www. tampabay.com/news/religion/without-walls-pastor-randy-white-steps-down-as-ex-wife-paula-white-steps-in/1017585).

Diener, Ed, Louis Tay, and David G. Myers. 2011. "The Religion Paradox: If Religion Makes People Happy, Why Are So Many Dropping Out?" *Journal of Personality & Social Psychology* 101(6):1278–1290.

Dillingham, Harry C. 1965. "Protestant Religion and Social Status." *American Journal of Sociology* 70(4):JAN.

Dobbelaere, Karel. 2002. *Secularization: An Analysis at Three Levels (Gods, Humans, and Religions)*. New York: Peter Lang Publishing.

Dobbelaere, Karel. 1987. "Some Trends in European Sociology of Religion: The Secularization Debate." *Sociological Analysis* 48(2):107–137.

Dobson, Keith, and Renée-Louise Franche. 1989. "A conceptual and empirical review of the depressive realism hypothesis." *Canadian Journal of Behavioural Science/Revue canadienne des sciences du comportement* 21(4):419–433.

Dolan, Paul, Tessa Peasgood, and Mathew White. 2008. "Do we really know what makes us happy A review of the economic literature on the factors associated with subjective well-being." *Journal of Economic Psychology* 29(1):94–122.

Donnison, Jon. 2010. "Palestinian blogger facing prison for Islam 'insults'." *BBC*, November 23. Retrieved November 13, 2011 (http://www.bbc.co.uk/news/world-middle-east-11820615).

D'Onofrio, B M, L J Eaves, L Murrelle, H H Maes, and B Spilka. 1999. "Understanding biological and social influences on religious affiliation, attitudes, and behaviors: a behavior genetic perspective." *Journal of personality* 67(6):953–984.

Dracos, Ted. 2003. *UnGodly: The Passions, Torments, and Murder of Atheist Madalyn Murray O'Hair*. First ed. Free Press.

Duck, Robert J., and Bruce Hunsberger. 1999. "Religious Orientation and Prejudice: The Role of Religious Proscription, Right-Wing." *International Journal for the Psychology of Religion* 9(3):157–179.

Dudley, Roger L., and Margaret G. Dudley. 1986. "Transmission of Religious Values from Parents to Adolescents." *Review of Religious Research* 28(1):3–15.

Duffy, John-Charles. 2003. "The Making of Immanuel: Brian David Mitchell and the Mormon Fringe." *Sunstone Magazine*, October 15, 34–45.

Dunford, C. Kent. 1992. "Light of Christ" edited by Daniel H. Ludlow. *Encyclopedia of Mormonism* 835.

Dunning, Brian. 2007. "Who Kills More, Religion or Atheism?" *skeptoid.com*. Retrieved September 2, 2012 (http://skeptoid.com/episodes/4076).

Durant, Will. 2011. *On The Meaning Of Life*. Literary Licensing, LLC.

Durkheim, Émile. 2008. *The Elementary Forms of Religious Life*. abridged ed. Oxford University Press, USA.

Ecklund, Elaine Howard. 2010. *Science vs. Religion: What Scientists Really Think*. Oxford University Press, USA.

Edgell, Penny, Joseph Gerteis, and Douglas Hartmann. 2006. "Atheists As 'Other': Moral Boundaries and Cultural Membership in American Society." *American Sociological Review* 71(2):211–234.

Egan, Matt, Carol Tannahill, Mark Petticrew, and Sian Thomas. 2008. "Psychosocial risk factors in home and community settings and their associations with population health and health inequalities: a systematic meta-review." *BMC Public Health* 8:239–251.

Emerson, Michael O., and David Hartman. 2006. "The Rise of Religious Fundamentalism." *Annual Review of Sociology* 32(1):127–144.

Enstrom, James E, and Lester Breslow. 2008. "Lifestyle and reduced mortality among active California Mormons, 1980-2004." *Preventive Medicine* 46(2):133–136.

Epley, Nicholas, Benjamin A Converse, Alexa Delbosc, George A Monteleone, and John T Cacioppo. 2009. "Believers' estimates of God's beliefs are more egocentric than estimates of other people's beliefs." *Proceedings of the National Academy of Sciences of the United States of America*. Retrieved December 24, 2009 (http://www.ncbi.nlm.nih.gov/pubmed/19955414).

Esau, Alvin J. 2005. *The Courts and the Colonies: The Litigation of Hutterite Church Disputes*. UBC Press.

Evans, John H. 2002. "Polarization in Abortion Attitudes in U.S. Religious Traditions, 1972–1998." *Sociological Forum* 17(3):397–422.

Feierman, Jay R. 2009. *The Biology of Religious Behavior: The Evolutionary Origins of Faith and Religion*. Praeger.

Ferraro, Kenneth F., and Jerome R. Koch. 1994. "Religion and Health Among Black and White Adults: Examining Social Support and Consolation." *Journal for the Scientific Study of Religion* 33(4):362.

Filkins, Dexter. 2009. "Afghan Girls, Scarred by Acid, Defy Terror, Embracing School." *The New York Times*, January 13. Retrieved March 11, 2012 (http://

www.nytimes.com/2009/01/14/world/asia/14kandahar.html).

Finkelhor, D. 1980. "Sex among siblings: a survey on prevalence, variety, and effects." *Archives of sexual behavior* 9(3):171–194.

Fleek, Sherman L. 2006. "The Church and the Utah War, 1857-1858." in *Nineteenth Century Saints at War*, edited by Robert C. Freeman. Provo, UT: Religious Studies Center, Brigham Young University.

Fletcher, Adam, Chris Bonell, and Annik Sorhaindo. 2011. "You are what your friends eat: systematic review of social network analyses of young people's eating behaviours and bodyweight." *Journal of Epidemiology & Community Health* 65(6):548–555.

Fobes, Catherine. 2004. "Maintaining the gender order: Using women, preferring men in an Episcopal Campus Chapel, 1927-1949." *Review of religious research* 46(1):72–87.

Fox, Nicole. 2012. "'God Must Have Been Sleeping': Faith as an Obstacle and a Resource for Rwandan Genocide Survivors in the United States." *Journal for the Scientific Study of Religion* 51(1):65–78.

Franzblau, Abraham Norman. 1972. *Religious Belief and Character Among Jewish Adolescents.* AMS Press.

Friends General Conference. 2012. "FAQs about Quakers." *fgcquaker.org*. Retrieved July 22, 2012 (http://www.fgcquaker.org/explore/faqs-about-quakers#pactifism).

Funk, Richard B., and Fern K. Willits. 1987. "College attendance and attitude change: A panel study, 1970–81." *Sociology of Education* 60(4):224–231.

Galea, Sandro, Melissa Tracy, Katherine J. Hoggatt, Charles DiMaggio, and Adam Karpati. 2011. "Estimated Deaths Attributable to Social Factors in the United States." *American Journal of Public Health* 101(8):1456–1465.

Galen, Luke W. 2012. "Does religious belief promote prosociality? A critical examination." *Psychological Bulletin* 138(5):876–906.

Galen, Luke W., and Jim Kloet. 2011. "Personality and Social Integration Factors Distinguishing Nonreligious from Religious Groups: The Importance of Controlling for Attendance and Demographics." *Archive for the Psychology of Religion / Archiv für Religionspsychologie* 33(2):205–228.

Garenne, Michel. 2004. "Age at marriage and modernisation in sub-Saharan Africa." *Southern African Journal of Demography* 9(2):59–79.

Garza-Gisholt, Ana Cecilia, Rodolfo Rivas-Ruiz, and Patricia Clark. 2012. "Maternal diet and vitamin D during pregnancy and association with bone health during childhood. Review of the literature." *Boletin Medico del Hospital Infantil de Mexico* 69(2):83–90.

Gavin III, James R., Kathleen M. Fox, and Susan Grandy. 2011. "Race/Ethnicity and gender differences in health intentions and behaviors regarding exercise and diet for adults with type 2 diabetes: A crosssectional analysis." *BMC Public Health* 11(1):533–540.

Geiger, Sarah Dee, Charumathi Sabanayagam, and Anoop Shankar. 2012. "The Relationship between Insufficient Sleep and Self-Rated Health in a Nationally Representative Sample." *Journal of Environmental and Public Health* 2012:518263.

Gershman, Bennett L., and and Joel Cohen. 2012. "When Rabbis Muzzle Sex Crime Victims, What's a Prosecutor to Do?" *Huffington Post*. Retrieved May 27, 2012 (http://www.huffingtonpost.com/bennett-l-gershman/rabbis-sex-abuse_b_1539613.html).

Gervais, Will M., and Ara Norenzayan. 2012. "Analytic Thinking Promotes Religious Disbelief." *Science* 336(6080):493–496.

Gervais, Will M, Azim F Shariff, and Ara Norenzayan. 2011. "Do you believe in atheists? Distrust is central to anti-atheist prejudice." *Journal of Personality and Social Psychology* 101(6):1189–1206.

Giles-Sims, Jean, Murray A. Straus, and David B. Sugarman. 1995. "Child, Maternal, and Family Characteristics Associated with Spanking." *Family Relations* 44(2):170–176.

Gill, Anthony, and Erik Lundsgaarde. 2004. "State Welfare Spending and Religiosity: A Cross-National Analysis." *Rationality and Society* 16(4):399–436.

Gill, R., C. K. Hadaway, and P. L. Marler. 1998. "Is Religious Belief Declining in Britain?" *Journal for the Scientific Study of Religion* 37(3):507–516.

Glass, Jennifer, Vern L. Bengtson, and Charlotte Chorn Dunham. 1986. "Attitude Similarity in Three-Generation Families: Socialization, Status Inheritance, or Reciprocal Influence?" *American Sociological Review* 51(5):685–698.

Glock, Charles Y., and Rodney Stark. 1966. *Christian Beliefs and Anti-Semitism*. 2nd Printing. Harper & Row, Publishers.

Glover, Rebecca J. 1997. "Relationships in moral reasoning and religion among members of conservative, moderate, and liberal religious groups." *The Journal of Social Psychology* 137(2):247–255.

Goldberg, Michelle. 2007. *Kingdom Coming: The Rise of Christian Nationalism*. W. W. Norton.

Goodstein, Laurie. 2012. "Catholic Church Puts Legal Pressure on Survivors' Network." *The New York Times*, March 12. Retrieved May 27, 2012 (http://www.nytimes.com/2012/03/13/us/catholic-church-pressures-victims-network-with-subpoenas.html).

Gould, Stephen Jay. 2002. *Rocks of Ages: Science and Religion in the Fullness of Life.* 1st Priting/1st Trade Paper Ed.2002. Ballantine Books.

De Graaf, Nan Dirk, and Manfred Te Grotenhuis. 2008. "Traditional Christian Belief and Belief in the Supernatural: Diverging Trends in the Netherlands Between 1979 and 2005?" *Journal for the Scientific Study of Religion* 47(4):585–598.

Greeley, Andrew. 1993. "Religion and Attitudes toward the Environment." *Journal for the Scientific Study of Religion* 32(1):19.

Greenberg, Jeff et al. 1990. "Evidence for terror management theory II: The effects of mortality salience on reactions to those who threaten or bolster the cultural worldview." *Journal of Personality and Social Psychology* 58(2):308–318.

Greven, Philip J. 1992. *Spare the Child: The Religious Roots of Punishment and the Psychological Impact of Physical Abuse.* Vintage.

Grundy, Emily M. D., and Cecilia Tomassini. 2010. "Marital history, health and mortality among older men and women in England and Wales." *BMC Public Health* 10:554–567.

Haan, N, M B Smith, and J Block. 1968. "Moral reasoning of young adults: political-social behavior, family background, and personality correlates." *Journal of personality and social psychology* 10(3):183–201.

Hadaway, C. Kirk. 1989. "Identifying American Apostates: A Cluster Analysis." *Journal for the Scientific Study of Religion* 28(2):201–215.

Hadaway, C. Kirk, Penny Long Marler, and Mark Chaves. 1998. "Overreporting Church Attendance in America: Evidence that Demands the Same Verdict." *American Sociological Review* 63(1):122–130.

Hadaway, C. Kirk, and Wade Clark Roof. 1979. "Those Who Stay Religious 'Nones' and Those Who Don't: A Research Note." *Journal for the Scientific Study of Religion* 18(2):194–200.

Hadley, Jack. 2003. "Sicker and Poorer—The Consequences of Being Uninsured: A Review of the Research on the Relationship between Health Insurance, Medical Care Use, Health, Work, and Income." *Medical Care Research & Review* 60(2):3S.

Haight, David B. 2003. "You Are Different." *New Era.*

Halman, Loek, and Veerle Draulans. 2006. "How secular is Europe?" *The British Journal of Sociology* 57(2):263–288.

Halverson, Richard R, and Michael S Pallak. 1978. "Commitment, ego-involvement, and resistance to attack." *Journal of Experimental Social Psychology* 14(1):1–12.

Hamman, Jaco. 2000. "The Rod of Discipline: Masochism, Sadism, and the Judeo-Christian Religion." *Journal of Religion and Health* 39(4):319–327.

Harrison, Michael I., and Bernard Lazerwitz. 1982. "Do Denominations Matter?" *American Journal of Sociology* 88(2):356–377.

Hauser, Marc. 2006. *Moral Minds: How Nature Designed Our Universal Sense of Right and Wrong.* 1st ed. Ecco.

Hayes, Bernadette C., and Yvonne Pittelkow. 1993. "Religious Belief, Transmission, and the Family: An Australian Study." *Journal of Marriage and the Family* 55(3):755–766.

Heaton, Tim B. 1986. "How Does Religion Influence Fertility?: The Case of Mormons." *Journal for the Scientific Study of Religion* 25(2):248–258.

Henry, P. J., Jim Sidanius, Shana Levin, and Felicia Pratto. 2005. "Social Dominance Orientation, Authoritarianism, and Support for Intergroup Violence Between the Middle East and America." *Political Psychology* 26(4):569–584.

Hill, Peter C., and Ralph W. Hood Jr, eds. 1999. *Measures of Religiosity.* 1st ed. Religious Education Pr.

Hochstetler, Andy, Heith Copes, and Matt DeLisi. 2002. "Differential association in group and solo offending." *Journal of Criminal Justice* 30(6):559.

Hoffmann, John E., and John E. Bartkowski. 2008. "Gender, Religious Tradition and Biblical Literalism." *Social Forces* 86(3):1245–1272.

Hoffmann, J. P. 1998. "Confidence in Religious Institutions and Secularization: Trends and Implications." *Review of Religious Research* 39(4):321–343.

Hoge, Dean R. 1981. *Converts, Dropouts, Returnees: A Study of Religious Change Among Catholics.* New York: Pilgrim Press.

Holden, Andrew. 2002. *Jehovah's Witnesses: Portrait of a Contemporary Religious Movement.* Routledge.

Holmes, Helen B., Betty B. Hoskins, and Michael Gross. 1980. *Birth control and controlling birth: women-centered perspectives.* Humana Press.

Hosseinpoor, Ahmad Reza et al. 2012. "Social Determinants of Self-Reported Health in Women and Men: Understanding the Role of Gender in Population Health." *PLoS ONE* 7(4):1–9.

Hout, Michael, and Claude S. Fischer. 2002. "Why More Americans Have no Religious Preference: Politics and Generations." *American Sociological Review* 67(2):165–190.

Hout, Michael, Andrew Greeley, and Melissa J. Wilde. 2001. "The Demographic Imperative in Religious Change in the United States." *American Journal of Sociology* 107(2):468–500.

Hoye, Sarah. 2012. "Philly priest gets 3 to 6 years in abuse case." *CNN.* Retrieved August 5, 2012 (http://articles.cnn.com/2012-07-24/justice/justice_pennsylvania -priest-abuse-sentencing_1_altar-boy-predator-priests-judge-m-teresa-sarmina).

Huijts, Tim, and Gerbert Kraaykamp. 2011. "Marital Status, National Marital Status Composition, and Self-Assessed Health." *European Societies* 13(2):279–305.

Hummer, Robert A., Richard G. Rogers, Charles B. Nam, and Christopher G. Ellison. 1999. "Religious Involvement and U.S. Adult Mortality." *Demography* 36(2):273–285.

Hunsberger, Bruce, Susan Alisat, S. Mark Pancer, and Michael Pratt. 1996. "Religious Fundamentalism and Religious Doubts: Content, Connections, and Complexity of Thinking." *International Journal for the Psychology of Religion* 6(3):201–220.

Hunsberger, Bruce E., and Bob Altemeyer. 2006. *Atheists: A Groundbreaking Study of America's Nonbelievers*. Prometheus Books.

Hunsberger, Bruce, Michael Pratt, and S. Mark Pancer. 2002. "A Longitudinal Study of Religious Doubts in High School and Beyond: Relationships, Stability, and Searching for Answers." *Journal for the Scientific Study of Religion* 41(2):255–266.

Iannaccone, Laurence R. 1990. "Religious Practice: A Human Capital Approach." *Journal for the Scientific Study of Religion* 29(3):297–314.

IslamToday.net. 2007. "Statement Regarding the 'Qatif Girl' Case." *IslamToday.net*. Retrieved September 2, 2012 (http://en.islamtoday.net/artshow-417-3017. htm).

Jacoby, Susan. 2005. *Freethinkers: A History of American Secularism*. Holt Paperbacks.

Janssen, Susan G., and Robert M. Hauser. 1981. "Religion, Socialization, and Fertility." *Demography* 18(4):511–528.

Jasilionis, Domantas, Evgueni M. Andreev, Tatyana L. Kharkova, and W. Ward Kingkade. 2012. "Change in marital status structure as an obstacle for health improvement: evidence from six developed countries." *European Journal of Public Health* 22(4):602–604.

Jelen, Ted G. 1993. "The Political Consequences of Religious Group Attitudes." *The Journal of Politics* 55(01):178–190.

Jelen, Ted G., and Clyde Wilcox. 2003. "Causes and Consequences of Public Attitudes Toward Abortion: A Review and Research Agenda." *Political Research Quarterly* 56(4):489–500.

Johnson, Byron R., David B. Larson, Spencer De Li, and Sung Joon Jang. 2000. "Escaping from the crime of inner cities: Church attendance and religious salience among disadvantaged youth." *Justice Quarterly* 17(2):377–391.

Johnson, Megan K., Wade C. Rowatt, and Jordan LaBouff. 2010. "Priming Christian Religious Concepts Increases Racial Prejudice." *Social Psychological and Personality Science* 1(2):119 –126.

Jost, John T. 2006. "The end of the end of ideology." *The American psychologist* 61(7):651–670.

Joyce, Kathryn. 2010. *Quiverfull: Inside the Christian Patriarchy Movement*. Beacon Press.

Kaczynski, Andrew T., Roger C. Mannell, and Stephen R. Manske. 2008. "Leisure and Risky Health Behaviors: A Review of Evidence about Smoking." *Journal of Leisure Research* 40(3):404–441.

Kahn, Joan R., and Kathryn A. London. 1991. "Premarital Sex and the Risk of Divorce." *Journal of Marriage and Family* 53(4):845–855.

Kalmijn, Matthijs. 2007. "Explaining Cross-National Differences in Marriage, Cohabitation, and Divorce in Europe, 1990-2000." *Population Studies* 61(3):243–263.

Kanazawa, Satoshi. 2010. "Why Liberals and Atheists Are More Intelligent." *Social Psychology Quarterly*. Retrieved July 29, 2012 (http://spq.sagepub.com/content/early/2010/02/16/0190272510361602).

Karnik, Sameera, and Amar Kanekar. 2012. "Childhood Obesity: A Global Public Health Crisis." *International Journal of Preventive Medicine* 3(1):1–7.

Kaufmann, Eric. 2008. "Human Development and the Demography of Secularization in Global Perspective." *Interdisciplinary Journal of Research on Religion* 4(1). Retrieved (http://www.religjournal.com/articles/article_view.php?id=22).

Keister, Lisa A. 2008. "Conservative Protestants and Wealth: How Religion Perpetuates Asset Poverty." *American Journal of Sociology* 113(5):1237–1271.

Kemp, Matthew W, Suhas G Kallapur, Alan H Jobe, and John P Newnham. 2012. "Obesity and the developmental origins of health and disease." *Journal of Paediatrics & Child Health* 48(2):86–90.

Kendler, Kenneth S, Margaret Gatz, Charles O Gardner, and Nancy L Pedersen. 2006. "A Swedish national twin study of lifetime major depression." *The American journal of psychiatry* 163(1):109–114.

Kirkpatrick, Lee A., and Ralph W. Jr. Hood. 1990. "Intrinsic-Extrinsic Religious Orientation: The Boon or Bane of Contemporary Psychology of Religion?" *Journal for the Scientific Study of Religion* 29(4):442.

Koenig, Harold G., Michael E. McCullough, and David B. Larson. 2001. *Handbook of Religion and Health*. 1st ed. Oxford University Press, USA.

Kohlberg, Lawrence. 1973. "The Claim to Moral Adequacy of a Highest Stage of Moral Judgment." *The Journal of Philosophy* 70(18):630–646.

Kohlberg, Lawrence, and Richard H. Hersh. 1977. "Moral Development: A Review of the Theory." *Theory into Practice* 16(2):53–59.

Kosmin, Barry A., and Ariela Keysar. 2006. *Religion in a Free Market Religious and Non-Religious Americans Who, What, Why, Where.* Paramount Market Publishing, Inc.

Kosmin, Barry A., Ariela Keysar, Ryan T. Cragun, and Juhem Navarro-Rivera. 2009. *American Nones: The Profile of the No Religion Population.* Hartford, CT: Institute for the Study of Secularism in Society and Culture.

Laband, David N., and Deborah Hendry Heinbuch. 1987. *Blue Laws: The History, Economics, and Politics of Sunday-closing Laws.* Think!

Lam, Pui–Yan. 2002. "As the Flocks Gather: How Religion Affects Voluntary Association Participation." *Journal for the Scientific Study of Religion* 41(3):405–422.

Larrimore, Mark. 2010. "Religion and the Promise of Happiness." *Social Research* 77(2):569–594.

Larson, E. J., and L. Witham. 1998. "Leading Scientists Still Reject God." *Nature* 394(6691):313.

Laythe, Brian, Deborah Finkel, and Lee A. Kirkpatrick. 2001. "Predicting Prejudice from Religious Fundamentalism and Right-Wing Authoritarianism: A Multiple-Regression Approach." *Journal for the Scientific Study of Religion* 40(1):1.

Leakey, Richard, and Roger Lewin. 1991. *Origins: The Emergence and Evolution of Our Species and Its PossibleFuture.* Penguin (Non-Classics).

Lee, Lois. 2012a. "Being Secular: Towards Separate Sociologies of Secularity, Nonreligion, and Epistemological Culture." PhD Dissertation, Cambridge, UK: Cambridge University.

Lee, Lois. 2012b. "Research Note: Talking about a Revolution: Terminology for the New Field of Non-religion Studies." *Journal of Contemporary Religion* 27(1):129–139.

Legkauskas, Visvaldas, and Džeralda Stankevičienė. 2009. "Premarital Sex and Marital Satisfaction of Middle Aged Men and Women: A Study of Married Lithuanian Couples." *Sex Roles* 60(1):21–32.

Lehrer, Evelyn L. 2004. "The Role of Religion in Union Formation: An Economic Perspective." *Population Research and Policy Review* 23(2):161–185.

Lerner, Gerda. 1987. *The Creation of Patriarchy.* Oxford University Press, USA.

Lesthaeghe, R., and K. Neels. 2002. "From the First to the Second Demographic Transition: An Interpretation of the Spatial Continuity of Demographic Innovation in France, Belgium and Switzerland." *European Journal of Population / Revue Européenne de Démographie* 18(4):325–360.

Lewis, Christopher Alan, and Sharon Mary Cruise. 2006. "Religion and happiness: Consensus, contradictions, comments and concerns." *Mental Health, Religion & Culture* 9(3):213–225.

Lewis, Michael, Kiyoko Takai- Kawakami, Kiyobumi Kawakami, and Margaret Wolan Sullivan. 2010. "Cultural Differences in Emotional Responses to Success and Failure." *International journal of behavioral development* 34(1):53–61.

Lindow, John. 2002. *Norse Mythology: A Guide to Gods, Heroes, Rituals, and Beliefs.* First ed. Oxford University Press, USA.

Lipset, Seymour Martin. 1997. *American Exceptionalism: A Double-Edged Sword.* W. W. Norton & Company.

Long, Theodore, and Jeffrey Hadden. 1985. "A Reconception of Socialization." *Sociological Theory* 3(1):39–49.

Louie, Grant H., and Michael M. Ward. 2011. "Socioeconomic and Ethnic Differences in Disease Burden and Disparities in Physical Function in Older Adults." *American Journal of Public Health* 101(7):1322–1329.

Luyster, Faith S, Patrick J Strollo Jr, Phyllis C Zee, and James K Walsh. 2012. "Sleep: a health imperative." *Sleep* 35(6):727–734.

Lynn, Richard, John Harvey, and Helmuth Nyborg. 2009. "Average intelligence predicts atheism rates across 137 nations." *Intelligence* 37(1):11–15.

Lyon, J. L., and S. Nelson. 1979. "Mormon Health." *Dialogue: A Journal of Mormon Thought* 12(3):84–96.

Macdonald-Wallis, Kyle, Russell Jago, Angie S Page, Rowan Brockman, and Janice L Thompson. 2011. "School-based friendship networks and children's physical activity: A spatial analytical approach." *Social science & medicine (1982)* 73(1):6–12.

Manning, Christel. 2010. "Atheism, Secularity, the Family, and Children." Pp. 19–42 in *Atheism and Secularity: Volume 1 - Issues, Concepts, and Definitions*, vol. 1, edited by Phil Zuckerman. Santa Barbara, CA: Praeger.

Marquis, Don. 1989. "Why Abortion is Immoral." *Journal of Philosophy* 86(4):183–202.

Marshall, Donald S. 1971. "Sexual Behavior on Mangaia." Pp. 103–162 in *Human Sexual Behavior: Variations in the Ethnographic Spectrum*, edited by Donald S. Marshall and Robert C. Suggs. Basic Books.

Martin, T C, and L L Bumpass. 1989. "Recent trends in marital disruption." *Demography* 26(1):37–51.

Martin, Todd F., James M. White, and Daniel Perlman. 2003. "Religious Socialization: A Test of the Channeling Hypothesis of Parental Influence on Adolescent Faith Maturity." *Journal of Adolescent Research* 18(2):169–187.

Marx, Karl. 1977. *Critique of Hegel's "Philosophy Of Right."*edited by Joseph O'Malley. Cambridge University Press.

Maselko, Joanna, Lisa M. Bates, Mauricio Avendaño, and M. Maria Glymour. 2009.

"The Intersection of Sex, Marital Status, and Cardiovascular Risk Factors in Shaping Stroke Incidence: Results from the Health and Retirement Study." *Journal of the American Geriatrics Society* 57(12):2293–2299.

Mason, Michael, Andrew Singleton, and Ruth Webber. 2008. *The Spirit of Generation Y: Young People's Spirituality in a Changing Australia.* John Garratt Publishing.

Mason, Oliver J., and Rebecca Holt. 2012. "Mental health and physical activity interventions: A review of the qualitative literature." *Journal of Mental Health* 21(3):274–284.

Max, Wendy. 2001. "The financial impact of smoking on health-related costs: a review of the literature." *American Journal of Health Promotion* 15(5):11.

McAllister, Ian. 1988. "Religious Change and Secularization: The Transmission of Religious Values in Australia." *Sociological Analysis* 49(3):249–263.

McBride Murry, Velma et al. 2005. "Parental Involvement Promotes Rural African American Youths' Self-Pride and Sexual Self-Concepts." *Journal of Marriage and Family* 67(3):627–642.

McCarthy, Bill, and Eric Grodsky. 2011. "Sex and School: Adolescent Sexual Intercourse and Education." *Social Problems* 58(2):213–234.

McLanahan, Sara, and Gary D. Sandefur. 1994. *Growing Up With a Single Parent: What Hurts, What Helps.* Harvard University Press.

McNamara, Patrick. 2009. *The Neuroscience of Religious Experience.* 1st ed. Cambridge University Press.

Melby, Christopher L., David G. Godflies, Gerald C. Hyner, and Roseann M. Lyle. 1989. "Relation between Vegetarian/Nonvegetarian Diets and Blood Pressure in Black and White Adults." *American Journal of Public Health* 79(9):1283–1288.

Merrill, R. M., and A. L. Thygerson. 2001. "Religious Preference, Church Activity, and Physical Exercise." *Preventive Medicine* 33(1):38–45.

Mooney, Chris. 2006. *The Republican War on Science.* Basic Books.

Morgan, S. Philip, and Bhanu B. Niraula. 1995. "Gender Inequality and Fertility in Two Nepali Villages." *Population and Development Review* 21(3):541–561.

Mosher, William D., Linda B. Williams, and David P. Johnson. 1992. "Religion and Fertility in the United States: New Patterns." *Demography* 29(2):199–214.

Mueller, Charles W., and Weldon T. Johnson. 1975. "Socioeconomic Status and Religious Participation." *American Sociological Review* 40(6):785–800.

Muennig, Peter, Peter Franks, Haomiao Jia, Erica Lubetkin, and Marthe R Gold. 2005. "The income-associated burden of disease in the United States." *Social Science & Medicine* 61(9):2018–2026.

Myers, Scott M. 1996. "An Interactive Model of Religiosity Inheritance: The Importance of Family Context." *American Sociological Review* 61(5):858–866.

Najman, Jake M. et al. 2010. "Family Poverty Over the Early Life Course and Recurrent Adolescent and Young Adult Anxiety and Depression: A Longitudinal Study." *American Journal of Public Health* 100(9):1719–1723.

Nielsen, Michael E., and Ryan T. Cragun. 2010. "Religious orientation, religious affiliation, and boundary maintenance: The case of polygamy." *Mental Health, Religion & Culture* 13(7):761.

Norenzayan, Ara, and Ian G. Hansen. 2006. "Belief in Supernatural Agents in the Face of Death." *Pers Soc Psychol Bull* 32(2):174–187.

Norris, Pippa, and Ronald Inglehart. 2011. *Sacred and Secular: Religion and Politics Worldwide*. 2nd ed. Cambridge University Press.

Nyborg, Helmuth. 2009. "The Intelligence-Religiosity Nexus: A Representative Study of White Adolescent Americans." *Intelligence* 37(1):81–93.

Olson, Maren E., Douglas Diekema, Barbara A. Elliott, and Colleen M. Renier. 2010. "Impact of Income and Income Inequality on Infant Health Outcomes in the United States." *Pediatrics* 126(6):1165–1176.

Opsasnick, Mark. 2000. "The Haunted Boy of Cottage City: The Cold Hard Facts Behind the Story That Inspired 'The Exorcist.'" *Strange Magazine*. Retrieved December 11, 2011 (http://www.strangemag.com/exorcistpage1.html).

Orrenius, Pia M., and Madeline Zavodny. 2009. "Do Immigrants Work in Riskier Jobs?" *Demography* 46(3):535–551.

Ouimet, Leanne. 2009. "Jeannine Lauber: Exploring the modern-day Shakers." *independentpub.com*. Retrieved August 5, 2012 (http://www.independentpub.com/story.asp?pubId=wi&artId=1260283348).

Pargament, Kenneth I. 2001. *The Psychology of Religion and Coping: Theory, Research, Practice*. 1st ed. The Guilford Press.

Park, Jerry Z., and Christian Smith. 2000. "'To Whom Much Has Been Given...': Religious Capital and Community Voluntarism Among Churchgoing Protestants." *Journal for the Scientific Study of Religion* 39(3):272.

Park, Jung Min, Angela R. Fertig, and Paul D. Allison. 2011. "Physical and Mental Health, Cognitive Development, and Health Care Use by Housing Status of Low-Income Young Children in 20 American Cities: A Prospective Cohort Study." *American Journal of Public Health* 101(S1):S255–S261.

Pasquale, Frank L. 2010. "A Portrait of Secular Group Affiliates." Pp. 43–88 in *Atheism and Secularity: Volume 1 - Issues, Concepts, and Definitions*, vol. 1, edited by Phil Zuckerman. Santa Barbara, CA: Praeger.

Pataki, Thomas. 2009. "Some Thoughts on Why I Am an Atheist." Pp. 204–210 in

50 Voices of Disbelief: Why We Are Atheists, edited by Russell Blackford and Udo Schuklenk. Wiley-Blackwell.

Paul, Gregory S. 2005. "Cross-National Correlations of Quantifiable Societal Health with Popular Religiosity and Secularism in the Prosperous Democracies." *Journal of Religion and Society* 7. Retrieved January 6, 2009 (http://moses.creighton.edu/JRS/2005/2005-11.html).

Paul, Gregory S. 2010. "The Evolution of Popular Religiosity and Secularism: How First World Statistics Reveal Why Religion Exists, Why It Has Been Popular, and Why the Most Successful Democracies are the Most Secular." Pp. 149–208 in *Atheism and Secularity: Volume 1—Issues, Concepts, and Definitions*, vol. 1, edited by Phil Zuckerman. Santa Barbara, CA: Praeger.

Pelone, F. et al. 2012. "Economic impact of childhood obesity on health systems: a systematic review." *Obesity Reviews* 13(5):431–440.

Perrin, Ellen C. 2002. "Technical Report: Coparent or Second-Parent Adoption by Same-Sex Parents." *Pediatrics* 109(2):341–344.

Pew Forum on Religion & Public Life. 2010. "U.S. Religious Knowledge Survey—Who Knows What About Religion." *pewforum.org*. Retrieved July 22, 2012 (http://www.pewforum.org/U-S-Religious-Knowledge-Survey-Who-Knows-What-About-Religion.aspx).

Phelps, Andrea C. et al. 2009. "Religious Coping and Use of Intensive Life-Prolonging Care Near Death in Patients With Advanced Cancer." *Journal of the American Medical Association* 301(11):1140–1147.

Pogue-Geile, Michael F., and Richard J. Rose. 1985. "Developmental genetic studies of adult personality." *Developmental Psychology* 21(3):547–557.

Pong, Suet-ling, Jaap Dronkers, and Gillian Hampden-Thompson. 2003. "Family Policies and Children's School Achievement in Single- Versus Two-Parent Families." *Journal of Marriage and Family* 65(3):681–699.

Popken, Ben. 2011. "MRI Shows Apple Stimulates Fan's Brain Like Religion." *The Consumerist*. Retrieved November 13, 2011 (http://consumerist.com/2011/05/mri-shows-apple-stimulates-fans-brains-like-religion.html).

Preyde, Michèle, and Kristie Brassard. 2011. "Evidence-based Risk Factors for Adverse Health Outcomes in Older Patients after Discharge Home and Assessment Tools: A Systematic Review." *Journal of Evidence-Based Social Work* 8(5):445–468.

Prothero, Stephen. 2007. *Religious Literacy: What Every American Needs to Know—and Doesn't*. HarperOne.

RCG. 2011. "Pat Robertson: Going Green is a Joke." *REepedia*. Retrieved September 2, 2012 (http://www.reepedia.com/archives/429).

Redden, Molly. 2011. "Whatever Happened to the Evangelical-Environmental Alliance?" *The New Republic*. Retrieved September 2, 2012 (http://www.tnr.com/article/politics/97007/evangelical-climate-initiative-creation-care).

Redlawsk, David P., Andrew J. W. Civettini, and Karen M. Emmerson. 2010. "The Affective Tipping Point: Do Motivated Reasoners Ever 'Get It'?" *Political Psychology* 31(4):563–593.

Rees, Tom. 2010. "Is Loss of Faith a Two-Generation Process?" *Free Inquiry* 30(4):17–18.

Regnerus, Mark D. 2007. *Forbidden Fruit: Sex & Religion in the Lives of American Teenagers*. 1st ed. Oxford University Press, USA.

Rest, James R., Darcia Narvaez, Stephen J. Thoma, and Muriel J. Bebeau. 2000. "A Neo-Kohlbergian Approach to Morality Research." *Journal of Moral Education* 29(4):381–395.

Richards, P. Scott, and Mark L. Davison. 1992. "Religious Bias in Moral Development Research: A Psychometric Investigation." *Journal for the Scientific Study of Religion* 31(4):467–485.

Richtel, Matt. 2007. "Thou Shalt Not Kill, Except in a Popular Video Game at Church." *The New York Times*, October 7. Retrieved July 29, 2012 (http://www.nytimes.com/2007/10/07/us/07halo.html).

Ricks, Shirley S. 1992. "Eternal Lives, Eternal Increase" edited by Daniel H. Ludlow. *Encyclopedia of Mormonism* 465.

Roberts, Laura. 2010. "Teenage Jehovah's Witness refuses blood transfusion and dies." *telegraph.co.uk*. Retrieved July 17, 2011 (http://www.telegraph.co.uk/health/healthnews/7734480/Teenage-Jehovahs-Witness-refuses-blood-transfusion-and-dies.html).

Robertson, John A. 1983. "Procreative Liberty and the Control of Conception, Pregnancy, and Childbirth." *Virginia Law Review* 69:405.

Roof, Wade Clark, and William McKinney. 1987. *American Mainline Religion: Its Changing Shape and Future*. Rutgers University Press.

Rossignol, D A, and R E Frye. 2011. "A review of research trends in physiological abnormalities in autism spectrum disorders: immune dysregulation, inflammation, oxidative stress, mitochondrial dysfunction and environmental toxicant exposures." *Molecular Psychiatry*. Retrieved December 11, 2011 (http://www.ncbi.nlm.nih.gov/pubmed/22143005).

Rowatt, Wade C., Alison Ottenbreit, K. Paul Nesselroade Jr., and Paige A. Cunningham. 2002. "On Being Holier-Than-Thou or Humbler-Than-Thee: A Social-Psychological Perspective on Religiousness and Humility." *Journal for the Scientific Study of Religion* 41(2):227.

Saltin, Bengt, Robert Boushel, Neils Secher, and Jere Mitchell. 2000. *Exercise and Circulation in Health and Disease*. 1st ed. Human Kinetics.

Santesso, N et al. 2012. "Effects of higher- versus lower-protein diets on health outcomes: a systematic review and meta-analysis." *European Journal of Clinical Nutrition* 66(7):780–788.

Sasaki, Masamichi, and Tatsuzo Suzuki. 1987. "Changes in Religious Commitment in the United States, Holland, and Japan." *The American Journal of Sociology* 92(5):1055–1076.

Schoen, Robert. 1975. "California Divorce Rates by Age at First Marriage and Duration of First Marriage." Retrieved August 5, 2012 (http://www.eric.ed.gov/ ERICWebPortal/detail?accno=EJ125594).

Schwadel, Philip. 2010. "Period and Cohort Effects on Religious Nonaffiliation and Religious Disaffiliation: A Research Note." *Journal for the Scientific Study of Religion* 49(2):311–319.

Shenhav, Amitai, David G. Rand, and Joshua D. Greene. 2011. "Divine intuition: Cognitive style influences belief in God." *Journal of Experimental Psychology: General* No Pagination Specified.

Shorter, Edward. 1973. "Female Emancipation, Birth Control, and Fertility in European History." *The American Historical Review* 78(3):605–640.

Sloan, Richard P. 2006. *Blind Faith: The Unholy Alliance of Religion and Medicine*. 1 Reprint. St. Martin's Griffin.

Smart, Tom, and Lee Benson. 2006. *In Plain Sight: The Startling Truth Behind the Elizabeth Smart Investigation*. Chicago Review Press.

Smith, Christian, and Melina Lundquist Denton. 2009. *Soul Searching: The Religious and Spiritual Lives of American Teenagers*. Reprint. Oxford University Press, USA.

Smith, George H. 1979. *Atheism: The Case Against God*. 1st paperback ed. Prometheus Books.

Smith, Ronald E., Gregory Wheeler, and Edward Diener. 1975. "Faith without works: Jesus people, resistance to temptation, and altruism." *Journal of Applied Social Psychology* 5(4):320–330.

Smith-Stoner, Marilyn. 2007. "End-of-life preferences for atheists." *Journal of Palliative Medicine* 10(4):923–928.

Smith, Tom W. 1987. *Classifying Protestant Denominations*. Chicago, Illinois: National Opinion Research Center. Retrieved March 25, 2012 (http://www. adherents.com/largecom/prot_classify.html).

Smith, Tom W., Peter Marsden, Michael Hout, and Jibum Kim. 2010. *General social surveys, 1972–2010*. Chicago: National Opinion Research Center.

Snoep, Liesbeth. 2008. "Religiousness and happiness in three nations: a research note." *Journal of Happiness Studies* 9(2):207–211.

Snowdon, David A., and Roland L. Phillips. 1985. "Does a Vegetarian Diet Reduce the Occurrence of Diabetes?" *American Journal of Public Health* 75(5):507–512.

Sousan, Abadian. 1996. "Women's autonomy and its impact on fertility." *World Development* 24(12):1793–1809.

Stark, Rodney, and William Sims Bainbridge. 1980. "Networks of Faith: Interpersonal Bonds and Recruitment to Cults and Sects." *American Journal of Sociology* 85(6):1376–95.

Stark, Rodney, and Roger Finke. 2000. *Acts of Faith: Explaining the Human Side of Religion.* 1st ed. University of California Press.

Stark, Rodney, and Charles Y. Glock. 1970. *American Piety: The Nature of Religious Commitment.* University of California Press.

Stayton, Donelda J., Robert Hogan, and Mary D. Salter Ainsworth. 1971. "Infant Obedience and Maternal Behavior: The Origins of Socialization Reconsidered." *Child Development* 42(4):1057–1069.

Steel, Piers, Joseph Schmidt, and Jonas Shultz. 2008. "Refining the relationship between personality and subjective well-being." *Psychological Bulletin* 134(1):138–161.

Steensland, Brian et al. 2000. "The Measure of American Religion: Toward Improving the State of the Art." *Social Forces* 79(1):291–318.

Stenger, Victor J. 2008. *God: The Failed Hypothesis. How Science Shows That God Does Not Exist.* Prometheus Books.

Stevens, Carey, Arthur M. Blank, and Greg Poushinsky. 1977. "Religion as a factor in morality research: A cross-sectional analysis of older adolescents, young adults, middle age and senior citizens." *Journal of Psychology & Judaism* 1(2):61–80.

Stolzenberg, Ross M., Mary Blair-Loy, and Linda J. Waite. 1995. "Religious participation in early adulthood: Age and family life cycle effects on church membership." *American Sociological Review* 60(1):84–103.

Sudeck, Gorden, and Oliver Höner. 2011. "Volitional Interventions within Cardiac Exercise Therapy (VIN-CET): Long-Term Effects on Physical Activity and Health-Related Quality of Life." *Applied Psychology: Health & Well-Being* 3(2):151–171.

Swatos, William H., Jr. 1998. *Encyclopedia of Religion and Society.* 1st ed. Altamira Press.

Taft, Ronald. 1955. "The ability to judge people." *Psychological Bulletin* 52(1):1–23.

Tajfel, H. 1982. "Social Psychology of Intergroup Relations." *Annual Review of Psychology* 33(1):1–39.

Teachman, Jay. 2003. "Premarital Sex, Premarital Cohabitation, and the Risk of Subsequent Marital Dissolution among Women." *Journal of Marriage and Family* 65(2):444–455.

The Associated Press. 2007. "Saudis: Rape victim deserved flogging for adultery." *USATODAY.com*. Retrieved September 2, 2012 (http://www.usatoday.com/news/world/2007-11-25-saudiarabia_N.htm).

The Associated Press. 2010. "West Bank: Blogger Arrested Over Posts Seen as Heresy for Satirizing Koran." *The New York Times*, November 11. Retrieved November 13, 2011 (http://www.nytimes.com/2010/11/12/world/middleeast/12briefs-Westbank.html).

The Barna Group. 2009. "Most American Christians Do Not Believe that Satan or the Holy Spirit Exist." *Barna.org*. Retrieved September 18, 2011 (http://www.barna.org/barna-update/article/12-faithspirituality/260-most-american-christians-do-not-believe-that-satan-or-the-holy-spirit-exis).

The Canadian Press. 2007. "Muslim leaders say teen's killing was domestic violence." *CBC News*. Retrieved July 14, 2011 (http://www.cbc.ca/news/canada/toronto/story/2007/12/14/aqsa-parvez.html).

The Church of Jesus Christ of Latter-day Saints. 1988. *Missionary Guide: Training For Missionaries*. Salt Lake City, UT: The Church of Jesus Christ of Latter-day Saints.

The Globe and Mail. 2010. "For the killers of Aqsa Parvez, 'culture' is no defence." *The Globe and Mail*. Retrieved September 2, 2012 (http://www.theglobeandmail.com/commentary/editorials/for-the-killers-of-aqsa-parvez-culture-is-no-defence/article579183/).

Thomas, M. Catherine. 1992. "Hell" edited by Daniel H. Ludlow. *Encyclopedia of Mormonism* 585–586.

Tittle, Charles R. 1977. "Sanction Fear and the Maintenance of Social Order." *Social Forces* 55(3):579–596.

Torpy, Jason. 2012. "Military Religious Demographics." *militaryatheists.org*.

Tracy, Jessica L, Richard W Robins, and Roberta A Schriber. 2009. "Development of a FACS-verified set of basic and self-conscious emotion expressions." *Emotion (Washington, D.C.)* 9(4):554–559.

Tracy, Jessica L., Azim F. Shariff, and Joey T. Cheng. 2010. "A Naturalist's View of Pride." *Emotion Review* 2(2):163–177.

U. S. Catholic Church. 1995. *Catechism of the Catholic Church*. First ed. Image.

Uslaner, Eric M. 2002. "Religion and Civic Engagement in Canada and the United States." *Journal for the Scientific Study of Religion* 41(2):239–254.

Voas, David. 2007. "The Continuing Secular Transition." Pp. 25–48 in *The Role of Religion in Modern Societies*, edited by Detlef Pollack and Daniel V. A. Olson. Routledge.

Wainright, Jennifer L., Stephen T. Russell, and Charlotte J. Patterson. 2004. "Psychosocial Adjustment, School Outcomes, and Romantic Relationships of Adolescents With Same-Sex Parents." *Child Development* 75(6):1886–1898.

Waller, Niels G., Brian A. Kojetin, Thomas J. Bouchard, David T. Lykken, and Auke Tellegen. 1990. "Genetic and Environmental Influences on Religious Interests, Attitudes, and Values: A Study of Twins Reared Apart and Together." *Psychological Science* 1(2):138–142.

Watch Tower Bible and Tract Society of Pennsylvania. 2008. "Benefit From the Best Education Available!" *Jehovah's Witnesses Official Web Site*. Retrieved July 29, 2012 (http://www.watchtower.org/e/20051015/article_02.htm).

Watch Tower Bible and Tract Society of Pennsylvania. 2006. "Blood—Vital For Life." *Jehovah's Witnesses Official Web Site*. Retrieved July 29, 2012 (http://www.watchtower.org/e/hb/article_01.htm).

Weber, Max. 1978. *Max Weber: Selections in Translation*. Cambridge University Press.

Werner, Carol M. et al. 1995. "Commitment, behavior, and attitude change: An analysis of voluntary recycling." *Journal of Environmental Psychology* 15(3):197–208.

White, Lynn. 1967. "The Historical Roots of Our Ecologic Crisis." *Science* 155(3767):1203–1207.

White, Paula. 2006. *First Fruits: From Promise to Provision*. 1st ed. Paula White Ministries.

Wicklund, Susan, and Alex Kesselheim. 2008. *This Common Secret: My Journey as an Abortion Doctor*. 1 Reprint. PublicAffairs.

Wikipedia contributors. 2012a. "I'd Like to Teach the World to Sing (in Perfect Harmony)." *Wikipedia, the free encyclopedia*. Retrieved September 2, 2012 (http://en.wikipedia.org/w/index.php?title=I%27d_Like_to_Teach_the_World_to_Sing_(in_Perfect_Harmony)&oldid=501356056).

Wikipedia contributors. 2012b. "Jeff Fenholt." *Wikipedia, the free encyclopedia*. Retrieved September 2, 2012 (http://en.wikipedia.org/w/index.php?title=Jeff_Fenholt&oldid=506491320).

Wilkinson, Toby A. H. 2001. *Early Dynastic Egypt*. New Ed. Routledge.

Winslow, Ben. 2010. "Rebuttal witnesses testify at Brian David Mitchell trial." *WTVR. com*, December 4. Retrieved February 16, 2012 (http://www.wtvr.com/news/local/kstu-elizabeth-smart-kidnapping-trial-final-days,0,6084937.story).

World Values Survey Association. 2009. *World Values Survey 1981-2008 Official Aggregate v.20090901*. Madrid, Spain: World Values Survey Association.

Zamboni, M. et al. 2005. "Health consequences of obesity in the elderly: a review of four unresolved questions." *International Journal of Obesity* 29(9):1011–1029.

Zuckerman, Phil. 2011. *Faith No More: Why People Reject Religion*. Oxford University Press, USA.

Zuckerman, Phil. 2010. *Society without God: What the Least Religious Nations Can Tell Us About Contentment*. NYU Press.

INDEX

ABOUT THE AUTHOR

Ryan T. Cragun is a husband, father, and sociologist of religion (in order of importance). The sixth of nine children, he was born and raised in Morgan, Utah. His family was (and largely still is) Mormon, and he was steeped in that tradition. In 1996, at age nineteen, he left on a two-year mission for the Mormon Church in Costa Rica. It was during his mission that he decided religion was an important issue in the modern world and that he really needed to better understand it. He tried to gear his undergraduate education at the University of Utah toward the study of religion, but there were very few social science courses on the topic. It wasn't until his last semester at the University of Utah that he came across a textbook on the sociology of religion. Reading that book convinced him of where his intellectual future lay. He married his wife, Debi, in December 1999, and they applied to graduate schools with PhD programs in sociology and master's programs in genetic counseling. They were both accepted at the University of Cincinnati, where they matriculated in 2001. A year of graduate education, much of which was unrelated to religion, was sufficient to lead Ryan to decide he needed to apply a scientific perspective to his religion. The summer of 2002 was a tumultuous one; Debi was away in Utah for an internship and Ryan was reading and studying Mormonism from a new, critical perspective. Together, they decided Mormonism was no longer a tenable belief system and they left the religion at the end of the summer.

Debi completed her degree in 2003 and then found employment as a genetic counselor in Cincinnati, while Ryan completed his PhD in sociology under the guidance of Rhys Williams. Upon his graduation in 2007, both found jobs at the University of Tampa, Ryan in a tenure-track position and Debi as a visiting professor of genetics for two years. During Debi's second year, they decided the time was right to have a child. Their son, Toren Marx Cragun, was born in June 2009. While pregnant, Debi applied for and was accepted into the PhD program in public health at the University of South Florida.

Ryan's research focuses on Mormonism and the nonreligious (i.e., atheists, agnostics, and nones), and is based in the theoretical framework of secularization. He has published more than a dozen articles in peer-reviewed journals, such as *Journal for the Scientific Study of Religion, Nova Religion, Sociology of Religion, Journal of Contemporary Religion, Journal of Religion and Health,* and *Dialogue: A Journal of Mormon Thought.* He is also the author of several book chapters, a variety of reports and magazine articles, including several in *Free Inquiry,* and the coauthor of the recently published book *Could I Vote for a Mormon for President? An Election-Year Guide to Mitt Romney's Religion.* He is also a founding editor of the new journal *Secularism & Nonreligion,* the world's first peer-reviewed journal dedicated to the study of all aspects of nonreligion. Several of his published articles were coauthored with his wife, who has also published close to a dozen articles in peer-reviewed journals.

When he's not working, he is typically spending time with his wife and son, watching science fiction, hiking, playing soccer, or tinkering with FOSS, Gnu/Linux, or computer hardware.

OTHER RECENT TITLES FROM PITCHSTONE

Attack of the Theocrats!:
How the Religious Right Harms Us All
—and What We Can Do About It
by Sean Faircloth

Candidate Without a Prayer:
An Autobiography of a Jewish Atheist in the Bible Belt
by Herb Silverman

PsychoBible:
Behavior, Religion & the Holy Book
by Armando Favazza, MD

Why Are You Atheists So Angry?:
99 Things That Piss Off the Godless
by Greta Christina

Why We Believe in God(s):
A Concise Guide to the Science of Faith
by J. Anderson Thomson, Jr., MD, with Clare Aukofer